High-Level Programmer's Guide
to the 68000

C. A. R. Hoare, Series Editor

BACKHOUSE, R. C., *Program Construction and Verification*
DEBAKKER, J. W., *Mathematical Theory of Program Correctness*
BARR, M. and WELLS, C., *Category Theory for Computing Science*
BEN-ARI, M., *Principles of Concurrent and Distributed Programming*
BIRD, R. and WADLER, P., *Introduction to Functional Programming*
BORNAT, R., *Programming from First Principles*
BUSTARD, D., ELDER, J. and WELSH, J., *Concurrent Program Structures*
CLARK, K. L. and McCABE, F. G., *Micro-Prolog: Programming in logic*
CROOKES, D., *Introduction to Programming in Prolog*
DROMEY, R. G., *How to Solve it by Computer*
DUNCAN, E., *Microprocessor Programming and Software Development*
ELDER, J., *Construction of Data Processing Software*
ELLIOTT, R. J. and HOARE, C. A. R., (eds.), *Scientific Applications of Multiprocessors*
GOLDSCHLAGER, L. and LISTER, A., *Computer Science: A modern introduction (2nd edn)*.
GORDON, M. J. C., *Programming Language Theory and its Implementation*
HAYES, I, (ed) *Specification Case Studies*
HEHNER, E. C. R., *The Logic of Programming*
HENDERSON, P., *Functional Programming: Application and implementation*
HOARE, C. A. R., *Communicating Sequential Processes*
HOARE, C. A. R., and JONES, C. B. (eds), *Essays in Computing Science*
HOARE, C. A. R., and SHEPHERDSON, J. C. (eds), *Mathematical Logic and Programming Languages*
HUGHES, J. G., *Database Technology: A software engineering approach*
HUGHES, J. G., *Object-oriented Databases*
INMOS LTD, *Occam 2 Reference Manual*
JACKSON, M. A., *System Development*
JOHNSTON, H., *Learning to Program*
JONES, C. B., *Systematic Software Development using VDM (2nd edn)*
JONES, C. B. and SHAW, R. C. F. (eds), *Case Studies in Systematic Software Development*
JONES, G., *Programming in occam*
JONES, G, and GOLDSMITH, M., *Programming in occam 2*
JOSEPH, M., PRASAD, V. R. and NATARAJAN, N., *A Multiprocessor Operating System*
KALDEWAIJ, A., *Programming: The Derivation of Algorithms*
KING, P. J. B. *Computer and Communication Systems Performance Modelling*
LEW, A., *Computer Science: A mathematical introduction*
MARTIN, J. J., *Data Types and Data Structures*
McCABE, F. G., *High-Level Programmer's Guide to the 68000*
MEYER, B., *Introduction to the Theory of Programming Languages*
MEYER, B., *Object-oriented Software Construction*
MILNER, R., *Communication and Concurrency*
MORGAN, C., *Programming from Specifications*
PEYTON JONES, S. L., *The Implementation of Functional Programming Languages*
POMBERGER, G., *Software Engineering and Modula-2*
POTTER, B., SINCLAIR, J., TILL, D., *An Introduction to Formal Specification and Z*
REYNOLDS, J. C., *The Craft of Programming*
RYDEHEARD, D. E. and BURSTALL, R. M., *Computational Category Theory*
SLOMAN, M. and KRAMER, J., *Distributed Systems and Computer Networks*
SPIVEY, J. M., *The Z Notation: A reference manual*
TENNENT, R. D., *Principles of Programming Languages*
TENNENT, R. D., *Semannnntics of Programming Languages*
WATT, D, A., *Programming Language Concepts and Paradigms*
WATT, D. A., WICHMANN, B. A., and FINDLAY, W., *ADA: Language and methodology*
WELSH, J. and ELDER, J., *Introduction to Modula 2*
WELSH, J. and ELDER, J., *Introduction to Pascal (3rd edn)*
WELSH, J. ELDER, J. and BUSTARD, D., *Sequential Program Structures*
WELSH, J. and HAY, A., *A Model Implementation of Standard Pascal*
WELSH, J. and McKEAG, M., *Structured System Programming*
WIKSTRÖM, Å., *Functional Programming using Standard ML*

High-Level Programmer's Guide to the 68000

Francis G. McCabe

Prentice Hall
New York   London   Toronto   Sydney   Tokyo   Singapore

First published 1992 by
Prentice Hall International (UK) Ltd
66 Wood Lane End, Hemel Hempstead
Hertfordshire HP2 4RG
A division of
Simon & Schuster International Group

Printed and bound in Great Britain
at Dotesios, Trowbridge, Wiltshire

Library of Congress Cataloguing-in-Publication Data

A CIP catalogue record for this book is
available from the Library of Congress

British Library Cataloguing in Publication Data

McCabe, Francis G.
  High-level programmer's guide to the 68000.
  I. Title
  005.13

  ISBN 0–13–388034-6

---

1 2 3 4 5   96 95 94 93 92

Contents

List of figures

For Mary Ann and Jessica

Aims and objectives

This book arose as a result of frustration in standard assembler course books which primarily teach assembler as 'yet another programming language' without adequately relating assembler level features to real applications.

The overall aim of the book is to allow you to gain an appreciation of the impact of computer architecture on software. Such an understanding is important even if you never again write an assembler program after finishing this course; since with this insight, you can appreciate the impact of the computer architecture on the programs you may write (or cause to be written) in other programming languages. On the other hand if you have a slightly 'queasy' feeling as you write and debug programs in high-level languages this may be because you do not feel that you are in full control of the resources you are using. Such queasy feelings disappear when programming in assembler (although they may be replaced by ones of frustration...)

We specifically do not, however, aim to teach assembler programming as yet another programming language. This is because very few applications need to be programmed in assembler, and therefore, few people program in assembler directly. Of course, in order to gain an appreciation of something it is necessary to know it at least a little. Therefore we will be learning about the programming concepts behind assembler language in general and the 68000 series in particular. The difference is in the perspective and the approach of this course.

What you should gain as a result of following this book is an understanding of what is in a modern computer, and how its various resources are used to implement programs written in modern programming languages. To this end we will see how data objects of various kinds are represented in the machine; for example we will see how various number systems arise and how they are manipulated to perform arithmetic. We will also see how some of the basic features of programs written in Pascal, LISP and Prolog are mapped onto the computers resources.

Just as we do not aim to teach assembler programming as another programming lanuage, nor do we aim to teach compiler construction. Although there is some overlap, in the sense that a compiler construction course would also cover details of code generation, our objective is to understand the code that is generated by high quality compilers, not how the code is actually generated.

CHAPTER ONE

Introduction

A reasonable question to ask at the beginning of this book is why anyone might ever program in assembler which is after all only a human-readable version of the computer's own language. Why then, should we be interested in programming computers in their own language? Most programs are written in high-level languages, such as 'C', COBOL and Pascal, which are then compiled down to the machine language by automatic compilers. High quality compilers exist which will generate code which is – on average – as good as if not better than the handwritten code produced by an average programmer in assembler.

On the other hand it *is* possible to produce programs in assembler that are faster and more compact than automatically generated code. Depending on the application it is possible to obtain improvements in performance compared to the equivalent programs written in Pascal or 'C' of between 100% to 500%. Whilst for many applications, this performance penalty is more than compensated for by faster program development, for some applications the difference can be very important: a classic application domain where performance is essential rather than desirable is in real-time control systems such as flight control systems or nuclear power station control systems. Other examples include language interpreters, parts of operating systems or some numerical algorithms in libraries (such as sorting or numerical solution techniques).

A second strong motivation for using assembler language is that it offers complete control of the machine. This control comes in two flavours. First, some of the physical resources of a typical computer – such as disk drives and modems for example – are not directly available in languages like Pascal. Standard Pascal provides logical input and output, so it is possible to access files but it does not allow access to specific sectors on specific tracks on a disk.

Therefore to access the physical level of input/output it is necessary to use assembler. This becomes crucial when designing drivers for I/O devices in an operating system or when a new type of device is to be added to an existing system: *someone* must implement the necessary functions to allow a computer to access disk drives and keyboards etc. Often, only a small amount of assembler 'glue' is needed to interface the main application program to the physical device; the bulk of any application can remain in Pascal.

The second form of control available to the assembler programmer, which is not available to the Pascal programmer, arises out of the very nature of assembler programming. While high-level languages such as Pascal impose a structure on programming and restrict the nature of possible programs, there are no 'rules' regarding the structure of an assembler program.

A classic example of this is the division between programs and data. Languages like Pascal impose a rigid boundary between programs and data which it is not possible to break. This is for a good reason – most of the time programs and data do not mix, and it is a source of errors that they can be confused. On the other hand, this boundary does not exist in assembler programs: an assembler program is represented in the computer as an array of data with a particular format that the computer can interpret as instructions to execute. The only difference between program memory and data memory is that the latter is not likely to produce useful results when executed: logically (and usually also physically) they are the same.

Such flexibility is used all the time in operating systems where, for example, application programs are loaded off disk into different parts of memory and then executed. The act of reading a program from a disk and storing it into memory is possible only by interpreting instructions as data which can be copied to and fro. The number of times an application programmer needs to write an operating system are admittedly rare but the ability to do so is none-the-less crucial to modern computers.

Not all programming languages have such a rigid boundary between programs and data – one of the reasons that symbolic languages like Prolog and LISP are so powerful is precisely that they do *not* have such a rigid boundary. A LISP program (or a Prolog program) is easily handled as a standard data object by other LISP programs (or even by itself...). So, it is easy, for example, to write a system in LISP (and Prolog) that edits LISP programs, transforms them in some way, *and executes the result* all within the same program.

Assembler programs are harder to build than equivalent programs in Pascal, COBOL, Prolog or LISP. This is because the programmer has to do more: there is normally no support in assembler for data structuring, control flow and other support structures found in a modern programming language. This extra work means that an assembler programmer may be some 10-15 times *less* productive than a 'normal' programmer. It also means that an application written in assembler will cost 10-15 times as much to build as one written in Pascal (say). The extra cost burden of writing in assembler might never be recovered by the investor.

A further 'problem' with writing an application in assembler is the inherent commitment to a single architecture. A program written in Pascal can be moved from one computer to another simply by recompiling it. In contrast, porting an assembler program from a 68000 to an 80386 (say) is almost as expensive as writing it from scratch. This further increases the cost of developing an application in assembler since the investment cannot be spread across different machines.

We would therefore argue that the decision to write an application in assembler is rare in practice and is taken only where the benefits outweigh the heavy cost penalties.

Whilst few programmers might ever write many programs in assembler this does not imply that it is not important to know about computer architectures and assembler programming. All programs in modern computers are mapped onto the assembler level either via compilers or interpreters. (A possible exception to this would be neural network computers which could not be said to be programmed in the normal sense of the word.) Thus all programs execute in assembler whether they were programmed originally at that level or not.

Programming languages also reflect the underlying computer architecture in the sense that constructs in the language reflect what the computer is capable of. Usually, the simpler an operation is to perform on a computer, the easier it is to express that operation in the programming language. Conversely, language designers are reluctant to build into their languages features which are known to be difficult or expensive to implement.

A good example of this is the tendency to restrict numbers in application programs to be fixed in size, say to 32 bits or 15 decimal digits. It is very easy to support fixed size numbers in a programming language since they are always directly supported by the computer. On the other hand it is harder to represent and manipulate numbers of an *arbitrary* size in the machine. The net result is that almost every programming language employs fixed length numbers and very few programming languages even allow the possibility of arbitrary size numbers. This same constraint typically propagates to the level of the application program – resulting, for example, in fixed size fields in databases and limited precision in spreadsheets.

In summary, an understanding of assembler level programming can complete the understanding of programming at the application language level. By seeing the way that programming language constructs are mapped onto a typical computer, the programmer can gain an insight into the various resources he is using; how expensive they are and where optimizations might be fruitful. The prime motivation of this book is therefore to increase your *understanding* of programs and programming by seeing how a computer is used to implement programs written in Pascal (say) rather than to teach you how to program in assembler as though that were yet another programming language.

1.1 Approach

Given our motivation for introducing assembler language programming an obvious approach is to see how a modern programming language is mapped onto a typical modern processor. We take Pascal as our primary example of a 'modern' programming language and the 680x0 series of processors as our modern computer.

Pascal is a reasonable choice as an application language even though it may not be the most popular programming language for professional programmers. This is because it contains features which are found in many other languages – which you are likely to use – such as types, records, arrays, recursion, scoped procedures etc. It is simple to see how other programming languages like 'C' are represented by viewing them as simple modifications to the basic scheme presented for Pascal.

As a target architecture, the 680x0 is appropriate since it is popular in real computers and it has a clean straightforward architecture. In seeing how Pascal is mapped to the 680x0 we can appreciate some of the architectural features that we find in the 680x0 (for example the use of separate address and data registers in the 680x0 register bank).

There are several models in the 68000 range of processors. Since we are primarily concerned with the basic instructions common to the whole range, we shall refer to the 680x0 when we mean any of them. Where a difference is important (in that it allows us to choose a different representation of a programming language construct) we will obviously highlight it. For example if there are restrictions which apply to the 68010 or 68000, or when we want to discuss additional features available on the 68020 or 68030 which are not available on the base 68000 model; in these circumstances we shall be more explicit.

Note that this is not a book about how to program; and we shall assume that you are already familiar with, and are reasonably comfortable writing programs in, Pascal. However, since it would be unnecessarily restrictive to make the same assumption about the assembler level, we will give a basic introduction to the architecture of the 680x0 series from a programmer's point of view. This includes introducing the concepts of registers, memory and so forth.

However, we will not be going into the details of the architecture of the 68000 that would be necessary for a computer designer. Thus we will not be dealing with issues relating to interfacing the 68000 to memory; nor will we be looking at some of the specialist assembler techniques needed for handling interrupts and other operating system functions.

There are a number of programming languages which do not fit into the Pascal mould. In particular symbolic languages such as Prolog and LISP are so different to Pascal that they require radically different representations in the machine. Therefore in the latter sections of this book we explore the features of these languages as well.

What we will do is examine the major components of the Pascal language and see how they are represented on the 680x0. We will do this by supposing that we ourselves are a reasonably clever compiler and we have the job of compiling Pascal programs onto the 680x0. We will often look at fragments of Pascal programs and see how they are mapped into the machine.

For example, by the time that we reach the end of Chapter 8, we will be able to look at the program fragment:

```
procedure  swap(var  i,j:integer);
var  k:integer;
begin
   k:=i;
   i:=j;
   j:=k;
end;
```

and we will see how programs like this can be represented by sequences of 680x0 assembler instructions such as:

```
swap   link    a6,#-2              ;allocate  k
       move.l  12(a6),a0
       move.w  (a0),-2(a6)         ;k:=i
       move.l  8(a6),a1
       move.w  (a1),(a0)           ;i:=j
       move.w  -2(a6),(a1)         ;j:=k
       unlk    a6                  ;deallocate  k
       rtd     #8                  ;clean  up  and  return
```

This is not a compiler construction course: therefore we will not cover at all such aspects of the compilation process as parsing, dictionaries, type checking etc. Our interest is in the end product of a compiler, not how the compiler goes about its business.

1.1.1 Structure of the book

This book is intended to be followed sequentially. The early material is quite basic whereas the latter parts are more advanced. The last two chapters on LISP and Prolog are optional in the sense that they refer to languages which are considerably less widespread in their use than the mainstream languages which are well represented by Pascal.

Most chapters are accompanied by exercises. These are intended to deepen your understanding of the text. Some of the exercises lead into areas which go beyond the scope of the book, and the reader is encouraged to follow this lead.

Chapter 2 concentrates on the issues involved in representing numbers in the machine. We look at how integers are represented, and the fundamental nature of computer arithmetic. We also see how algorithms for multiplication and division can be implemented. It is important to get to grips with numbers in computers because they appear extremely frequently within programs.

Quite apart from their role in application programs, multiplication and division represent the most complex operations which are necessary to support features of Pascal itself. Other, more complex operations such as cosine and square root are important for applications but are not needed to access and generate data structures.

Chapter 3 introduces the basic structure of the 680x0 series of processors. The aim of this chapter is to familiarize you with the registers and operations available to the assembler programmer. We also see exactly what goes into an assembler program, and how they are assembled.

By the end of Chapters 2 and 3 you should be aware of the major components of the 680x0 and the kind of data objects that are prevalent in an assembler program. This provides a base for the following chapters in which we explore the use of 680x0 features to support Pascal.

Chapter 4 looks at the representation of scalar values and expressions. Some techniques for implementing expressions are presented based on converting into reverse polish notation and using the system stack and registers. We also look at the role of run-time errors in making sure that programs only execute normally when the arithmetic performed is safe: i.e. it is within the limits set by the program.

Chapter 5 concentrates on non-scalar or compound data structures. We cover how records are laid out in memory and how fields of records are accessed. We also see how arrays are mapped onto the machine and how array elements are indexed and accessed.

The more advanced Pascal data structures such as packed structures and sets are covered in Chapter 6. We illustrate the large difference between accessing normal or unpacked structures and packed structures. In this case, and generally, we show the instructions necessary to access structures both in standard 68000 instructions and in 68020/68030 instructions (where their additional instructions and addressing modes can make the tasks simpler).

In Chapter 7 we tackle the issues of Pascal's control features. We see how the various basic control structures such as conditional statements and loop statements are supported by the 680x0. We conclude this chapter with a section on performance oriented assembler programming.

The procedure and function statements merit a separate chapter: Chapter 8. In this chapter we see how procedures are called, parameters are passed to them and how local variables are allocated. This chapter also examines the complexities of scoped procedures and implementing **goto** in the context of scoped procedures.

In Chapter 9 we leave Pascal and look at a completely different style of programming language, namely LISP. Implementing LISP brings additional complications over Pascal; in particular we look at how recursive data structures are represented and garbage collection.

Chapter 10 introduces some of the mechanisms needed to support Prolog. Prolog and LISP are quite a lot further from the machine's level than Pascal. This increased gap is reflected in the relatively long sequences of instructions needed to implement simple LISP and Prolog programs.

The two appendices A and B provide reference material on the 680x0 machine. These are primarily intended to support the text, but should also be helpful beyond the immediate scope of this book.

Appendix A summarises the addressing modes available on the 680x0 range, and Appendix B lists all the instructions which are referred to in the text and others which are related. This listing is not a complete listing of the 680x0 instruction set, however it does include all the instructions which are likely to be used in applications level programming. (There are a number of instructions which are primarily of interest to systems programmers and are not really relevant to normal programming.)

1.1.2 Exercise

1. Please complete the following in ten words or less:

    'It is important that I know assembler language programming because...'

CHAPTER TWO

Bits, bytes and numbers

It is a common misconception that computers are mostly about numbers. In fact, they are as much about characters and symbols as they are about numbers. The most fundamental type of object manipulated by a computer is the bit pattern. It is *our interpretation* of the behaviour of the computer which assigns meaning to the bit patterns as they are transformed from one form to another. As far as the internal electronic circuits within the computer are concerned *there are only bit patterns*, there are no 'numbers' or 'characters' within the machine's memory.

The interpretation that we associate with a given bit pattern depends on the context and use that is being made of it: it can be a number, a character, a program instruction, a set, a packed record: the list of possibilities is endless. Any particular interpretation of a pattern is primarily in the mind of the programmer, not within the machine. On the other hand, since it is always possible to interpret a bit pattern as an integer, we often use numbers to write down bit patterns even if there is no intention to denote an integer.

A bit pattern is simply a sequence of ons and offs, 1s and 0s. Most computers manipulate bit patterns in fixed length chunks – normally they cannot easily deal with a quantity smaller than a **byte**. A byte is a sequence of 8 bits. A byte in memory can be said to have a value – the pattern of the state of the 8 switches or bits it contains. Some values that a byte might take on are:

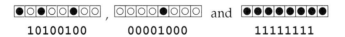

In all, there are 2^8 or 256 possible patterns that 8 bits can take. By associating each of these patterns with a number we can represent any one of 256 different numbers in a byte, usually written as the range 0...255 although the range could be represented by any range of 256 integers:

-128...127 or even 1012...1267. Although we might present the bit pattern in a byte as a number it is not to be confused with the number itself: a bit pattern is just that – a pattern.

Bytes are a convenient size because we can represent a character from the ASCII character set (say) easily in a single byte and character processing applications are extremely common and important in computing. It should be said that some character sets – especially the Japanese characters – require two bytes per character.

Larger groupings of bytes are also common: typically a modern computer will group two bytes together to form a **word** (sometimes called a half-word) and two 16 bit words together form a **long word**. A 16 bit word can represent up to 2^{16} numbers, for example in the range 0...65535. A long word is 32 bits long and can represent 2^{32} numbers, for example integers in the range -2,147,483,648...2,147,483,647.

Having said that the fundamental structure in a computer is a bit pattern, it is also fair to say that the representation of numbers and of arithmetic play an extremely important role in computer applications. This is not simply in obvious areas such as spreadsheet programs and graphics but also within the execution of any program. For example, each byte that is held in memory, or on disk, has an address associated with it. That address is also a number; and address arithmetic is vital in accessing data within the machine.

So, we shall explore some of the issues involved in the representation of various kinds of numeric values. In particular we look at integers, how negative numbers are arrived at and how arithmetic is performed using strings of bits. We also explore other kinds of number systems such as fixed point and floating point numbers. In this way, we can prepare ourselves for the issues of representing data in general in computers.

2.1 Representing numbers in a machine

A number is an abstract mathematical entity which is not tied to a particular representation or defining instance. Thus a number should not be confused with written representations of the number. For example, the following expressions are all equivalent:

sixty five thousand five hundred and thirty six   English decimal
65536   Decimal
$10000   Hexadecimal
10000000000000000B   Binary
LXVDXXXVI   Roman numerals

These expressions are all equivalent in the sense that they denote the same number: they are **numerals**. A numeral is an expression which denotes a number.

The decimal notation that we are familiar with is a shorthand notation for an expansion into a sum of terms, each of which is a multiple of a power of 10. Each digit in the numeral corresponds to the factor in a different term in the expansion; where the position of the digit indicates which power of 10 is referred to.

For example, we can expand the number 'sixty five thousand five hundred and thirty six' into a sum of powers of 10; and we can also expand it as a sum of powers of 16 or 2:

$$
\begin{aligned}
65536 \quad &= 6*10^4+5*10^3+5*10^2+3*10^1+6*10^0 \\
&= 1*16^4+0*16^3+0*16^2+0*16^1+0*16^0 \\
&= 1*2^{16}+0*2^{15}+...+0*2^0
\end{aligned}
$$

All these equations refer to the same number, a slightly different expansion will give a different number:

$$
\begin{aligned}
65535 \quad &= 6*10^4+5*10^3+5*10^2+3*10^1+5*10^0 \\
&= 0*16^4+15*16^3+15*16^2+15*16^1+15*16^0 \\
&= 0*2^{16}+1*2^{15}+...+1*2^0
\end{aligned}
$$

The so-called *positional notation* is used today, in preference over the Roman system of numbers, because it is useful: we can easily perform arithmetic on numbers by manipulating their decimal numerals. The positional notation is so powerful that we can, for example, teach our children mechanical techniques such as long multiplication and long division to allow them to multiply and divide numbers beyond the scope of simple mental recall.

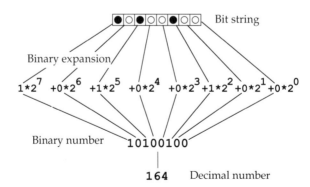

Figure 2.1 *Bit strings and binary expansions*

Each term in a binary expansion of a number is either a 0 or a 1; which we can represent as a switch or a bit (≡ **binary digit**). Just as with decimal notation, the *position* of a bit in a bit string determines the corresponding term in the binary expansion. The decimal expansion series notation for numbers is convenient for ten fingered people, a binary expansion series is similarly convenient for two fingered computers!

From our perspective, the most important property of binary numbers is that it is easy to build circuits that can perform arithmetic by using simple manipulations of the binary bit patterns. These manipulations are analogous to the manipulations that we make on decimal strings and which we call (decimal) arithmetic with the added advantage that the binary versions are often considerably simpler than the familiar decimal ones. In the rest of this chapter we explore some of basic properties of binary numbers and see how binary arithmetic can be performed.

2.2   Arithmetic in fixed length bit strings

In a computer with a fixed length word, we do not do normal arithmetic, instead we do **modulo** arithmetic. Modulo arithmetic has the property that the sum of two numbers (or any other arithmetic operation for that matter) always lies in the same finite range of numbers.

A common example of modulo arithmetic in everyday use is the 12 hour clock. On the 12 hour clock face there are only 12 hours; and therefore there is no direct equivalent of 13 o'Clock (say): only 1 o'Clock. In order to perform a calculation in hours, such as adding 3 hours to 10 o'Clock, we perform the calculation in the normal way and then take the remainder after dividing by 12. 13 remainder 12 is 1, so 10 o'Clock plus 3 hours is 1 o'Clock.

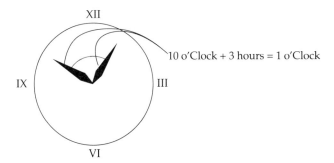

Figure 2.2 *Modulus arithmetic on a clock*

In a byte we can represent 256 numbers, so if we are doing arithmetic within the space of a byte then the most natural form is arithmetic modulo 256. Since it is useful to be able to have a zero in our arithmetic, the range of numbers in modulo 256 is usually described as being from 0...255 rather than from 1...256 as would be analogous to the 12 hour clock. So, if we add 10 to 20 in byte arithmetic we get the answer 30 as expected; but if we add 100 to 200 we get 44 rather than 300 because 300 remainder 256 is 44, or

$$\left|300\right|_{256}=44$$

Although modulo arithmetic has a necessarily limited accuracy/range of representable numbers, it *is* possible to represent arbitrarily large numbers (though not infinitely large numbers). This is done by linking together more than one word/bit pattern to represent the pattern for the whole number. This form of arithmetic is often called multi-precision or *big num* arithmetic. Arithmetic using big nums is much like long arithmetic as taught in school except that the underlying number system is binary rather than decimal. We shall return to this topic when we look at LISP big nums.

2.2.1 Negative numbers

In decimal notation there are several ways that have been used to represent negative numbers. For example, in accounting practice it is common to indicate a negative number by enclosing it in parentheses: (10) is -10 to a bookkeeper. In normal scientific notation we use a special character, the minus '-' sign, to represent a negative number. We could also do something similar in binary notation: we could allocate one of the bits in a bit pattern to signify whether a pattern represents a positive or a negative number. This bit is called the *sign bit*. However, for reasons we shall see below, normally a different notation is used.

There is just one defining property of negative numbers; namely that adding X and $-X$ gives zero as the result:

$$X + -X = 0$$

In modulo N arithmetic all numbers are within the range 0...N-1; including the negative numbers. This means that negative numbers appear to map onto positive numbers; for example if we subtract 4 hours from 2 o'Clock we get 10 o'Clock rather than -2 o'Clock. To form the negative of a number in modulo arithmetic we subtract it from the modulus (12 in this case). For example, to get $|{-4}|_{12}$ we subtract 4 from 12 which gives 8 as the negative of 4. This is because $|4+8=12|_{12}=0$.

There are some particular properties of modulo numbers when combined with a binary representation which make negative values easy to determine. We saw above that we can represent numbers such as 35 as expansions of powers of 2:

$$35 \quad = 0*2^7+0*2^6+1*2^5+0*2^4+0*2^3+0*2^2+1*2^1+1*2^0$$
$$= 00100011B$$

The negative of 35, $|{-35}|_{256}$, is 221, and if we look at the binary expansion of 221 we get:

$$221 \quad = 1*2^7+1*2^6+0*2^5+1*2^4+1*2^3+1*2^2+0*2^1+1*2^0$$
$$= 11011101B$$

Suppose that instead of binary arithmetic in 8 bits we were to use 9 bits. In 9 bits we can get 512 different numbers, so we use modulo 512 arithmetic. As before, we can see that $|{-35}|_{512}$ is 477, and the expansion of 477 is:

$$477 \quad = 1*2^8+1*2^7+1*2^6+0*2^5+1*2^4+1*2^3+1*2^2+0*2^1+1*2^0$$
$$= 111011101B$$

This expansion has the same terms as the expansion for 221, except for an additional term at the beginning. We can repeat this for any number of terms to get an expansion of -35 in any number of bits, so in 16 bit arithmetic (i.e. arithmetic modulo 65536), $|{-35}|_{65536} = 65501$, and the expansion for 65501 is:

$$65501 \quad = 1*2^{15}+1*2^{14}+ \quad \ldots +1*2^6+0*2^5+1*2^4+1*2^3+1*2^2+0*2^1+1*2^0$$
$$= 1111111111011101B$$

The rightmost 8 bits are identical in the representations of 65501, 477 and 221. This is true no matter how many bits we choose to represent our numbers *provided that there are sufficient bits to represent them and their negatives*. We would get into trouble, for example, trying to represent -35 in a 6 bit system. In modulo 64 arithmetic, -35 is equivalent to 29, and this means that we cannot separate the numbers 29 and -35 in a 6 bit system (just as we cannot distinguish -35 and 221 in an 8 bit system); we would have to choose which one the pattern represented. But there is not much point in having a system which allows us to represent -35 but not to represent 29 since $\left|-29\right|_{64} = 35$. In effect we *overflow* a 6 bit representation if we want to represent numbers outside the range -31...31 in 6 bit arithmetic.

Notice that the bit pattern corresponding to -35 is almost exactly complementary to the bit pattern for 35 (assuming that we have enough bits to represent them both faithfully): where there was a 1 we have a 0, and vice versa.   There is, in fact, a simple algorithm for forming the negative of a number in a binary modulo arithmetic system.

If we look at the binary expansion of a number, complement each of the factors in the expansion: i.e. if a factor is 1 then set it to 0 and if it is 0 then set it to 1, and then add 1 to the resulting number then we form the negative of the original number.   So, for example, we can see how to take the negative of 35:

$$35 \qquad = 0*2^7+0*2^6+1*2^5+0*2^4+0*2^3+0*2^2+1*2^1+1*2^0$$

We complement each of the factors in the expansion to get:

$$1*2^7+1*2^6+0*2^5+1*2^4+1*2^3+1*2^2+0*2^1+0*2^0$$

finally we add 1 to the number and we get the new expansion:

$$1*2^7+1*2^6+0*2^5+1*2^4+1*2^3+1*2^2+0*2^1+1*2^0$$

which is the expansion for 221, which we already know is equivalent to -35 in modulo 256 arithmetic.

A good question to ask is given that we can represent -128, what happens to 128?   In fact the 8 bit pattern for -128 is identical to the pattern for 128; this means that we cannot represent both in 8 bits.   All the negative numbers in the range -127...-1 have the most significant bit set in their binary numerals, 128 and -128 also have the most significant bit set. If we choose -128 to be in accord with the other negative numbers, then we have a simple test for negative numbers: their most significant bit is set.

The signed form of representation is called *2's complement*, and arithmetic using this representation is called *2's complement arithmetic*. Nearly all modern computers use this type of arithmetic as the basic form of integer arithmetic.   Integer arithmetic may be supplemented by some form of fractional arithmetic, typically floating point, but even that is sometimes based on 2's complement arithmetic.

Typically, in a computer, we often mix our use of numbers – sometimes we regard a bit string as representing unsigned numbers, and at other times it is interpreted as signed.   In both forms the interpretation is the same for positive numbers (i.e. numbers in the range 0...127 for byte arithmetic).   In fact, the operations needed to perform simple arithmetic (addition and subtraction) are identical regardless of whether the pattern is a signed number or an unsigned number. This is useful for computer designers in that it reduces the complexity of the processor.

2.2.2 Multiplication of binary numbers

After addition and subtraction the most common arithmetic operation occurring in programs is multiplication. Also, in addition to those occasions where we explicitly use multiplication, there are other less obvious situations where multiplications are implied. For example, in order to access entries in vectors and matrices it is often necessary to perform a multiplication to convert an index into an offset within the memory area allocated to the vector or matrix data.

Whilst many micro-processors have a multiplication instruction, some do not; furthermore general purpose multiplication tends to be one of the more expensive operations. If we know in advance the multiplier in a multiplication – as we typically would in an array access – then we can convert the multiplication into a sequence of simpler operations which use much faster instructions.

Suppose that we wanted to multiply an unknown number **I** by a known multiplier **M**. We can express this as the product of the binary expansion for **M** multiplied by **I**.

$$\mathbf{M} \qquad = m_0 * 2^0 + m_1 * 2^1 + \ldots + m_n * 2^n, \text{ where each } m_i \text{ is 0 or 1.}$$

$$\begin{aligned} \mathbf{M*I} \quad &= m_0 * 2^0 * I + m_1 * 2^1 * I + \ldots + m_n * 2^n * I \\ &= m_0 * I * 2^0 + m_1 * I * 2^1 + \ldots + m_n * I * 2^n \end{aligned}$$

In binary arithmetic, we can multiply a number by 2 by shifting its bit pattern one place to the left. Such an operation is extremely cheap to compute on a computer since the bit manipulation involved is very simple. In general, a shift expression such as X<<Y refers to the value X left shifted by Y places, meaning that the bit pattern which makes up X is moved Y places to the left and the vacated bits on the right are filled with zeros. Any bits which 'fall off' the left hand end are lost (except for the last such bit which is often kept in a special flag).

Using this, we can rewrite the multiplication as a sum of shifts:

$$\mathbf{M*I} \quad = m_0 * (I<<0) + m_1 * (I<<1) + \ldots + m_n * (I<<n)$$

In effect, in this breakdown of the multiplication of two numbers, we are using the bit pattern of the multiplier to control the accumulation of shifted multiplicand terms. For example, if we wanted to represent the expression: `i*10` we get:

$$i*10 \quad = i*8+i*2 \qquad \text{since } 10=\mathbf{1}*2^3+\mathbf{0}*2^2+\mathbf{1}*2^1+\mathbf{0}*2^0$$
$$= i<<3 + i<<1$$

This expression, involving two shifts and an add, is often twice as fast compared to using a general purpose multiply instruction to perform the same multiplication.

General purpose multiplication

We can also see how a general purpose multiplication algorithm can be constructed from this principle. Notice that in order to multiply **I** by **M** we successively add together terms of the form

$$I<<k$$

depending on whether the corresponding term $\mathbf{m}_k$ in the expansion for **M** is a 1 or 0. We can organize a loop whereby in each iteration we form the next term of the form `I<<k+1`, and add it to the result so far if the corresponding $\mathbf{m}_{k+1}$ is a 1. We can find the successive $\mathbf{m}_k$'s by using a *shift* operation on the number **M**: in each iteration of the loop we *divide* the multiplicand by 2. The remainder of this division is either a 1 or 0 depending on the value of the least significant bit:

$$\mathbf{M} \quad = \mathbf{m_0}*2^0+\mathbf{m_1}*2^1+...+\mathbf{m_n}*2^n$$

$$\mathbf{M}\div 2 \quad = (\mathbf{m_0}*2^0+\mathbf{m_1}*2^1+...+\mathbf{m_n}*2^n)\div 2$$
$$= \mathbf{m_1}*2^0+...+\mathbf{m_n}*2^{n-1} + \mathbf{m_0}\div 2$$

which might be better expressed as

$$= \mathbf{m_1}*2^0+...+\mathbf{m_n}*2^{n-1} + \text{remainder } \mathbf{m_0}$$

This amounts to a shift of the multiplier to the right with the remainder term dropping from the right hand end of the number. We use the remainder term to decide whether or not to add the current `I<<k` term to the result so far. So, each iteration of the loop performs three operations:

1)   Divide multiplier by 2, taking the remainder into C:

$$\mathtt{M:=M\div 2;} \quad \mathtt{C:=}remainder;$$

This can be done in a single step on most computers because a division by 2 can be achieved with a *right shift*. The bit pattern in the number is shifted one position to the right; the leftmost bit position is filled with a zero, and the rightmost bit which is lost from the bit pattern is typically stored in a special 1 bit register or flag. We can test this C flag and...

2)   if C = 1 then add current multiplicand to answer so far:

   `A:=A+I;`

3)   We compute the next multiplicand term `I<<k+1` by multiplying the current one by 2, i.e. by shifting it one bit to the left:

   `I:=I<<1.`

We perform this loop for however many significant bits there are in the expansion of the multiplier; and the algorithm is initialized by setting the answer A to 0. Figure 2.3 illustrates how the algorithm applies if we let M=5 and I=10:

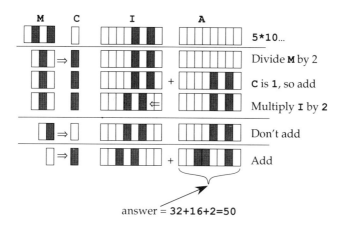

answer = 32+16+2=50

Figure 2.3 *The multiplication of 5 by 10*

If the numbers involved are 32 bits long (say) then we know that after doing the loop 32 times there can be no more significant bits in the multiplier, so the loop is performed no more than 32 times.

In general, the result of the multiplication may have as many significant bits in it as are in the multiplier and multiplicand together – that is why the multiply instructions on a processor tend to produce double precision answers: a 16 bit multiply generates a 32 bit answer.

The algorithm as we have stated it is only correct for positive numbers. However, it is a simple matter to extend it to signed multiplication by noting the equality:

$$\texttt{x*y} \quad = \quad \texttt{sign(x)*sign(y)*abs(x)*abs(y)}$$

We can separately multiply the signs and the absolute quantities of **x** and **y**. The sign multiplication is a simple calculation:

$$\texttt{s(x)*s(y)} \quad = \quad \texttt{(s(x)} \wedge \texttt{s(y))} \quad \vee \quad \texttt{(}\overline{\texttt{s(x)}} \wedge \overline{\texttt{s(y)}}\texttt{)}$$

where **s(x)** is **0** if **x** is positive, and **1** if **x** is negative. This multiplication algorithm is the basis for hardware multiplication instructions.

2.2.3 Division of binary numbers

If we want to see how division is performed in the computer it is useful to go back to school, and see how long division is done there; for the division of binary numbers borrows greatly from school level arithmetic. A classic 'sum' that we might do in school is:

$$1989 \div 16$$

which, using standard long division has, as its first step, the division of 19 by 16:

```
        1
   16  1989
        16
       ----
        3
```

The quotient of this division step – 1 – is also the first digit of the quotient of the whole calculation, and the remainder – 3 – is used in the rest of the division. The next step in the long division is to divide 38 by 16:

```
        12
   16  1989
        16
       ----
        38
        32
       ----
         6
```

The quotient and remainder of this division – 2 and 6 respectively – form the next digit of the complete quotient and the new rest-of-dividend. The calculation continues to remove digits from the dividend until we have run out of digits. The remainder of the last sub-division is the remainder of the whole division:

```
            124
      16  1989
            16
            38        1989÷16 = 124  remainder  5
            32
            69
            64
             5
```

We can see why long division works by looking at the first step a little more closely. In particular to divide 1989 by 16 we split it into a most significant part and a least significant part:

$$1989÷16 = (19÷16)*100 + (89÷16)$$

we can now divide 19 by 16 to get

$$= (1+3÷16)*100+(89÷16)$$

because 19÷16 = 1 rem 3. Unpacking the expression gives us

$$= 100 + 300÷16+89÷16$$

We can now merge the two divisions

$$= 100 + 389÷16$$

because 300÷16+89÷16 = (300+89)÷16

The most significant decimal digit of 100 – i.e. 1 – is both the quotient of the sub-division of 19÷16 *and* the most significant digit of the full quotient. As a result of this last step, the whole calculation of 1989÷16 is reduced to the smaller one of 389÷16 the quotient of which is guaranteed to be less than 100.

In general, in each step of the long division, we split the dividend – $\mathcal{D}$ – into two parts: the dividend-so-far $\mathcal{D}_a$ and the rest-of-the-dividend $\mathcal{D}_b$ such that

$$\mathcal{D} = \mathcal{D}_a*10^i + \mathcal{D}_b \qquad \text{for some } i, \text{ where } \mathcal{D}_b<10^i$$

we can choose i so that dividing $\mathcal{D}_a$ by the divisor $\mathcal{V}$ results in a single digit quotient:

$$0≤\mathcal{D}_a÷\mathcal{V}≤9$$

We can now perform a single step of the long division of $\mathcal{D} \div \mathcal{V}$ abstractly:

$$
\begin{aligned}
\mathcal{D} \div \mathcal{V} \quad &= \quad \mathcal{D}_a * 10^i \div \mathcal{V} + \mathcal{D}_b \div \mathcal{V} \\
&= \quad (\mathcal{D}_a \text{ div } \mathcal{V}) * 10^i + (\mathcal{D}_a \text{ rem } \mathcal{V} * 10^i + \mathcal{D}b) \div \mathcal{V}
\end{aligned}
$$

where $\mathcal{D}_a$ div $\mathcal{V}$ refers to the quotient of $\mathcal{D}_a \div \mathcal{V}$ and $\mathcal{D}_a$ rem $\mathcal{V}$ refers to the remainder. Referring to our example, we get:

$$
\begin{aligned}
1989 \div 16 \quad &= \quad 19 * 10^2 \div 16 + 89 \div 16 \\
&= \quad 1 * 10^2 + (3 * 10^2 + 89) \div 16
\end{aligned}
$$

Since $(\mathcal{D}_a$ rem $\mathcal{V}) < \mathcal{V}$, and $\mathcal{D}_b < 10^i$, we are guaranteed that $(\mathcal{D}_a$ rem $\mathcal{V} * 10^i + \mathcal{D}_b) \div \mathcal{V} < 10^i$ also. Subsequent steps, which involve the term $\mathcal{D}_a$ rem $\mathcal{V} * 10^i + \mathcal{D}_b$, cannot affect the quotient digits calculated so far.

The most significant digit of the full quotient is obtained from this sub-division, and the remainder is used to form the next dividend-so-far $\mathcal{D}_a{'}$ and the next rest-of-dividend $\mathcal{D}_b{'}$:

$$
\begin{aligned}
\mathcal{D}_a{'} &= (\mathcal{D}_a \text{ rem } \mathcal{V}) * 10 + d \\
\mathcal{D}_b{'} &= \mathcal{D}_b \text{ rem } 10^{i-1}
\end{aligned}
$$

where d = most significant digit of $\mathcal{D}_b$, and $\mathcal{D}_b{'}$ is the rest of $\mathcal{D}_b$.

When, finally, $\mathcal{D}_b{'}$ becomes zero, and there are no more digits left in the dividend, then the corresponding $\mathcal{D}_a{'}$ is the remainder of the whole division and the quotient can be extracted from the intermediate quotient digits computed along the way.

In each step of the long division we can concern ourselves with only the most significant part of the dividend – in particular we can rely on the property that the quotient of the sub-calculation is a single digit. The full quotient is calculated one digit at a time. For school children of all ages it is easier to perform such divisions than full divisions involving multi-digit quotients and this is equally true for computers.

We can apply the same kind of reasoning to long division using binary expansions for numbers as well as for decimal expansions. As with binary multiplication, the use of binary expansions considerably simplifies the procedures needed to perform long division.

If we know that the quotient of $\mathcal{D}_a \div \mathcal{V}$ is a single *binary* digit – 0 or 1 – then we also know that

$$0 \le \mathcal{D}_a < 2 * \mathcal{V}$$

Performing the sub-division $\mathcal{D}_a \div \mathcal{V}$ amounts to a subtraction: if $\mathcal{D}_a - \mathcal{V} \ge 0$ then the quotient of is 1, and it is 0 if $\mathcal{D}_a < \mathcal{V}$. Thus at the heart of binary long division is a simple subtraction and comparison. The binary version of our example above is:

```
10000B⌐11111000101B
```

The very first step in this long division would be to attempt the division: 1÷1000B, which is, of course, 0. Thus the leading binary digit of the quotient is 0. The next step would be to add an extra digit from the rest of the dividend and try again: 11B÷1000B, which also has a zero quotient. The first step which results in a non-zero quotient digit is:

```
          00001
10000B⌐11111000101B
       10000
        1111
```

In the step that follows this one, we can compute the next dividend-so-far by left shifting the remainder by one bit. The *least* significant bit of the new dividend-so-far can be obtained from the *most* significant bit of the rest-of-the-dividend. This is done by shifting the rest-of-the-dividend to the left and extracting the bit that 'drops off'; this bit is then inserted into the dividend-so-far as it is shifted to the left. The effect of this bit twiddling is to bring down the next binary digit from the rest-of-dividend into the current dividend.

The new dividend looks like:

```
          000010
10000B⌐11111000101B
       10000
        11110
        1110
```

The complete binary division sum looks like:

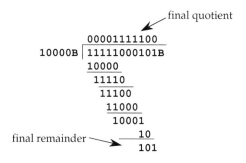

final quotient

```
              00001111100
10000B⌐11111000101B
       10000
        11110
         11100
          11000
           10001
            10
            101
```

final remainder

We can implement binary long division using bit strings in registers. We use one register (R) to represent the dividend-so-far, which in each step is compared against the divisor (V), and a third register holds the rest-of-the-dividend (D). A left shift of the rest-of-the-dividend into the dividend-so-far mimics the action of moving a digit from the dividend to the right of the current remainder:

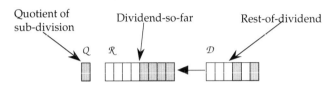

If we want to accumulate the digits of the quotient we can do so by setting the least significant bit of a quotient register to the quotient digit obtained at each step, and then left shifting it along with the dividend-so-far and rest-of-dividend between steps. The rest of the complete division, in terms of comparisons and left shifting can be seen though the sequence:

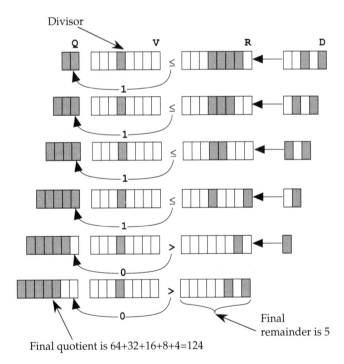

Figure 2.4 *The division of 1989 by 16*

When the last digit has been shifted out of the the dividend then the algorithm stops, and the quotient register contains the full quotient, and the remainder is held in the dividend-so-far register.   The complete division algorithm is:

Set $\mathcal{R}$ to zero and set Q to zero; $\mathcal{D}$ to dividend and $\mathcal{V}$ to divisor.

Repeat for each bit in the dividend:

1)   Left shift $\mathcal{D}$ by one bit, shifting its most significant bit into x;
Left shift $\mathcal{R}$ by one bit, shifting x into $\mathcal{R}$'s least significant bit.

2)   If $\mathcal{V} \leq \mathcal{R}$ then
          set x to 1, and subtract $\mathcal{V}$ from $\mathcal{R}$
     else
          set x to 0.

3)   Left shift Q by 1, shifting x into Q's least significant bit.

As with binary multiplication, this algorithm is only correct for unsigned division; in order to perform signed division we can convert it into an unsigned division together with an appropriate sign calculation.

2.2.4 Exercises

1.   a)   What is the binary expansion for 1000?

     b)   What is the value of $\left| -1000 \right|_{65536}$?

2.   How many bits are needed to faithfully represent all the integers in the range 20...26?

3.   Show how the 2's complement procedure of 'complementing bits and adding 1' for negating numbers can be deduced from the negation axiom and modulo arithmetic applied to binary numbers.

Hint: Take the binary expansion of an arbitrary number, subtract it from the binary expansion of the modulus.

4.   Show the intermediate products involved in multiplying 35 by 24

5.   Use the division algorithm to divide 10 by 0. What answer would you
     have expected? What happens when you divide 0 by 0?

6.   If the complexity of a 32 bit addition is 32 (from 32 separate bit-wise
     additions plus carry), then the complexity of a 32 bit multiply is
     essentially 32 additions, i.e. 32^2. In general, when counting the
     complexity of bits, a multiply of N bits is $O(N^2)$.

     We can do rather better than this when multiplying 2^n bit numbers.
     Suppose we want to multiply a $\times$ b each of which is a 2^n bit number,
     then we can re-express the multiplication as follows:

     $a = a_0 + E \times a_1$

     and

     $b = b_0 + E \times b_1$ where $E = 2^{n/2}$

     To multiply a and b then, we can form four separate multiplications
     and three additions:

     $a \times b \quad = (a_0 + E \times a_1) \times (b_0 + E \times b_1)$
     $\qquad\quad = a_0 b_0 + (a_0 b_1 + a_1 b_0) \times E + a_1 b_1 \times E^2$

     Since each of a_0, a_1, b_0 and b_1 have half as many bits as a and b
     respectively, the complexity of their multiplication is $0.25 \times O(n^2)$
     which does not achieve very much since we have four of them to do.
     However, we can save one multiplication based on the observation
     that

     $a_0 b_1 + a_1 b_0 = (a_0 + a_1)(b_0 + b_1) - a_0 b_0 - a_1 b_1$

     We already need the calculation of $a_0 b_0$ and $a_1 b_1$ to compute a$\times$b; so
     these two sub-multiplications are shared.

     Show how to implement a bit-wise multiplication algorithm based on
     a recursive version of this split. I.e. at each level of the recursion, split
     the numbers, multiply the parts and combine the results.

     What is the complexity of the recursive algorithm for multiplication?

2.3 Other kinds of numerals

Whilst integers are obviously very important to computer programmers and users, there are many applications where they are not sufficient. For their sake we look at numeral systems which allow fractional numbers to be represented; in particular we are interested in fixed point numbers and floating point numbers.

2.3.1 Fixed point numbers

Perhaps the simplest extension to integers is the system of so-called fixed point numbers. As the term suggests, a fixed point number consists of a number with a fixed position of the binary point within the number; i.e. with a fixed number of digits allocated to the integral and fractional parts. For example, we might choose to have a fixed point number with 16 bits for the integral part and 16 bits for the fractional part:

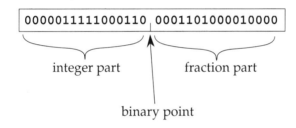

Figure 2.5 *Fixed point representation of 1990.1018*

The number of bits that we allocate to the integral part of a fixed point number determines the *range* of numbers that can be represented; the number of bits allocated to the fraction part determines the *accuracy* of the resulting number. In the example here, where we have allocated 16 bits for the integral part and 16 bits for the fraction part, we can approximate numbers in the range -32768..32767 with a fraction accuracy of one part in 65536.

Notice that the fixed point concept includes the case of integers: simply set the number of bits allocated to the fractional part to zero and the result is an integer.

Binary fractions

Recall that in the standard positional notation for integers, each bit stands for the coefficient of a power term. The same applies for the fractional part of a number, except that we use negative powers: each successive power term in the fraction represent a smaller magnitude number rather than a greater magnitude number. So, for example, the fractional number 0.275 can be expanded:

$$0.275 \quad = 0*2^0 + 0*2^{-1} + 1*2^{-2} + 0*2^{-3} + 1*2^{-4}$$

So, the binary expression of 0.275 becomes

$$0.275 \quad = 0.0101B$$

The main difference between expanding integers and expanding fractions is that many expanding series of fractions are infinite. Worse than this, some fractions are infinite in binary, even if they are finite in decimal. For example, the decimal fraction 0.3 becomes, in binary:

$$0.3 \quad = 0*2^0 + 0*2^{-1} + 1*2^{-2} + 1*2^{-3} + 0*2^{-4} + 0*2^{-5} + 1*2^{-6} + 1*2^{-7} \ldots$$
$$= 0.011001100110011\ldots B$$

On the other hand, there are no finite binary fractions which cannot be represented exactly as a finite decimal fraction. (This is because any term of the form 2^{-x} can be expressed as a finite sum of powers of 10.)

Fixed point arithmetic
We can perform fixed point arithmetic using many of the same operations that are used when performing integer arithmetic. This is because we can effectively factor out the existence of the fractional part in the number.

For example, suppose that we wanted to add 12.34 to 5.67 in a system of decimal fixed points in which we have allocated four digits for the integer part and two digits to the fraction. Since the decimal point is fixed, we can re-express these numbers as products of significant integers and a known power of 10:

$$12.34 \quad = \quad 1234 * 10^{-2}$$

$$5.67 \quad = \quad 567 * 10^{-2}$$

With this in mind we can perform our fixed point arithmetic separately on the significant integer and the powers of 10:

$$12.34 + 5.67 \quad = \quad 1234*10^{-2} + 567*10^{-2}$$
$$= \quad (1234+567)*10^{-2}$$
$$= \quad 1801*10^{-2}$$
$$= \quad 18.01$$

Thus, to add two fixed point numbers we can simply add up their bit patterns as though they represented integers. As we shall see, this procedure is somewhat simpler than that for adding two floating point numbers and this simplicity is the reason that fixed point numbers are computationally efficient.

Multiplying two fixed point numbers is slightly more complicated than adding them because we are also required to multiply the two powers of 10:

$$
\begin{aligned}
12.34 * 5.67 \quad &= \quad 1234*10^{-2} * 567*10^{-2} \\
&= \quad (1234*567)*10^{-4} \\
&= \quad 699678*10^{-4} \\
&= \quad 69.9678
\end{aligned}
$$

Since this product has four digits in the fraction and in our fixed point format we only allow two decimal digits for the fraction, we must adjust the result. This adjustment is accomplished by dividing the result of the integer multiplication by 100 and ignoring the remainder. The result of this division is that we 'lose' the two least significant digits to produce an answer with the same represented accuracy as the two operands:

$$12.34 * 5.67 \quad \approx \quad 69.96$$

This loss of accuracy is inevitable with a fixed point number system since we must always ensure that the result has its decimal point in a fixed place.

The arithmetic for binary fixed point numbers is exactly the same as for decimal fixed point numbers; except that in order to adjust the result after a multiplication (and division) we have to divide by a power of 2 rather than a power of 10. Such a division is easily achieved on a computer by a shift instruction.

Fixed point numbers are only slightly more complicated to manipulate than integers. As a result they are very fast, considerably faster on most computers than floating point numbers for example. For those applications where it is relatively easy to predict the required range of numbers, and that range is not very great, then fixed point numbers are very suitable.

There are many applications that fall into that category. For example, in a real-time radar tracking application, the input data is likely to consist of pairs of angles and distances. The angular data will consist of numbers in the range 0...360 and will therefore all be of a similar size. The distance information is likely to have a larger range but may still be in a relatively manageable band. The effect of this constraint is that a fixed point system may well be sufficient to represent and manipulate the angle and distance data.

On the other hand, given the loss of accuracy that results when multiplying two fixed point numbers together, and given the difficulty of predicting the suitable allocation of bits to the integer and fraction part of a fixed point number, few programming languages provide direct support for fixed point numbers. Instead, effort is concentrated on floating point numbers which are more stable in their accuracy.

2.3.2 Floating point numbers

We saw above that when two fixed point numbers are multiplied together (or divided) we lose some digits of accuracy simply because of the fixed point format. It would only require a few multiplications in succession for the accuracy of a fixed point calculation to be totally compromised. There are many applications where that would be unacceptable.

We can partially avoid the problem by storing the position of the binary/decimal point *explicitly* along with the significant digits which make up the number. With this arrangement, it becomes clear what to do when we multiply two numbers: instead of an artificial division to ensure the fixed point, the floating point is adjusted instead.

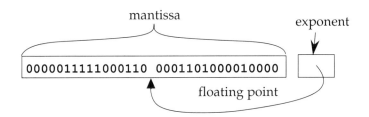

Figure 2.6 *Floating point representation of 1990.1018*

We call the string of digits which form the significant digits of the number the *mantissa* or *fraction* and the number which indicates the position of the floating point the *exponent*.

One immediate point to notice here is that the binary point need not be within the mantissa: it can be outside it. That is, we can also represent very large numbers (by having the pointer to the right of the mantissa) and numbers which are close to zero (by having the pointer to the left of the mantissa).

An alternative way of understanding the binary point pointer is that it is a multiplier: the floating point number is represented as a mantissa multiplied by a power of 2 (or 10 in the case of decimal floating point systems or even 16 in the case of some early floating point systems). Hence the term exponent for the binary point pointer. A formal way of describing a floating point number is that it is the value of the expression:

$$\mathcal{F}.p \quad = \quad mantissa \star 2^{\,exponent}$$

The exact interpretation of the mantissa varies with different systems. Some systems, in particular early Burroughs computers, interpret the mantissa as a 2's complement integer. In this system, an exponent of zero indicates a normal integer value being held in the floating point number. This arrangement simplifies the arithmetic and allows an integer to be physically a subset of a floating point number. However, most floating point formats, and the IEEE floating point standard in particular, normally regard the binary/decimal point as being on the left of the mantissa.

In fact, for reasons that we shall see shortly, the standard representation of the mantissa is 'sign and magnitude': a separate bit is used to represent the sign of the number and the magnitude of the mantissa is represented as a positive number. So, the full expression of a floating point number is:

$$I.\mathcal{E}.\mathcal{F}.p \quad = \quad (\text{-}1)^{\,sign} \star mantissa \star 2^{\,exponent}$$

If the number of significant digits of a number is less than the supported accuracy (i.e. less than the number of possible digits in the mantissa) then there are several configurations possible:

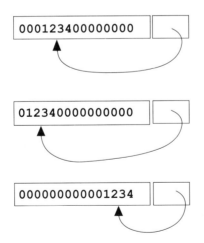

Figure 2.7 *Different floating point representations of* `12.34`

Given that, when multiplying numbers there is a tendency for digits to grow, it is convenient to arrange to shift the significant digits of a number so that the most significant digit is at one end of the mantissa (usually the left end). This way we can leave room for the number of digits to expand:

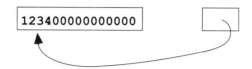

Figure 2.8 *Normalized representation of 12.34*

Such numbers, where the leftmost digit of the mantissa is guaranteed to be non-zero, are called *normalized*. We can gain a further benefit from normalizing numbers in a binary system.

Since, in a normalized number, the leading bit in a *binary* floating point number is always going to be a '1' then we do not actually need to store that bit. This has the effect of giving an extra bit of accuracy for 'free' in our representation, and we can represent twice as many numbers.

The problem of multiple representations of a number is considerably magnified when it comes to representing floating point zero. Clearly, the mantissa of zero is also zero; however, the exponent could be any value. However, to ease comparison it makes obvious sense to standardize on an exponent of zero. This has the added benefit that integer zero and floating point zero have the same bit pattern.

The exponent is an unusual number in that a very negative value does not imply a negative floating point value, but rather a very small one. If we stored the exponent as a simple number, then small numbers would look quite different from zero:

Figure 2.9 *Floating point zero*

looks quite different to:

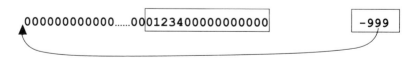

Figure 2.10 *A very small floating point number*

This discontinuity between very small numbers – whose exponents are very negative – and zero suggests that a smoother system might *bias* the exponents by adding a large value to them. If we bias the exponent by an amount equal to the greatest exponent, then a bit pattern in the exponent field of zero really represents a very small number, and a value of 128 (say in a system with an eight bit binary exponent), represents an exponent multiplier of unity. This system is called biassed exponent for obvious reasons.

So, the conventional floating point format looks something like:

Figure 2.11 *Floating point number:* $(-1)^s \times 1.mantissa \times 2^{exp-bias}$

We have a sign bit, an exponent which is biassed by the maximum possible exponent, and a mantissa which holds the significant digits of the floating point value. The mantissa is normally adjusted so that the leading bit is non-zero; a fact that we use to avoid storing that most significant bit.

Floating point arithmetic
In order to add two floating point numbers together, it is not sufficient to simply add up their mantissae. We must first adjust them so that their respective exponents are equal, and only then we can add up the mantissae. Of course, to maintain the correct value of the floating point numbers any adjustment of the exponents also involves adjusting the mantissae. So, adding one to the exponent of a floating point number would need to be compensated by dividing the mantissa by 10 (or 2 in the case of binary floating points). Similarly, if we subtracted three from the exponent, we would need to multiply the mantissa by 10^3 (or 2^3).

For example, to add up $0.1234*10^2$ and $0.567*10^1$ we must adjust the numbers so that their exponents match. We could do this by multiplying 0.1234 by 10 so that the first number becomes $1.234*10^1$; then, since both exponents would match, the addition would proceed giving $1.801*10^1$ as the result.

However, multiplying the mantissa by a power of 10 (or by a power of 2 in the case of binary floating points) involves a left shift, and in a fixed field this left shift is likely to cause the most significant digits of the mantissa to be shifted out of the number. This would compromise the accuracy of the result. If instead, we *divide* the smaller of the two operands by 10 we could also align the numbers:

$$0.567*10^1 = 0.0567*10^2$$

Now if we add up the numbers we get $0.1801*10^2$; but, more importantly, any digits which might be lost by dividing the mantissa by 10 are the *least significant* digits from the smaller of the two numbers. This will minimize any errors arising from the addition.

Many floating point systems further reduce any errors by adding one or more guard digits. Guard digits are not stored with the number but are used to collect the last digits that were shifted out of the number as a result of aligning it in order to perform the addition. These guard digits are used during the calculation and only afterwards, when the result is stored in the normal format, are the guard digits finally lost.

After adding the two mantissae, it is possible that the result is no longer normalized. Therefore, after the addition has taken place the number must be re-normalized. This could mean that the guard digits reappear if normalization implies that the mantissa is shifted to the right. If normalization means that the mantissa must be left shifted – i.e. if the addition resulted in a carry being generated – then the guard digits are really lost. That should not concern us so much since we are storing the result as accurately as possible in the given number of bits.

Floating point multiplication is less complicated than addition since we do not need to align the numbers before performing the multiplication. Instead, we can separately multiply the mantissae and *add* the exponents:

$$0.1234*10^2 * 0.567*10^1 = (0.1234*0.567)*10^{(2+1)}$$
$$= 0.0699678 * 10^3$$

Again, we potentially need to adjust the result to ensure that it is normalized, and this may mean a shift to the left (as in this case). If we had used some guard digits to hold the extra digits generated as a result of the multiplication then some of these would be shifted back into the number during normalization:

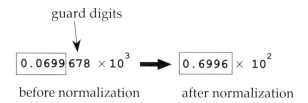

Figure 2.12 *Guard digits in normalization*

IEEE Floating point numbers

We have mentioned a few times the IEEE floating point standard. This standard arose out of the proliferation of different methods of representing floating point numbers (for example where to put the binary point, how many bits to allocate to the exponent etc.) Unlike 2's complement arithmetic for integers, there is no particular mathematical reason for choosing one format over another and this has led to great variety of formats.

The IEEE standard imposes a particular representation of floating point numbers. It standardises on the layout, on the number of bits allocated to the exponent versus the mantissa (or *fraction* as it is called in the standard) and on a minimal set of operations that can be performed on floating point numbers.

Over and above this, it uses some of the bit patterns to represent other numbers: in particular $\pm\infty$ and a special type of number called a NaN (or Not a Number). NaNs serve a special role to indicate that the result of a computation is not representable as a number, for example dividing any number by zero will result in a NaN.

NaNs have the peculiar property that any calculation involving a NaN leaves a NaN as its result. The effect of this is to propagate the error condition through any calculation that generates the nonsense result. In particular, if an error occurs deep in a calculation the final result will still show an error. Using a NaN rather than some apparently correct number allows the calculation to proceed and yet not result in erroneous results.

2.3.3 Hexadecimal notation

Although the natural system of numbers for a computer is binary, writing down numbers using only binary digits uses a lot of digits: a 16 bit number may require up to 16 binary digits even though the same number in decimal will only require up to 5 digits (possibly plus a sign). A variation on binary which allows a more compact representation is hexadecimal. There are 16 digits in hexadecimal arithmetic written as 0,1,2,...,9,A,B,C,D,E,F corresponding to the decimal numbers 0,1,2,...,9,10,11,12,13,14 and 15 respectively. So, for example, the decimal number 35 would be 23 in hexadecimal notation. To distinguish between decimal, binary and hexadecimal numbers we prefix hexadecimal numbers with an '$' and suffix binary numbers with a 'B'. Another common convention for hexadecimal numbers is to suffix them with an 'H'. This convention also requires – in many compilers and assemblers – that the first digit of a hexadecimal number be a decimal digit. If it would normally be a letter, for example decimal **211** is **DD** in hexadecimal, then a leading zero is added: **0DDH**.

Hexadecimal is arguably the most natural number system for assembler programmers; many assembler level tools – such as debuggers and monitors – print internal numbers in hexadecimal as the default.

The real reason that hexadecimal is convenient is that a single hex digit corresponds exactly to 4 binary digits. Thus we can easily convert between binary and hexadecimal as needed. This is not the case for pure decimal – there is no easy match between binary digits and decimal digits. Furthermore two hex digits form a byte which is usually the smallest addressable unit in the machine.

2.3.4 Exercises

1. Suppose that we had a system of decimal fixed point numbers, with two digits of accuracy. If we start with an initial value of **0.50**, it would take just three successive squares before we ended up with a value of zero:

    $$0.50^2 \;\Rightarrow\; 0.25 \qquad\qquad \text{no lost digits}$$

    $$0.25^2 \;\Rightarrow\; 0.06 \qquad\qquad \text{lose '25'}$$

    $$0.06^2 \;\Rightarrow\; 0.00 \qquad\qquad \text{lose '36'}$$

    How many iterations would be required to reduce **0.5** to zero in a binary fixed point system with 16 bits allocated to the fraction?

    If the same 16 bits were used to represent the mantissa in a floating point system, how many squares would then be needed before the result degenerated into zero?

2. Give a simple procedure for performing fixed point division; using as a basis integer division. What sources of error are introduced by the fixed point notation?

3. Prove that any number of the form 2^{-x} – where x is a positive integer – can be represented as a finite decimal fraction.

CHAPTER THREE

The 680x0 programmer's model

For us to be able to understand how Pascal programs are implemented on a real computer it is necessary to establish how it is programmed at its own level. This involves understanding the kinds of data objects, variables and statements available to the assembler programmer.

The Pascal programmer has a particular model of the world. This model consists of the legal types of data that can be described, the legal types of program that can be constructed and various programming techniques and algorithms that can be used. Together, these form the grammar and vocabulary of a language which defines the programs that can be written. Although this language is limited when compared to a normal natural language such as English, it is somewhat richer than the native machine language which assembler directly reflects.

The assembler programmer's view of the world can be expressed in similar terms to the Pascal programmer's view: there are a fixed number of global variables called *registers* and a single array called the *memory* of fixed size cells. Unlike Pascal variables, whose names and types are chosen by the programmer, registers nearly always have a fixed name (something interesting like **A0** or **CX**) and a fixed size. There is also a small collection of statement types – called instructions – each of which is usually much simpler than a Pascal statement. A typical processor will have from 100 to 200 different instructions; called collectively the processor's instruction set.

The complete combination of registers, memory and instruction set also forms a language – assembler language – and it is the task of the compiler (us in this case) to translate programs expressed in one into the other. All of the Pascal language constructs must be built from these simple objects.

Registers are an important resource for the assembler programmer; as well as being involved in arithmetic calculations, registers are often used to access the memory array. In addition registers are much faster than memory: it can be 2-10 times faster to access a quantity held in a register compared to memory. For this reason, registers are also used to hold frequently accessed values and variables.

Given the fact that there are only a few registers – the 680x0 has 16 general registers, and there are rarely more than 32 – and because registers can be accessed quickly there is a strong desire to use registers to represent a Pascal program's variables, these register variables must change their meaning from time to time within the program. It is one of the assembler programmer's greatest tasks to keep track of the precise meaning of a register in the various parts of the program.

3.1 The 680x0 registers

The 680x0 has 16 general purpose registers which are split into two banks – the data registers (identified as **d0** through to **d7**) and the address registers (**a0** to **a7**). All these registers are 32 bits long: i.e. sufficient to hold a long word bit pattern.

The 680x0 also has some special purpose registers; in particular the program counter (**PC**) and the condition codes register (**CCR**). If a floating point co-processor is attached to the computer, then there are, in addition, eight floating point registers and a floating point control register. There are a number of other special registers on the 680x0, particularly in the 68020/68030, but they do not normally affect the way that we write general purpose programs.

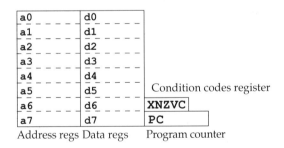

Address regs Data regs   Program counter

Figure 3.1 *Programmer's registers on the 680x0*

The split of the 16 registers into 8 data and 8 address registers roughly reflects a separation of address and data found in Pascal programs The data manipulated by an application program falls into two aspects: literal data values – such as the characters in a string or the numbers in an expression – and the locations or addresses of those values in memory. The two types of data require different kinds of operation and that is reflected in their separation in the 680x0.

The data registers are used to hold the arguments and results of operations. So, for example nearly every arithmetic operation requires at least one of the operands to be in a data register; with the other being in memory or in another data register.

The data registers can be accessed and manipulated as 32 bit registers, or as 8 or 16 bit registers. In the latter cases the least significant 8 or 16 bits of the data register are used and/or affected by an operation. This flexibility reflects the different natures of the data commonly processed: 8 bits are often used for text processing applications for example.

The address registers are most often referred to in the calculation of where data is. So we shall see below – as in the various addressing modes of the 680x0 – that the address registers are often used to establish where the various values are located in memory. It is as though they form a set of 8 pointer variables where the data registers are integer variables. The address registers also have a limited computational power associated with them: mainly the ability to add and subtract into them.

One of the address registers – **a7** – has an additional interpretation: it is the *system stack pointer*. It is sometimes also referred to as **sp**. This pointer is used by the processor as the address to which to save the state of the machine during certain instructions. All of the address registers can be used to implement stacks, but **a7** is used by the processor when *it* needs a stack.

So, when a subroutine or function is called, the stack pointer register indicates where to store the address of the next instruction to be executed so that it can be returned to when the subroutine has completed. We shall see later that we can use this stack for many other purposes: we can use it for allocating space for local variables and for holding temporary values during complex computations.

The 680x0 also has a special *shadow register* of the **a7** register. This shadow **a7** register is used by the operating system as a second stack pointer during the processing of special events such as interrupt processing and virtual memory handling. This allows the operating system to provide a separate memory area which is guaranteed to be sufficient to process interrupts and other operating system events without cluttering up the user's workspace.

In fact, some of the models in the 680x0 range have many other specialized registers. The 68030 has some 30 odd further registers which are used to implement operating system functions such as virtual memory. If a floating point co-processor is attached then there are 8 more floating point registers and three more control registers making a grand total of 64 registers in the 68030. However we will only be concerned with 18 of them – the 16 address and data registers, the condition codes register and the program counter.

It is not *logically necessary* to split registers into data and address registers: one could easily imagine a scheme where there were 16 truly generally purpose registers which did not have a predefined association of being 'data' or 'address'. Not all applications have such an easy separation between addresses and values as is typical of Pascal programs. For example, in language interpreters such as Prolog or LISP interpreters, addresses *are* the data that is most often being manipulated. For programs in these languages, the split into two banks of data and address registers can lead to seemingly awkward programming.

3.1.1 The condition codes register

In most modern processors a special register is set aside to hold the various flags which indicate the state of the machine. In the 680x0 the **condition codes register** (CCR) performs this function. The five principal flags stored in the CCR which are available to the application level assembler programmer are shown in Fig. 3.2:

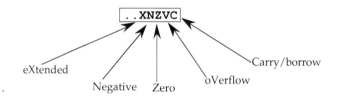

Figure 3.2 *The 68000 condition codes register*

The Carry flag is set whenever the last arithmetic operation resulted in a value which could not be correctly represented in 8/16/32 bit modulo arithmetic (depending on the size of the operation). For example, in 8 bit arithmetic, if we add 100 to 200, then the result will be 44; this is because the true answer – 300 – is represented as 44 in modulo 256 arithmetic. The fact that there was an overflow is signalled by the carry flag being set. The carry flag is also used in the shift operations where it holds the last bit that was shifted out.

The oVerflow flag is set when the last operation resulted in a value that could not be faithfully represented as a signed number in 2's complement. For example, if we add 100 to 50 in 8 bit arithmetic then the result will be 150. But this is a negative number in 2's complement and so the oVerflow flag is set.

The oVerflow flag is important for calculations involving *signed* arithmetic whereas the Carry flag is reflects the result of *unsigned* arithmetic.

The **Z**ero flag is set if the last data value processed was zero. This is often used in comparisons, for example. A comparison is implemented as a subtraction where the result is used only to set flags. If the result of the subtraction was zero then the two values were equal.

The **N**egative flag is set whenever the last value computed was a negative number in 2's complement. In practice that means that the Negative flag tracks the most significant bit (i.e. the sign bit) of values computed in the processor.

The e**X**tend flag is similar to the Carry flag except that it is used in implementing multi-precision arithmetic. Therefore it is also *input* to certain instructions as well as being generated by them.

The individual flags in the CCR are rarely used on their own. Instead various combinations of them are used which represent more meaningful *conditions*. These are the conditions which are directly available to the programmer in instructions such as branch conditional (**b**$_{cc}$) where $_{cc}$ refers to one of the 16 conditions listed below:

Unsigned arithmetic conditions	CC	carry clear	CS	carry set
	HI	high	LS	low or same
	EQ	equal/zero	NE	not equal/non zero
	F	false/never	T	true/always
Signed arithmetic conditions	MI	minus	PL	plus
	VC	overflow clear	VS	overflow set
	GE	greater or equal	LT	less than
	GT	greater than	LE	less or equal

Although nearly all processors have some equivalent to the CCR, an important feature of the 680x0 is that the flags in the CCR are affected by some non-arithmetic operations as well as arithmetic ones. In particular any data transfer to/from memory or a data register will affect them (except for the move multiple **movem** instruction which saves/reloads registers without affecting the flags). This is in contrast with processors such as the Intel 80x86 series, whose condition codes are set only by arithmetic operations such as addition or comparison. On the other hand no transfer to an address register will affect the flags.

3.2 The 680x0 memory architecture

The memory array is the single data structure into which all of the application program, its data and application variables must be mapped. As a result of this, it is necessary to attach different meaning to different parts of the memory array – some of it contains the code itself, other parts of it contain the data and still other parts belong to the operating system... However, from the point of view of the machine itself, there is only a single interpretation of the memory – it is an array of fixed length bit patterns arranged as words or cells.

Each memory cell has an index which we call its *address*. The address of a memory cell is not part of the memory cell itself, but it allows us to uniquely identify the cell.

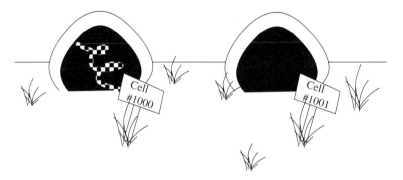

Addresses, like array indices, are just numbers. Such numbers can be stored in memory cells just as any numbers can be. This allows us to have some cells 'point' to other cells by allowing them to contain the number of the target cell's address:

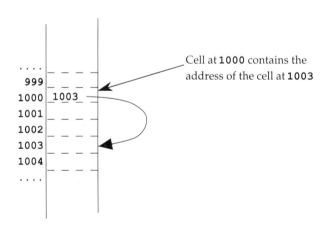

Cell at **1000** contains the address of the cell at **1003**

Pascal also has the concept of a pointer. In Pascal a pointer is a variable which contains the address of a value of a given type, usually a record structure; in assembler all pointers contain addresses of cells in the memory.

Addresses and pointers are used rather more often in assembler programming than in Pascal. For example, in order to map out the memory array into its different components of program, data etc. the *addresses* of these areas will frequently appear in registers of the machine. In fact, pointers are the data structuring equivalent of the **goto** statement: just as compound statements such as loop control statements can be built from simpler statements using **goto** statements, so most data structures involve the use of addresses in their implementation.

The memory architecture of the 680x0 consists of an array of bytes. Each byte in the memory array has a unique address, the 680x0 is therefore termed a byte-addressed machine. Other machines, especially older machines such as the CDC6x00 series and modern RISC computers, may be word addressed. In these machines the memory consists of an array of words each of which might contain several bytes.

Although the memory of the 680x0 is organized as a collection of bytes, it can also be addressed as a collection of 16 bit words and 32 bit long words. Two contiguous bytes in memory might be addressed as a single word and four contiguous bytes may be addressed as a long word.

On the 68000/008/010 word and long word addresses are restricted to be even; i.e. it is not permitted to access a word or long word using an address which is odd. This restriction does not apply to the later models in the range –the 68020 and 68030. Even so, addressing words on even byte boundaries is more efficient on these machines also. Furthermore all instruction words and the system stack must be on even byte boundaries in all the machines. We will assume that words and long words are always on even address boundaries.

The address range determines the largest possible physical embodiment of the memory of a computer; if this number is too small then the underlying architecture can be overtaken by progress in the technology of computer memory – on the other hand, if the address range is too large it may result in an architecture which is un-economic because large addresses occupy more memory than small addresses.

The 68000 has an address of 16 Megabytes of memory, hence addresses in this machine are 24 bits long; although an address register is 32 bits long. Only the lower 24 bits of an address register in the 68000 have any significance: the upper 8 bits are ignored by the processor when forming an address. The 68008, which is really an 8 bit version of the 68000, can address one megabyte, therefore its memory addresses are 20 bits long, leaving 12 bits unused in the address registers. Some compiler writers make use of the fact that an address on these processors is shorter than a full long word to store type information with addresses.

The later models are true 32 bit computers which can theoretically address 4 Gigabytes (4096 Megabytes) of memory with a full 32 bit address.

It is quite rare for a computer to possess 4 Gigabytes of physical memory. On the other hand, with virtual memory techniques a reasonable approximation of this much memory is possible.

3.3 Simple assembler programming

An assembler program consists of a sequence of assembler statements, nearly always one statement per line of source. Most of these statements represent *instructions* to be performed by the processor; although a significant minority are *directives* such as equates (see below) and define storage commands.

A single instruction is typically equivalent to much less than a single statement in a high-level programming language like Pascal. For example, the simple Pascal statement

```
a:=a+b*c;
```

where **a, b** and **c** are integer variables, could be represented by the instructions:

```
move.w   c,d0
muls     b,d0    ;multiply  b*c
add.w    d0,a    ;add  to  a
```

The only point to note here is that a single Pascal statement often requires many assembler instructions to implement. The result is that assembler programs usually contain many more lines than their Pascal equivalents.

Apart from the difference in the granularity of assembler statements compared to statements in high-level languages, the other main difference is the restricted nature of the data that can be manipulated directly. A Pascal program variable can range in type from a single boolean value to complex structures such as arrays of records each containing a sub-array... By contrast, in an assembler program we are always dealing with the contents of registers or of individual memory locations.

Perhaps one of the simplest assembler programs we might think of takes two numbers, adds them together and places the result in a third location. We could do this with the instructions:

```
move.w   1000,d1
add.w    d1,d0
move.w   d0,1002
```

The first instruction moves the contents of the word whose location in memory is **1000** into the data register **d1**. The size specifier '**.w**' which we have attached to the **move** instruction indicates that we are interested in an operation involving a 16 bit word. If we had specified '**.l**' instead then this would indicate a long or 32 bit word operation and if we had specified '**.b**' then a byte sized move would be indicated. It is important to understand that this instruction *does not* put the value **1000** into **d1**, if we had intended that we should have used:

```
move.w  #1000,d1
```

If, just prior to executing this instruction, the memory location at address **1000** had **35** in it, then the **d1** register will have **35** in it after the **move**.

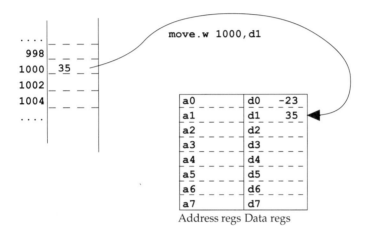

Figure 3.3 *Move the contents of location 1000 to d1*

The second instruction adds the contents of data register **d1** to the register **d0**, overwriting it in the process. So, if **d0** previously contained **−23** in it, then after the **add** instruction it will contain **13**:

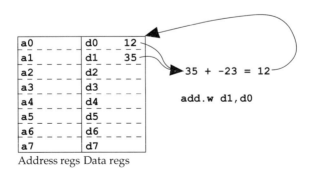

Figure 3.4 *Add the contents of d1 to d0*

Again, the '.**w**' specifier in the **add** instruction indicates that we want to use 16 bit addition. The final **move** instruction overwrites the memory contents at location **1002** with the contents of register **d0**, i.e. with the result of the addition:

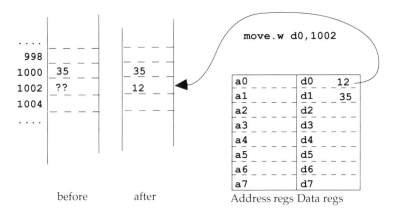

Figure 3.5 *Move the contents of d0 to location 1002*

3.3.1   The 680x0 instruction set

In all there are ten groups of instructions in the 680x0: data movement, integer arithmetic, logical, shift and rotate, bit manipulation, bit field manipulation, binary coded decimal arithmetic, program control, system control and multi-processor control. The bit field and multi-processor control instructions are particular to the 68020 and later models.

By far the most important groups of instructions are the data movement and program control instructions. Together these make up more than 60% of a typical application's code. Generally, we shall introduce an instruction as and when we need it to implement some feature of Pascal programming. For a complete list of the instructions used in the text, together with associated instructions where appropriate, refer to Appendix B where we list and summarise the 680x0 family instructions.

The operational/data transfer instructions typically have the format:

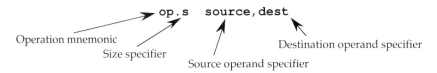

where **op** determines the operation performed between **source** and **dest**, leaving any result in **dest**.

The operation mnemonic indicates what the instruction does. This is the main keyword by which we identify the statement type, and what the instruction will do. On most of the instructions which modify or transfer data there is a *size specifier*. This is a single letter which indicates the size of the calculation or data movement to take place. This can either be **b**, **w** or **l** (for byte, word and long word operations respectively). If the size specifier is omitted from an instruction that requires one then **w** (i.e. word length) is assumed.

There is nothing to stop us using different size specifiers in subsequent instructions – the processor would not notice if we performed a 16 bit **move** followed by a 32 bit **add** for example. It is up to us as programmers to ensure that the manipulations we perform in our instructions match the data movements that we have requested. Getting the sizes of operands 'wrong' is a constant source of errors in assembler programs, both those written by novices and those written by highly experienced professionals. On the other hand, there are a few occasions when a 32 bit addition following a 16 bit **move** is exactly what we want to perform.

There are instructions with zero, one or two operands or address specifiers. Most of the instructions have one or two operands. In the case of a zero operand instruction the location of the data or address to be manipulated is *implied* or fixed by the instruction. For example the **rts** instruction does not have an explicit operand, instead it takes its data from the stack which is addressed via the **a7** register.

The program control instructions usually have the format:

Operation mnemonic

Branch size specifier

Program label specifier

The program control instructions may also have a size specifier, in which case it specifies whether a short or long jump (**goto**) is to be taken. The existence of this specifier allows the programmer to select the size of instruction needed to encode a particular jump. Since the program control instructions are extremely frequent in assembler programs most computer designers attempt to optimise their representation – a short branch is shorter (occupies less space) than a long one. Some assemblers can calculate this specifier automatically since the target address or label is always known; however most assemblers require at least some assistance.

The 680x0 addressing modes

An addressing mode is a specification of an operand to an instruction. It specifies how the operand of the instruction is to be computed. We have already seen some addressing modes: register direct for example, where the operand is a data register, absolute address mode, where the operand is in a fixed location in the memory, and immediate mode, where the operand is part of the instruction itself.

There are some 10 addressing modes on the 68000 itself with a further four new addressing modes and four extensions of 68000 addressing modes on the 68020/68030. This means that in the specification of an instruction there may be up to 18 ways of determining where an operand is. However each mode is quite limited and the collection is not nearly as rich as the essentially unlimited number of ways of specifying data in Pascal (we can have arrays of records of pointers to arrays etc.).

The richness of a processor's suite of addressing modes governs the compactness of an application's code: a rich set of addressing modes means that fewer instruction will be needed to implement complex data movements. However, rich addressing modes are also complex to implement and can result in slower processors. The 680x0 range has one of the richest set of addressing modes of popular processors; but some trends indicate a return to simpler more efficient instruction sets with correspondingly simpler addressing modes.

We shall introduce each of these addressing modes as we come across them in examples of instructions; they are all summarised in Appendix A.

3.3.2 Assembling and running programs

For a sequence of instructions to be executed it is necessary to *assemble* them into a sequence of *instruction patterns* or *instruction words* – usually expressed as word-length numbers. These instruction words must then be loaded into some appropriate part of the memory and then, in order to execute the program, the program counter of the machine must be set to point to the portion of memory where it was loaded.

The process of assembling, loading and executing programs written in assembler is exactly analogous to the process of compiling, linking and executing Pascal programs. The difference is that each one of our source statements corresponds to the single machine instruction that we have specified ourselves, whereas a single Pascal statement may correspond to an arbitrary number of instructions and the Pascal programmer may not know what they are.

Like compilers, assemblers can usually be made to generate a listing as part of the process of assembling the program. In the case of an assembler program, this listing would not only identify any errors produced, but will also indicate the actual bit patterns generated for each instruction. Listing formats vary with different assemblers, however a typical assembler might generate the following for our simple three line program:

```
Filename:  test.asm                                    Page  1


1:00000000                          list      1
2:                     ;
3:                     ;            a  sample  program
4:                     ;
5:00000000  323803E8               move.w     1000,d1
6:00000004  D041                   add.w      d1,d0
7:00000006  31C003EA               move.w     d0,1002
8:0000000A                         end

Code  size  =  10
Number  of  errors  =  0,  number  of  warnings  =  0
```

Figure 3.6 *A sample listing of an assembled program*

If we look at one of the lines in this listing in more detail, we can see what information the assembler produces:

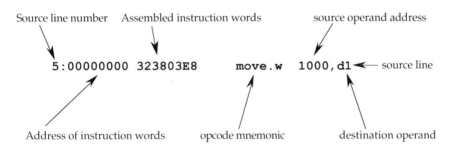

Figure 3.7 *Anatomy of a line of listing*

The original source line echoes the exact contents of the file being assembled. This is further identified by the number of the line in the file.

Immediately adjacent to the line number is the address (in hexadecimal) into which this instruction is being assembled. On a modern computer, this address is rarely the real address of the instruction in the memory, but rather its *relative* location within the program. When the assembled program is loaded into the machine, these addresses are adjusted to indicate where it has been loaded into the memory.

The hexadecimal number which follows the instruction address is the actual instruction word(s) generated by the assembler. This number will be loaded into the memory and executed subsequently by the processor. This bit pattern encodes the function code (a **move** instruction), the source address (in this case the memory contents at location **1000**) and the destination (in this case the data register **d0**).

The lines in the program which begin with a ';' are comments and are not interpreted by the assembler. The detailed syntax of comments varies with different assemblers, we shall use the convention that the rest of any line after a semi-colon is treated as a comment.

Since an assembler program is so close to the machine, and since that is likely to be a much lower level than the programmer's intent, it is quite important to provide good comments in an assembler program. It is good practice to include one comment on *each* line of assembler source. We suggest, however, that the programmer avoids the classic novitiate comment of repeating in English the meaning of the assembler statement itself!

The exact encoding of 680x0 instructions is rather detailed and we do not really need to elaborate it completely in this book. However, we can get the principle of instruction encoding by looking at the **move** instruction in more detail. The bit pattern which represents an encoded instruction is like a packed Pascal record, with different bit fields within the instruction determining its meaning.

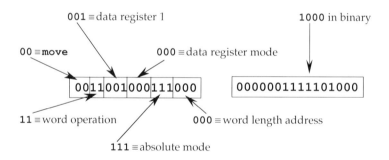

Figure 3.8 *Encoding a* **move** *instruction*

The first 16 bit word of an instruction determines both the opcode and the major aspects of operand addressing used in the instruction. In this case, the two most significant bits of the instruction word are zero, which indicates a **move** instruction. The next two bits determine the size of the **move** (**01** would signify a byte operation, **10** would signify a long operation and **00** signifies a completely different instruction). The next 6 bits determine the destination of the **move** – **d1** here – and the least significant bits determine that a **move** from an actual memory location is specified. The memory address to read from is in the next word of the instruction.

The length of a 680x0 instruction depends on the complexity of the addressing being specified: the shortest instructions are one 16 bit word, whereas the longest instruction on the 68020 occupies 11 words!

Symbols, names and assembler directives

Most assemblers allow us to give names to constants and addresses; this avoids the continual appearance in our programs of 'magic numbers' whose meaning tends to become obscured with time. So, for example, the instruction below compares the lowest byte in register **d0** with **32**, which also happens to be the code for an ASCII space character:

```
cmp.b    #32,d0
```

The operand **#32** is the source operand and it is an *immediate operand* (indicated by the presence of the '**#**' character in front of the literal number), and the destination operand – **d0** – is an example of the *register direct addressing* mode.

The effect of executing this **cmp** instruction is to compare data register **d0** with the literal quantity **32**. Only the least significant 8 bits in **d0** take part in the comparison since the size specifier is '**.b**'.

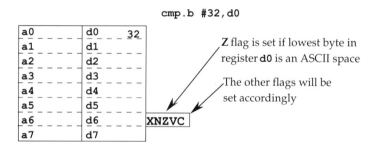

Figure 3.9 *The* cmp *instruction*

If it was our intention to compare the value in **d0** with a space then instead of using the number **32** in the **cmp** instruction, we could have written:

```
space equ     32              ; 'declare' space
      ...
      cmp.b   #space,d0
```

The first of these statements is an *assembler directive*. A directive is an assembler statement which provides some information to the assembler itself; some directives also cause some actions to be performed. (Cf. an instruction statement which represents an individual instruction to the processor.) The directive that we have here is called an *equate*; its function is to declare to the assembler that the name **space** has a value **32**. No 680x0 instructions are generated by an equate but thereafter we can use **space** instead of **32** whenever a number is legal in an assembler statement.

The careful reader might have detected another assembler directive in the short listing above. The **end** statement is really a directive informing the assembler that the source program has ended. The **end** directive dates from an era when computers were 'fed' data via decks of 80 column punched cards and the program to be assembled would be incorporated in a card deck together with operating system control information. Usually, assemblers assume that the end of the source is indicated by the end of the file containing the source.

An assembler will normally also have a syntax for denoting ASCII characters. This would consist of the characters themselves surrounded by quotes, e.g. 'a' or "a". So another alternative way of writing the **cmp** instruction could have been:

```
cmp.b    #' ',d0
```

It may also be necessary to allocate parts of memory for variables. Rather than the programmer being required to assign explicitly where in memory each variable is, it is possible to inform the assembler that *there is* such a location, give it a name and leave it up to the assembler (or even the link loader) to determine the address of the variable.

This is done with another assembler directive: the *define storage* directive: **ds**. If space for a variable is declared with the define storage statement the programmer thereafter can refer to the variable by its symbolic name rather than the numerical value of its address:

```
store ds.l    1       ;reserve 1 long word

      ...

      move.l  store,d4
```

The **ds.l** directive does not generate any 680x0 instructions – its function is to ensure that the assembler reserves some space (one long word in this case). *There is no requirement that this long word in memory has an initial value.* If it is required for a variable to have an initial value, or if it is necessary to have a constant literal in the assembler program (a literal with a specific location as well as value) then we use the related directive: the define constant – **dc** – statement. For example, a statement such as:

```
space_c          dc.b  ' '  ;constant  space
```

declares a pre-filled byte-sized location with the symbolic name **space_c** with an initial value of 32.

Assemblers lend an additional hand by allowing the programmer to assign symbolic labels to program addresses. The programmer can then use symbolic names for subroutines etc. without having to determine in advance where they lie in memory.

It is good programming practice to avoid the use of explicit numbers altogether in the main body of an assembler program. In fact, the number of times a programmer *has* to use a number for any operand is so rare that it almost always signals an error in the program!

Executing assembler programs

Since the instructions that we have been discussing are the actual instructions obeyed by the processor, and since a processor is always executing one instruction or another, we must also be concerned about what happens in the machine *after* it has completed our program. Most often, an assembler program will be called as part of a larger application program which is written in another language. In this case, when the assembler procedure has terminated, control will normally return to the application program that called it; just as though the program had called a Pascal procedure. However, it is possible that the entire application program is written in assembler, in which case we must address what happens at the end of the program.

In our simple example earlier, we had just three instructions, and we must ensure that something sensible happens after those three instructions have been executed. If we assemble our three statements and execute them, then after performing the addition the processor will execute whatever follows next in the memory after our three instructions. It is unlikely that what does follow is particularly meaningful. This is true whether or not the program is called as a procedure from a Pascal program or directly as a stand-alone application.

Except in the circumstance when a program is executing on a bare computer we always run programs in the context of an operating system. So, when we request the execution of our program the operating system loads the program instructions into memory and starts executing them. After the program is complete it is the responsibility of the programmer to ensure that control is returned to the operating system so that the user can continue to use the machine.

The exact way in which control is returned to the operating system after executing an assembler program varies from one operating system to another. One common convention is for the operating system to call the program as though it were a procedure call. Another common convention is to provide 'program termination' as one of the standard services that any operating system offers to a program – so a program would terminate by requesting termination in a similar manner to which some input/output function might be requested.

In this book, we shall assume that the operating system has called our program, so that all we need to do to ensure a tidy return to the operating system is to return from a procedure:

```
move.w  1000,d1
add.w   d1,d0
move.w  d0,1002
rts
```

The **rts** instruction would also be used to return to an application program.

3.3.3 Exercises

1. Explain the difference between the instructions

    ```
    move.l  10,d0
    ```

    and

    ```
    move.l  #10,d0
    ```

2. What would you expect to be left in register **d1** after the instructions

    ```
    move.l  #100000,d0
    move.l  #200000,d1
    move.w  d0,d1
    ```

    have been executed?

3. Write a short sequence which has the effect of exchanging the contents of register **d0** and **d1** using a third register.

4. The instruction **eor** performs an 'exclusive or' operation, as defined by the truth function:

$$0 \oplus 0 \rightarrow 0 \qquad 1 \oplus 1 \rightarrow 0$$

$$1 \oplus 0 \rightarrow 1 \qquad 0 \oplus 1 \rightarrow 1$$

Write a sequence of instructions which exchanges **d0** and **d1** using no other registers or memory locations.

The exclusive or is sometimes referred to as a 'pre-add' function since the answer is also the result of adding two bits together. To construct a full adder, a carry input has to be incorporated and a carry output generated.

3.4   Input and output in assembler

One feature to notice about our assembler programmer's model is that, compared with a Pascal programmer's model, or indeed a physical model of a computer, input and output do not figure all that directly. Although the assembler programmer generally has complete control of the machine for normal application code, input and output from an assembler level program is normally left to the operating system to perform.

In a typical system environment performing input or output may require hundreds if not thousands of instructions to be executed. In order to perform an input or output function the assembler programmer invokes a subroutine either from a library of input/output functions or directly from the operating system. By packaging the input/output functions in this way its true complexity is largely hidden from the assembler programmer (and the corresponding burden is removed also).

Of course, there are times when this is not possible. For example, if a new physical device driver is to be built, then it will almost certainly have to be built in assembler. Moreover, that driver program will be performing real input/output functions. Such a device driver is often to be found as part of the operating system rather than being embedded in an application program. In order to build a device driver, the assembler programmer must know about the characteristics of the device (such as what sequence of commands the device requires to perform an operation).

Apart from understanding the physical device, complete knowledge is also required of how the device is logically connected to the computer (for example, which input/output ports or memory locations correspond to the control ports of the device). Given that level of knowledge, implementing a device driver consists of writing a set of functions to manipulate those input/output ports or memory locations to achieve the required effects.

Once embedded into the operating system, a driver can be invoked by the operating system in order to open the associated peripheral device, read and write data to it and otherwise control its behaviour. The connection between the processor and the physical device, be it a printer, screen or disk drive, is implemented as part of the electronic design of the computer.

It is beyond the scope of our book to discuss how the physical input and output are accomplished in computers. On the other hand, the principles that guide the building of input/output libraries and device drivers are not that different from building any other kinds of program.

CHAPTER FOUR

Representing Pascal expressions

Data values in Pascal are built from a set of primitive data types – called scalar types – and a set of methods for combining and structuring the data. So we have, for example, integers, 'real' numbers and characters as scalar types in Pascal. These can be combined into arrays, records and sets or various combinations of these.

Intimately associated with these data types are the variables which can have them as values. A Pascal 'variable' is best thought of as a named location in the computer's memory. The different values that a variable can take on, through being assigned to, are reflected by the different contents of the variable's location. Furthermore the structure of a variable's location will depend on its type.

Apart from simply *representing* variables and values, it is also necessary to show how expressions can be computed, how variables can be assigned to, and how components of complex data structures can be accessed and updated. In effect, this chapter is concerned with the implementation of a single type of Pascal statement: the assignment statement; in particular, we concentrate on expressions involving scalar values and variables.

Although we will look in later chapters at the explicit control aspect of programs, it is fair to say that we are also interested in control in this chapter. On the whole though, the control referred to whilst accessing data is *automatic*: i.e. it is only indirectly specified by the programmer through the use of expressions.

4.1 Scalar values and variables

A primitive or scalar value is one which has no discernible internal structure. For example, in Pascal, integers and reals are scalar; of course we have seen that the representation of numbers is not trivial in a computer: a word which hold integers does indeed have a structure – the bit pattern corresponding to the binary expansion of the integer. However, on the whole, the internal structure of integers is not seen by the programmer.

From the point of view of the Pascal and assembler programmer a scalar quantity is also treated as a whole and its structure is not normally inspected. In practice a stricter interpretation of scalar is also used in computing – a scalar quantity is one which can reside in a machine register. This is a more restricted view than the mathematical definition; for example, the set of integers has infinitely many elements, but a 680x0 register can only handle integers in the range -2,147,483,648…2,147,483,647; which though it is large it is not an infinite range: larger numbers have to be constructed from sequences of integers within the range that can be handled directly.

There are three different types of scalar in the Pascal language – ordinals which includes sub-ranges of the integers, characters and booleans; pointers; and the real numbers.

In fact, computer 'real' numbers are not Real but floating point numbers which are really fractions. There are an uncountably infinite number of reals, most of which would require an infinitely large amount of computer storage to represent – just *one* real number π has infinitely many digits in its decimal (or binary) expansion. Therefore it is not really practical to have *real* real numbers!

However reals are a primitive type in Pascal and are treated as scalar. In assembler, floating point numbers are not primitive as they have an internal structure consisting of exponent, mantissa and sign bit.

4.1.1 Ordinals

An ordinal scalar type expresses a sub-range of some other (possibly infinite) type. The most fundamental example of this is the type consisting of the representable integers; other examples include the characters and the enumerated types. Although intended for different uses, the different types of ordinal types are handled by Pascal programs in similar ways and can all be represented in the machine using common techniques.

These are some example Pascal definitions of ordinal types, together with the typical number of bits required to represent values in them:

```
boolean  =  (false,true)                { 1 bit }
byte  =  0..255                          { 8 bits }
signed_byte  =  -128..127                { 8 bits }
weekday  =  (monday,tuesday, ..., sunday) { 3 bits }
word  =  -32768..32767                   { 16 bits }
integer  =  -maxint..maxint              { ? bits }
```

maxint is a system defined constant in Pascal which denotes the largest integer that can be represented in a variable of type **integer**. **-maxint**, which is not strictly legal Pascal, is intended to denote the most negative `integer`.

Since the smallest addressable quantity in the 680x0 is a byte, it is convenient to allocate space for variables in multiples of bytes. If a scalar value requires less than 8 bits to represent it then a byte is used none-the-less. If a scalar requires between 8 and 16 bits to represent it then a 16 bit word will be used. For example, a number of the sub-range type -512..512 occupies the same space as a number of sub-range type -32768..32767. Similarly if a scalar quantity needs more than 16 bits then the whole 32 bits are used to represent values of that type.

Later we shall investigate packed data structures where it is essential to use the least possible amount of space. In a packed structure we make an effort to use only the absolute minimum number of bits needed to represent each value; for example, if data items of a particular type only need 9 bits to represent it then 9 bits are used. This will mean that there may be more than one data item represented within a word, and even that an individual item may be spread across word boundaries. However, since the processor does not easily access such odd size quantities there is a consequent increase in complexity in accessing packed data.

Characters

Logically the character scalar type is also a sub-range: characters from systems such as the ASCII characters form a subset of all the possible characters. There are several different character sets in common use including ASCII, EBCDIC and the various Japanese Katakana/Kanji character sets; some of these character sets are more common than others.

There are 128 characters in the standard ASCII character set, including 32 control characters. Since we can represent 128 patterns in 7 bits we typically use a single byte to represent a given character. There are some variations on the 7 bit ASCII character set: for example there is an 8 bit ASCII character set, the IBM PC character set and the Apple Macintosh® character set.

Character processing is extremely important in computing. Characters and the ability to manipulate them are essential in applications ranging from word processing to databases. It can be argued that the primary motivation to have a byte oriented memory structure in processors such as the 680x0 is the desire to optimise character and string processing.

®   IBM PC and Macintosh are trademarks of IBM and Apple respectively.

4.1.2 Pointers

A pointer is a quantity which is a reference to another value. We would
call it a scalar value since it has no internal structure even though we can
use a pointer to access the value identified by it. Pointers are also very
important in programming; although a major desire in the design of
programming languages is to make them either transparent – in the case
of LISP and Prolog – or to make their definition and use disciplined – as is
attempted in Pascal.

On a computer such as the 680x0 a pointer is represented as a memory
address; which is of course a number which can be placed into an address
register. The effective size of this number is different in the 68000 and in
the 68020 and 68030 (24 bits and 32 bits respectively). However, most
compilers devote a full 32 bit long word for a pointer whether the target
machine is a 68000 or a 68020.

4.2 Scalar expressions

One of the earliest 'features' ever introduced into a high-level
programming language was the expression or formula: Fortran (which is
an acronym for FORmula TRANslation) was the first programming
language which had expressions and it was first introduced in the 1950's.
Expressions are a key component of modern high level languages: they
can appear in many different places, for example expressions appear in
assignments, as arguments to procedures and functions and in array access
computations. However there is no direct support for evaluating an
arbitrary expression in the 680x0 instruction set; this means that we must
be able to implement an arbitrary expression as a sequence of 680x0
instructions.

Possibly the single most common assignment statement ever found in
Pascal programs – or any programming language for that matter – is
something like:

```
x   :=  x+1;
```

where **x** is an integer variable. We can implement this Pascal statement
with a single 680x0 instruction:

```
add.w   #1, x
```

The **add** instruction adds the integers in its source and destination – **1**
and x respectively – and stores the result in the destination – x. The effect

of this instruction is to increment χ by 1. The **.w** size specifier indicates that we want a 16 bit addition to be performed.

Notice that we have used the original variable name χ in our assembler instruction. We cannot use this instruction as written. Before it can be assembled and executed χ must be resolved to one of the standard addressing modes available on the 680x0. On the other hand, we cannot do that until we know where χ is located. If, ultimately, we resolve χ to be located in the data register **d7** (say), then the instruction needed to implement the Pascal assignment is:

```
add.w    #1,d7
```

In general, it may require additional instructions to address a variable.

Later on we shall examine more closely the allocation of variables – how they are assigned to registers and/or memory. For the moment, however, whenever we have a reference to a variable we shall use the name of the variable in our assembler instructions. This is in full knowledge of the fact that they may not be complete, but we shall use this 'shorthand' whilst we look at other aspects of Pascal programs. To emphasise the fact that we sometimes write partially specified instructions, we use a different *font* to denote such variables.

4.2.1 Evaluating complex expressions

Normally expressions are too complicated to implement in a single instruction. In particular, unlike arithmetic operators in Pascal, the operands of an individual assembler instruction *must* be numeric. This rules out, for example, implementing any kind of nested expressions using just one instruction. If we have to evaluate a complex expression then we must arrange the execution of instructions so that each operator is applied to numeric values rather than arbitrary expressions. We require a systematic method for arranging the evaluation of expressions to ensure that each operator is applied to numeric values.

For example, the Pascal statement:

```
x:=(x*y+z**2)/(x-y);
```

where **x**, **y** and **z** are integer variables, is much too complicated to implement as a single 680x0 instruction. (We have taken the liberty of using a non-standard Pascal operator ****** here. An expression of the form **u**v** is intended to mean 'u raised to the power v'.)

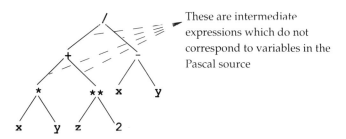

These are intermediate
expressions which do not
correspond to variables in the
Pascal source

Figure 4.1 *The parse tree of* **(x*y+z**2)/(x-y)**

The parse tree shown in Figure 4.1 highlights the dependencies between
the various parts of the expression and the variables and constants
involved. It also shows where there are intermediate points within the
expression which are not directly associated with a variable or numeric
value. We shall see that although these points have no identifiers
associated with them in the Pascal expression, we do have to explicitly
identify them when we come to map the expression into assembler
instructions.

Reverse polish notation

There is a way of writing expressions which has the crucial property that
we can easily evaluate them in such a way that as we apply each operator
the operands have already been evaluated. This is the so-called *reverse
polish form*. In this notation we write the operator of an expression *after*
writing the operands. So, for example, the expression

$$x+y*z$$

becomes in reverse polish form:

$$x \quad y \quad z \quad * \quad +$$

The meaning of this expression is

'apply ***** to **y** and **z**, and apply **+** to the result of that and **x**'

More complicated reverse polish form expressions often have several
operators in sequence being applied to larger and larger sub-expressions.
Our initial expression would be written in reverse polish form as:

$$x \quad y \quad * \quad z \quad 2 \quad ** \quad + \quad x \quad y \quad - \quad /$$

Another important observation to make about this form of expression is that there are no parentheses: the relative priorities of sub-expressions is guided entirely by the ordering of operators.

It can take some adjustment to become fluent in reading reverse polish form expressions, however they are often used as *the* main way of writing expressions. Indeed some calculators use reverse polish form to enter calculations.

It is relatively simple to convert from the normal infix form of an expression to its reverse polish form. The process involves recursively moving the operator of an expression to the right of its sub-expressions, after applying the conversion to each of the sub-expressions. So, for example, the expression

> **x+y**

is converted to: x y +

A more complex expression is converted recursively, by first converting sub-expressions:

> u * v + x * y
>
> ⟹   u v *   + x * y
>
> ⟹   u v *   + x y *
>
> ⟹   u v * x y * +

I.e. for any expression of the form:

> L op R

we recursively map **L** to L , and we map **R** to R and then move the operator to the end to get L R op .

If we apply the conversion to our original expression we get the transformations:

> (x*y+z**2)/(x-y)
>
> ⟹   (x y *   + z**2)/(x-y)
>
> ⟹   (x y *   + z 2 **)/(x-y)
>
> ⟹   (x y *   + z 2 **)/ x y -
>
> ⟹   x y * z 2 ** + / x y -
>
> ⟹   x y * z 2 ** + x y - /

Any rules that we have regarding associative operators must be followed during this conversion process. For example, if we want to convert the expression

$$x-y-z$$

we have first to decide whether this refers to

$$(x-y)-z$$

or

$$x-(y-z)$$

Both interpretations are possible, though they lead to different, non-equivalent, reverse polish forms:

$$\boxed{x \quad y \quad - \quad z \quad -}$$

and

$$\boxed{x \quad y \quad z \quad - \quad -}$$

Evaluating reverse polish form expressions
We can evaluate reverse polish form expressions with the aid of an expression stack. This stack is used to hold the temporary intermediate values generated during the evaluation and as a source of operands for the arithmetic operators.

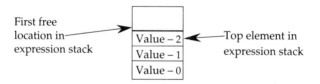

In order to evaluate an expression in reverse polish form we follow a simple rule: proceeding from left to right, we examine each symbol, and

a)   if we encounter a constant literal or a variable we push its value onto the stack and continue to the next symbol in the expression;

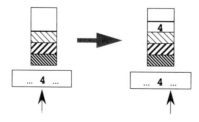

b) if we encounter a binary operator (such as **+**) we remove its two operands from the expression stack, apply the operator to them and place the result back on to the expression stack. We then continue to the next symbol.

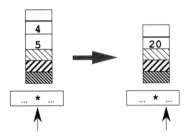

c) In general, on encountering an *n*-ary operator, we remove *n* operands from the stack, apply the operator and place the result back on the stack.

d) After the last symbol in the expression has been processed, the expression stack contains a single value: the value of the expression as a whole.

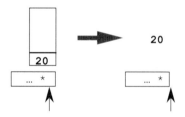

Most arithmetic operators are *binary* – they take two arguments – but some are *unary* – square root for example – and there may even be some ternary operators such as **if-then-else** (though not in standard Pascal).

Using our procedure, we can see how to evaluate the simple expression

Proceeding from left to right we push **x** onto the stack,

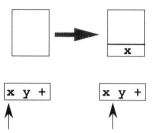

and then push **y** on to the expression stack,

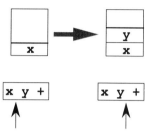

On reaching the + symbol, we take the top two items from the stack, add them together and put the result back on the stack. This is the last symbol in the expression so the single value remaining is the value of the expression.

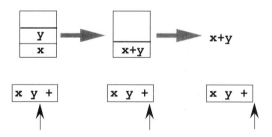

The only difference, in principle, between a simple expression and a complex one is that the stack gets a little deeper when evaluating the complex expression:

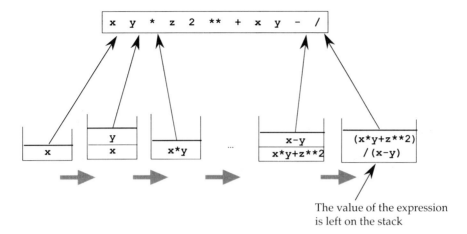

Figure 4.2 *The evaluation of (x*y+z**2)/(x-y)*

If there are insufficient operands on the stack to apply an operator, or if there is more than one value left on the expression stack at the end of the evaluation, then the reverse polish expression was not *well-formed*. Since we are primarily interested in the reverse polish form to aid the evaluation of complex expressions that we already know to be well-formed we regard it to be beyond the scope of this book to explore ill-formed expressions in general.

Expression stacks on the 680x0
The 680x0 has good support for expression stacks, indeed it has special purpose addressing modes which can be used for pushing items onto stacks and popping them off again. An expression stack can be involved as the source or destination (but not both) of any arithmetic instruction.

We can model an expression stack by allocating an array of memory to it, and using a pointer variable within the array to address the top of the stack. Conventionally, stacks 'grow' downwards in memory; that is, as a new element is pushed onto the stack, the stack pointer is *decremented* and the new memory location is used to place the value on the top of the stack:

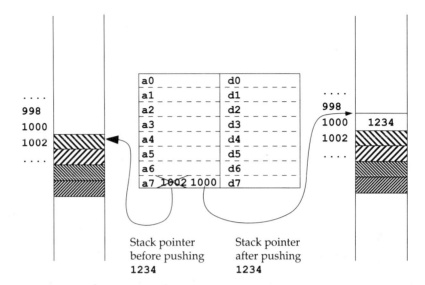

Figure 4.3 *The system stack as an expression stack*

It is quite convenient to use the *system stack* (which is addressed by the **a7** register) as our expression stack when processing a reverse polish expression. In order to push a constant literal or the value of a variable onto the system stack we use an instruction similar to the

move.w #*const*,**-(a7)** or   **move.w**   *var*,**-(a7)**

instructions.

The addressing mode we have used here **-(a7)** – is the *address register indirect with pre-decrement* mode. In this mode, the address register is *decremented* and the value contained in the address register is then used as the address of the operand. The amount that the address register is decremented depends on the size of the data transfer; in this case it is two since the **.w** specifier indicates a word length transfer. The aim behind the pre-decrement addressing mode is to always ensure that the stack pointer is in an appropriate place to place new values on the stack. Without this addressing mode we would have to adjust the stack pointer explicitly with extra instructions.

The pre-decrement mode can be used to specify either a source operand or, as in this case, a destination operand, i.e. where to store the *var* on the expression stack. If *var* was identified with the data register **d0**, we could implement a push onto the expression stack with

move.w **d0,-(a7)**

which would save the lower word contents of data register **d0** on the system stack.

Every time we encounter a binary operator in our processing of a reverse polish expression we are required to take off two operands from the stack, apply the operator and replace the result onto the stack. In order to take an entry off the system stack we use an instruction such as:

```
move.w  (a7)+,d0
```

Here we have used *address register indirect with post-increment* addressing mode as the source operand of the **move** instruction. This addressing mode is analogous to the pre-decrement mode except that the address register is incremented after it is used to determine the address of the operand. Again, since a word length **move** is specified, **a7** is incremented by 2.

With these two addressing modes we can construct the sequence of instructions to evaluate the complete reverse polish form expression:

$$\boxed{\text{x \ y \ +}}$$

for which we can use the instruction sequence:

```
move.w  x,-(a7)     ;push  x  on  the  stack
move.w  y,-(a7)     ;push  y  on  the  stack
move.w  (a7)+,d0    ;pop off  y
add.w   (a7)+,d0    ;pop  x & add to  y
move.w  d0,-(a7)    ;place  result  on  stack
```

The instruction sequence for our simple expression is somewhat more clumsy than the single instruction that we used to implement **x:=x+1;** however the procedure we have followed to generate it is guaranteed to be able to implement *any* expression.

We can, in fact, take advantage another of the 68000's addressing modes and shorten the sequence to:

```
move.w  x,-(a7)     ;push  x  as  before
move.w  y,d0        ;pick  up  y  into  d0
add.w   d0,(a7)     ;add  and  replace
```

This relies on the fact that we can add 'into memory' with the **add** instruction using the *address register indirect* addressing mode. This mode, which is written as **(aₙ)** where **aₙ** is an address register, uses the contents of an address register as the address of the operand without changing the value in the address register. So, the instruction:

```
add.w   d0,(a7)
```

adds the lower 16 bit contents of **d0**, together with the 16 bit word addressed by **a7** (which is **x** in this case), and replaces the word in memory by the result. In effect we have replaced the old copy of **x** on the stack with **x+y** in a single 680x0 instruction.

Notice that if we knew more about where the variables **x** and **y** were located in memory, if either was in a data register for example, then the code sequence could be further shortened to a single instruction:

$$\textbf{add.w} \quad x, y$$

Finally, we are now in a position to convert our original expression – using the same minor optimizations – into 680x0 instructions. If we do, then we get the sequence of instructions:

```
move.w    x,-(a7)       ; x
move.w    y,d0          ; y
muls.w    (a7)+,d0      ; x*y
move.w    d0,-(a7)      ; replace
move.w    z,-(a7)       ; z
move.w    #2,-(a7)
<exponentiate>          ; z**2
move.w    (a7)+,d0
add.w     d0,(a7)       ; x*y+z**2
move.w    x,-(a7)
sub.w     y,(a7)        ; x-y
move.w    (a7)+,d0
move.w    (a7)+,d1
ext.l     d1
divs.w    d0,d1         ; (x*y+z**2)/.
move.w    d1,-(a7)      ;   (x-y)
move.w    (a7)+,x       ; x:=...
```

This rather long sequence of instructions illustrates graphically the difference in granularity and detail between a simple Pascal statement and the machine instructions needed to implement it.

The third instruction in the sequence is a signed multiply instruction: **muls**. This instruction is unusual in that the destination (which must be a data register) is different in size to the source. In general multiplication can double the number of significant digits; for example, multiplying 75×45 is 3375 which has twice the number of digits of either operand. The same applies to binary multiplication which is why the **muls** instruction takes two 16 bit operands and returns a 32 bit answer. However, we are only saving 16 bits of the result in this sequence so we run a risk of generating erroneous results.

On the other hand, division has the opposite phenomenon to multiplication: generally the number of significant digits is reduced by a division. Thus the **divs** instruction accepts a 32 bit dividend and a 16 bit divisor to generate a 16 bit quotient and 16 bit remainder (the 68020 and 68030 also have long forms of multiplication and division which accept and generate 32 bit operands). It is for this reason that we inserted an **ext.l** instruction, which extends a 16 bit number into a 32 bit number, just prior to the division. We could, of course, have preserved the full 32 bit result from the multiplication and possibly gained some accuracy in the process. The 32 bit result would then be already formatted for the subsequent division.

We have so far omitted the code fragment for exponentiation. Since there is no direct exponentiation instruction on the 680x0, we have two choices to implement the operator: we can call a sub-routine which will perform the exponentiation, or we can insert a loop into the code sequence which will implement exponentiation directly:

```
            move.w  (a7)+,d1    ;# of times  to  multiply
            sub.w   #1,d1       ;1=2-1
            move.w  (a7),d0     ;z
    @1      muls.w  (a7),d0     ;d0  :=  d0*z
            sub.w   #1,d1       ;d1:=d1-1
            bne.s   @1          ;done  multiplying?
            move.w  d0,(a7)     ;push  result  back
```

The **bne** instruction that we have used here is a program control instruction, and its effect is to branch to the label **@1** if the result of the last operation – **sub.w #1,d1** – was non-zero. Register **d1** will be zero when the last multiplication has taken place, in other words, when we have decremented the exponent counter to zero. In effect we have implemented exponentiation by repeated multiplication and we use the power to raise **z** by as the control variable in the loop.

Notice that we have used a label with a rather strange syntax: **@1**. This is an example of a *local label* . Local labels are a feature found in many assemblers which allow the programmer to economise on the invention of meaningful names. A typical assembler program will have hundreds if not thousands of labels simply because it is much lower level – and hence has a finer level of detail – than Pascal. Making sure that all these labels are unique is a considerable chore for the assembler programmer. A local label has a limited scope – it is only valid between two 'meaningful' labels. Two local labels which are separated by an ordinary label are logically different even if they look the same; so the programmer can re-use the same local labels again and again. The syntax of a local label may vary, here we assume that a local label is of the form **@nnn** where **nnn** is a number.

Since the power to which we are raising **z** is a constant known at compile time, we have an alternative to building in a loop to implement the exponentiation: we can 'unfold' the loop into an explicit sequence.

Doing this unfolding nearly always results in faster program execution but it can lead to greatly expanded code. In this case the saving in instructions executed is spectacular; the loop *and* the initial stack pushes can be replaced by the sequence:

```
move.w  z,d0
muls.w  d0,d0
move.w  d0,-(a7)
```

Notice that when we implemented our stack moves – stack pushes and stack pops – we used pre-decrement addressing as the destination when pushing a value onto the stack, and post-increment addressing as the source when popping a value from the stack. This results in a downwards growing stack: that is the stack's address register *decreases in value* as more is pushed onto the stack.

We could just as easily use post-increment as the destination and pre-decrement as the source; in which case the resulting stack would be an 'upwards growing stack' – with increasing memory addresses as more is pushed onto it. However the system stack – as addressed by **a7** – is assumed to be a 'down' stack by the processor; and therefore it would be extremely unwise to use **a7** to construct an upward stack.

We can use the pre-decrementing and post-incrementing addressing modes with any of the 680x0's address registers; this means that we can have stacks pointed at by any address register. It is possible, for example, to have more than one expression stack – the **a7** register points to the system stack and we could use **a4** (say) to point to a different stack.

One limitation of implementing stacks in the way that we have, is that there is no bounds checking. Unless extra checking instructions are used to make sure that the stack pointer remains within the memory allocated to the expression stack there is a danger of stack overflow or underflow. Not unusually for assembler programming it is the responsibility of the programmer to ensure that stacks do not stray outside their allocated space and overwrite neighbouring areas of memory; this is usually achieved by allocating a large enough space for the stack and hoping that it will never overflow when running the application.

Evaluating an expression using registers

Just as we can unfold a bounded loop into a sequence of its bodies, so we can unfold the various stack operations – instead of using the system stack for intermediate results we can *simulate* a stack by using data registers.

In such a scheme we might use **d7** for the first stack push; and if there is a second stack push without there being a stack pop first then we use register **d6** for the second level of the stack. We can use **d5** for the third level of the stack and so on down to **d3** (say). Provided that the data registers **d3** to **d7** are not needed for other purposes this technique would allow us to simulate a stack with 5 levels; this is enough for most of the expressions that are likely to be encountered in a Pascal program.

Using the data registers to simulate a stack allows further scope for optimization – we can eliminate some of the stack movement instructions altogether since data registers can be used directly as the source/destination for arithmetic instructions. Instead of a sequence such as:

```
move.w   x,-(a7)      ;x
move.w   y,d0         ;y
muls.w   (a7)+,d0     ;x*y
move.w   d0,-(a7)
```

to implement the sub-expression **x*y**, we would use:

```
move.w   x,d7
muls.w   y,d7
```

Applying this technique to the whole expression gives a somewhat shorter and more efficient sequence than we had before:

```
move.w   x,d7         ;x
muls.w   y,d7         ;x*y
move.w   z,d6         ;z
muls.w   d6,d6        ;z**2
add.w    d6,d7        ;x*y+z**2
move.w   x,d6
sub.w    y,d6         ;x-y
ext.l    d7
divs     d6,d7        ;value in d7
move.w   d7,x
```

4.2.2 Error checking

A Pascal programmer has a safety net that is not available directly to the assembler programmer – the Pascal compiler/run-time system makes sure that the expressions computed during the execution of a program are valid. This is different to *type checking* which is generally a static verification of the program that the types of data being processed are consistent. A run-time test is used to verify that correct *values* are being computed.

For example if a division is to be performed then the compiler will ensure that the divisor is non-zero; if it is then an error is signalled to the programmer when the program is executed. The purpose of error checking is to pin-point errors in the program as closely as possible to the statement(s) that generated the erroneous value.

It should be pointed out that, in current compiler technology, the most that automatic error detection can achieve is to make sure that the values computed in a program statement, or the result of an expression, can be faithfully represented in the computer. No compiler can make sure that an expression or statement is an accurate reflection of the programmer's intention.

The 'detectable errors' are mainly range errors – attempting to put an out-of-range value into a variable for example, overflow errors arising from adding too large numbers together for example, and arithmetic errors – as in dividing by zero. These errors are detected by the compiler inserting checking instructions at suitable points in the evaluation of expressions.

If we look at our original statement there are a number of places within it where an error can be generated:

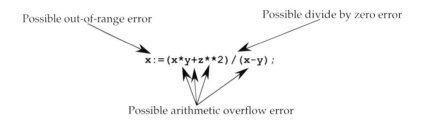

Figure 4.4 *Sources of error in an expression*

If we are to correctly implement the assignment statement then we must insert extra instructions to check that the calculation is proceeding within bounds. So, for example, instead of simply having the pair of instructions:

```
move.w   x, d7
muls.w   y, d7
```

to represent the sub-expression **x*y**, we should add an instruction which checks the state of the flags in the condition codes register and reports an error if a problem arises:

```
move.w   x, d7
muls.w   y, d7
bvs      overflow_line_xxx
```

The **bvs** instruction checks the **ccr** register for the overflow condition, and if the multiply resulted in an overflow then the branch is taken. The **bvs** (and the **bne**) instructions are special cases of the **b_cc** instruction which branches on any of the test conditions. See Appendix B for a more detailed description of **b**_{cc}.

The label **overflow_line_xxx** is at some suitable place in the program which would contain the necessary instructions to report the error and allow the programmer to be aware that an overflow error occurred at line **xxx** of the Pascal program. If we repeat this exercise for the whole statement we see that some 50% of the instructions are error checking code!

```
move.w   x, d7           ; x
muls.w   y, d7           ; x*y
bvs      overflow_xxx
move.w   z, d6           ; z
muls.w   d6, d6          ; z**2
bvs      overflow_xxx
add.w    d6, d7          ; x*y+z**2
bvs      overflow_xxx
move.w   x, d6
sub.w    y, d6           ; x-y
bvs      overflow_xxx
beq      zero_divide_xxx
ext.l    d7
divs     d6, d7          ; value in d7
bvs      overflow_xxx
cmp.w    #max_for_x, d7  ; x in range?
bgt      range_error_xxx
cmp.w    #min_for_x, d7
blt      range_error_xxx
move.w   d7, x
```

The last four instructions prior to the final **move** instruction implement a range check – they test that the value of the expression is in the type range of the variable x. We can slightly optimise this sequence on the 68020/68030 by using a single instruction to perform both comparisons for **x** during the assignment. We can use the **cmp2** instruction which compares a register against *two* quantities:

```
        cmp2.w   x_bnd, d7
        bcs      range_error_xxx
        ...
x_bnd   dc.w     min_for_x
        dc.w     max_for_x
```

The two literal constants **min_for_x** and **max_for_x** define the minimum and maximum values that **d7** is to be compared with. The **cmp2** instruction compares its destination operand with both bounds and if the number is out of range than the Carry flag is set – hence the **bcs** instruction. The constants **min_for_x** and **max_for_x** can be located elsewhere within the program.

In practice it may be possible, by using 32 bit arithmetic instead of 16 bit arithmetic, to reduce the error checking instructions inserted. For example, if two single precision numbers are added together they might overflow the single precision; if they are converted to double precision and added we can guarantee that the double precision calculation cannot overflow. This allows us to delay testing for overflow, possibly until the assignment has to be executed; thus eliminating many of the test instructions. Some compilers automatically perform *all* expression evaluation in double precision. However it may not always be possible to double the precision of the arithmetic; for example when the original type is already 32 bit.

4.2.3 Exercises

1. Given that the Pascal variables **u**, **v**, **w**, **x** and **y** are 16 bit integers, show the reverse polish form of the expression

    ```
    u-v-w+x-y
    ```

    assuming that '-' and '+' are left associative: i.e. that

    ```
    a-b-c  =  (a-b)-c
    a+b+c  =  (a+b)+c
    ```

    Show a sequence of 680x0 instructions that implements this expression using the system stack.

2. a) Given that the Pascal variables **u** and **v** are 16 bit integers show the reverse polish form of the expression:

    ```
    (u+v)/(u-15)
    ```

    b) Show the 680x0 instructions that implement this expression using the system stack.

    c) Show what instructions would be needed if registers **d7**, **d6** and **d5** were available to simulate a stack.

3. Assuming that **w** is an *unsigned* 8 bit quantity, and that **u** and **v** are 16 bit quantities, generate the instruction sequence (including error checking code) to evaluate the expression:

    ```
    ((u*32)+(u/v))**w
    ```

Pascal compound structures

In Pascal structured data, such as vectors, matrices, stacks and queues, are primarily represented using combinations of records and arrays; in LISP and Prolog compound structures are formed, in a higher level way, using lists and trees. Here, it is our intention to examine the representation and manipulation of Pascal compound structures such as records, arrays and sets.

The 680x0 is, like most conventional processors, a fundamentally *scalar* machine: an individual instruction can only manipulate scalar quantities: bytes, words and long words. The largest objects routinely handled by processors as scalar objects are typically floating point numbers; even here the main 680x0 processor does not have any specific floating point instructions – instead a co-processor is linked to perform floating point arithmetic.

The key to handling compound structures in the 680x0 is the observation that they are nearly always represented – in memory – as *collections* of bytes and words. Although the 680x0 cannot deal directly with a compound structure as a single entity we will see that we can manipulate expressions involving them a 'piece at a time'.

5.1 Records

A Pascal record cannot be held entirely in a single 680x0 register. Record values are represented *only* in memory: as a collection of bytes – in fact as a *contiguous concatenation* of the component parts of the record.

Each component part of a record has a size: this size is pre-determined for scalar types (i.e. the number of bytes needed to represent the scalar variable) and the size of a compound structure is found by adding up the sizes of each of the component parts of the structure:

```
foobar  =  record
   foo:integer;          {2  bytes}
   bar:record
      a:integer;         {2  bytes}
      b:char;            {1  byte}
   end;                  {a  filler  byte}
   foop:^foobar;         {4  bytes}
   end;                  {total:  10  bytes}


fb:foobar;               {variable  uses  10  bytes}
```

The total space occupied by a value of type **foobar** is 10 bytes, therefore any variable of that type – including **fb** – will also occupy 10 bytes.

Notice that we have indicated a byte-sized *filler* – which holds no data – immediately after the byte sized field **bar.b**. We use a filler because we want to ensure that the pointer field **foop** is always on an even address boundary. With the filler, if the record as a whole starts on an even boundary then each word or long word length field in the record is also on an even address boundary. This is required for the 68000, but even on the 68020/68030 it is advisable since it is more efficient to access words and long words on even boundaries.

Knowing the sizes of each of the component parts of a record, we can determine the offset of each component from the start of the record:

```
foo     equ    0           ;the  0th  byte
bar     equ    foo+2       ;the  2nd  byte
bar_a   equ    bar         ;0th  within  bar
bar_b   equ    bar+2       ;2nd  within  bar
foop    equ    bar+6       ;last  entry
foo_len equ    foop+4      ;total  length
```

Notice that we have set up the equates to refer to symbolic values defined in earlier equates. Each equate only had to 'know' the size of the previous element in the record description. Putting the equates in this form makes the layout of complex records more manageable.

Since we can't access a record structure directly in a 680x0 register we have to do so indirectly through the memory. This means that in order to access or modify a component of a record we establish a pointer to the record in an address register, and then we can use offsets from that address to access the record's fields.

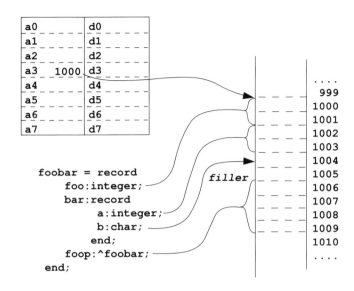

Figure 5.1 *The layout of a Pascal record in memory*

A typical Pascal statement which involves accessing a variable of type **foobar** might be:

        fb.bar.b:='9';

For us to be able to implement a statement like this we must first determine where the variable **fb** is in the memory. However, for the moment, we shall assume that we have already done this, and that address register **a3** has been loaded with the address of **fb**. To store the character **'9'** into **fb** we use this register as a base, and we add the pre-determined offset **bar_b** which gives us the location of **bar.b** within **fb**. The 680x0 provides us with a convenient way of doing this with the *address register indirect with displacement* addressing mode:

        move.b #'9',bar_b(a3)

In general, the address register indirect addressing mode is written as **Off(a_n)** or **(Off,a_n)**, where the offset **Off** is a number in the range -32768...32767. This addressing mode uses the value contained in the address register added together with **Off** as the address of the operand. So, in this case, the contents of **a3** (i.e. 1000) is added to the offset (which is 4 since **bar_b** has been **equ**ated to 4) to form the address of **fb.bar.b** as being 1004:

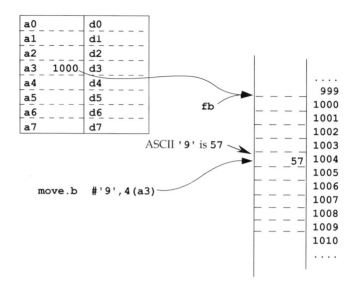

Figure 5.2 *Assigning to a field in a record*

5.1.1 Assignment of a record variable

We have seen that we can assign a scalar variable with essentially a single instruction. We may need several instructions to compute the value to be assigned, and we will often also need extra instructions to compute exactly *where* the scalar variable is located in memory so that we can update it, but the assignment itself can be performed in a single instruction.

In the case of a record variable, like the **fb** variable above, we cannot assign to the whole variable in one instruction because it is 10 bytes long which is larger than the contents of an individual register. We can assign to *components* of **fb** but not the whole of **fb** itself in a single instruction. If we want to assign a record variable as a whole, then we will need to use several instructions.

```
jb:foobar;    { another  foobar  variable}
   ...
        jb:=fb; { assign  a  whole  record  }
```

This assignment will require three instructions to implement. If we can again assume that register **a3** has been set up to point to the **fb** variable, and if we can also assume that address register **a2** has been set to point to **jb** then the assignment can be implemented as three **move** instructions:

```
move.l  0(a3),0(a2)
move.l  4(a3),4(a2)
move.w  8(a3),8(a2)
```

Notice that we can use these three instructions *no matter how many fields there were in* **foobar** providing that its length was still 10 bytes. The sequence of **move** instructions in the assignment does not relate to the individual fields in the records but rather to the total number of bytes needed to be moved. Indeed in this case one of the fields – **foop** – is moved in two pieces across the second and third instructions. We can do this because assignment is an *atomic* action from the point of view of the Pascal programmer and the state of the memory is consistent both before and after the assignment sequence (although not necessarily during it).

If the record is very large then the iterated sequence of move instructions might lead to a large number of instructions. We could, instead, implement the record assignment as a loop:

```
        move.w  #foo_len-1,d0   ;record  size
 @0     move.b  (a3)+,(a2)+     ;byte  transfer
        dbra    d0,@0
```

Here we are using a byte sized transfer together with the post-increment addressing mode to copy the record across. The address registers **a3** and **a2** are successively incremented in each pass of the loop so that they are always pointing at the next byte to copy. At the end of the loop, when all the bytes have been copied, **a3** and **a2** will point to the first byte *after* the **fb** and **jb** variables respectively. In practice of course, we wouldn't use a byte transfer – we would probably use a word or long word transfer – and have fewer passes round the copying loop.

The **dbra** instruction decrements the bottom half of the data register **d0** and if the result is **-1** then the loop terminates and execution continues with the next instruction. Otherwise, the processor jumps to the label **@0** and the loop is re-entered. Since the loop finishes when **d0** reaches **-1** we have initialized the counter **d0** with one less than the length of the record.

5.1.2 Pointers and pointer manipulation

In Pascal, records and record variables are often associated with pointers. A pointer is a scalar quantity which can address a variable of its associated type which may or may not be scalar. So, for example, this statement declares two pointers to **foobar** records:

```
fbp,jbp:^foobar;
```

and we might use the **jbp** variable to update a component in the record addressed by **fbp**:

```
fbp^.foop:=jbp;
```

Notice that while **fbp** is a scalar variable, **fbp^** is a record variable which would have to be manipulated via its address – but we can obtain that from the scalar **fbp**. The record element **fbp^.foop** is once again a scalar that can be processed directly. As we come to implement this Pascal statement we no longer need to assume that **fbp^** has somehow been loaded into **a3** – we can do this directly by loading it from the **fbp** variable:

```
move.l  fbp,a3        ;a3 is fbp^
move.l  jbp,foop(a3)
```

There are a number of programming clichés which are commonly used in pointer manipulation algorithms; two of which are *pointer following* and *pointer exchange*. A typical pointer following loop is:

```
while fbp^.foop<>nil  do
    fbp:=fbp^.foop;
```

The pointer assignment within this loop can be implemented in a fairly short sequence of instructions:

```
move.l  fbp,a0        ;pick up fbp
move.l  foop(a0),a0    ;fbp^.foop
cmp.l   #nil,a0         ;valid pointer?
beq     access_nil_line_xxxx
move.l  a0,fbp         ;assign
... ... ...             ;continue
```

A pointer exchange operation is used, for example, when a linked list is updated to add a new element – identified, in this example, by the **nw** variable:

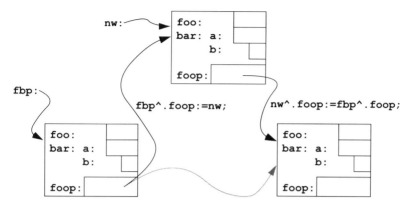

Figure 5.3 *Inserting an element into a list*

The old value in **fbp^.foop** is copied to the new element's **foop**, before being updated to point to the new element:

```
nw^.foop:=fbp^.foop;
fbp^.foop:=nw;
```

We can implement this fragment with the sequence:

```
move.l   fbp, a0
move.l   nw, a1
move.l   foop(a0),foop(a1)
move.l   a1,foop(a0)
```

5.1.3 The **with** statement

The **with** statement is used in Pascal to temporarily 'declare' the components of a record variable within its scope. For example, if we had to update all of the values of some record which is addressed by a pointer we could do so with the Pascal fragment:

```
nw^.foo:=10;
nw^.bar.a:=nw^.foo*23;
nw^.bar.b:='0';
nw^.foop:=nil;
```

In these statements there are many occurrences of the sub-expression **nw^**. This is both ugly and can easily lead to less than optimal code. We can use a **with** statement to find a neater way of expressing these separate assignments to the same record. The **with** statement temporarily declares the components of the records **nw^** and **nw^.bar** to be in scope, in effect defining new variables:

```
with nw^, bar do
begin
    foo:=10;
    a:=foo*23;
    b:='0';
    foop:=nil;
end;
```

If we were a naïve compiler, then the first set of statements would involve repeatedly computing the address **fbp^** as we accessed and stored values into the record. However in the second formulation, we can take the hint of the **with** statement and allocate an address register **a3** (say) to temporarily hold the addresses of **fbp^** and **fbp^.bar**. If we do this, then when we map the statement sequence, we can assume that we know where the variables **foo, a, b** and **foop** are in relation to **a3**:

```
move.l   nw,a3         ;the  with
move.w   #10,foo(a3)
move.w   foo(a3),d0
muls.w   #23,d0        ;foo*23
move.w   d0,bar_a(a3)
move.b   #'0',bar_b(a3)  ;b:='0'
move.l   #nil,foop(a3)
```

After the completion of the **with** statement then we can 'release' the address register **a3** for other roles.

Recall that we constructed the assembler symbols for the offsets of the elements of the **foobar** record by means of a series of equates. With a large program it is quite possible to accumulate large numbers of equates relating to the various records and other constants. Unless carefully managed, this can result in some confusion, especially if there are records with duplicate field names in them. A few assemblers have a more elaborate way of declaring record layouts which reduces this problem by isolating each record description. The technique is reminiscent of declaring storage:

```
barr    record  incr
a       ds.w    1       ;integer  word
b       ds.b    1       ;character  byte
        endr
```

together with a similar declaration for **foobar** itself:

```
foobar  record  incr
foo    ds.w    1      ;foo is an integer
bar    ds      barr   ;the bar record
foop   ds.l    1      ;long word foop
length equ     *      ;= size of record
       endr
```

The **ds.w** statements within the **record/endr** statements do not define storage: they simply define some symbolic names; it is as though we had the **equ** statements:

```
barr.a          equ    0
barr.b          equ    2

foobar.foo      equ    0
foobar.bar.a    equ    2
foobar.bar.b    equ    4
foobar.foop     equ    6
foobar.length   equ    10
```

The symbolic names that are introduced with this notation can be used instead of offsets; so for example, a Pascal statement such as

```
fbp^.foop:=nil;
```

can be written in assembler as the instruction:

```
move.l  fbp,a3
move.l  #nil,foobar.foop(a3)
```

The main advantage of using such record descriptors in assembler programs is that the names which are declared within the record are not global: a normal **equ**ate directive would declare a symbol for the whole of the remainder of the source file. With record declarations, we could describe several records, with possibly overlapping field names, and reduce the risk of confusion.

The record descriptions can be used to give a similar kind of support to the assembler programmer as Pascal does with the **with** statement. The assembler **with** directive 'declares' that the symbols within a record description are made directly available. Using field names within the scope of an assembler **with** directive would be automatically converted into the appropriate offset values. The scope is terminated by a matching **endwith** directive.

It is still however the programmer's responsibility to ensure that an address register has been appropriately loaded with the base address of the record. Our original initializing sequence can now be expressed as:

```
with      foobar              ;assembler  with
move.l    nw,a3               ;the  'real'  with
move.w    #10,foo(a3)         ;foo within  nw
move.w    foo(a3),d0
muls.w    #23,d0              ;foo*23
lea       bar(a3),a2
with      barr                ;nested  with
move.w    d0,a(a2)
move.b    #'0',b(a2)          ;b:='0'
endwith                       ;end  nested  with
move.l    #nil,foop(a3)
endwith                       ;end  outer  with
```

We also have a new instruction here: the load effective address – **lea** – instruction. This is an interesting and important instruction which loads the *address of an operand* into an address register rather than the *value addressed by the operand*. In this case the instruction

```
lea       bar(a3),a2
```

is equivalent to the pair of instructions:

```
move.l    a3,a2
add.l     #bar,a2
```

We can use any memory addressing mode as the source of this instruction – there is no numeric value for the address of a register however, so it is not possible to load its effective address!

The **add** instruction above is really an **adda.l** instruction which is a version of **add** which adds to an address register as opposed to a data register, but most assemblers automatically substitute **adda** for **add** when the destination is an address register.

5.1.4 Exercises

1. To delete the element identified by the expression: **fbp^.foop** from a list, we would use the Pascal statement:

    ```
    fbp^.foop:=fbp^.foop^.foop;
    ```

    Assuming that **fbp** is a pointer variable to a **foobar** record as seen above, show the sequence of 680x0 instructions which implements this assignment.

2. Show the sizes of the record types below, and determine the numerical offsets of the components:

```
d_entry  =  record
      mark:boolean;
      t:(a_tag,b_tag);
      n:^d_entry;
      end;
```

and

```
e_entry  =  record
      mark:boolean;
      n:^e_entry;
      t:(a_tag,b_tag);
      end;
```

Which record occupies less space? Why? Would you recommend that a compiler performed an automatic optimization of one to the other?

5.2   Representing arrays

Like records, arrays are not scalar objects, and therefore cannot be processed other than as structures in memory. Generally the elements of an array are laid out consecutively with the first element followed by the second and so on. For example, if we had the array declaration:

```
ai:array[1..10]  of  integer;
```

then the array **ai** would be laid out in memory as:

Figure 5.4 *The layout of an array in memory*

In order to access an element of an array we need to be able to convert the *index* of the element into an address in memory. This is done by computing the element's *offset* from the base of the array and adding in the array's base address.

   There are three aspects to computing the offset of an array element: we need to ensure that the index is valid, i.e. that it is within the bounds of the array; we need to map the index into a new range so that the first index is mapped to the first element of the array – which is always at offset 0 – and then we need, in general, to *multiply* the shifted index by the size of each element of the array:

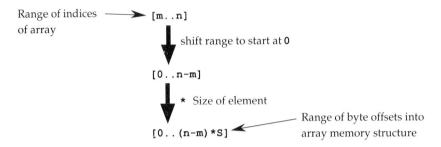

For example, if each element of an array occupies 10 bytes then the 3rd element in the array is 2*10 bytes from the beginning of it.

In the **ai** array above, each element is an integer, which we are assuming to be a 16 bit integer. Thus in order to convert an index into an offset we need to multiply the index by 2. For example, the Pascal assignment statement:

```
ai[x]:=32;
```

where **x** is an integer variable, can be mapped to the instruction sequence:

```
lea      ai,a2
move.w   x,d0
sub.w    #1,d0      ;array  starts  at  1
muls.w   #2,d0      ;convert  to  offset
add.l    a2,d0      ;add  in  offset
move.l   d0,a0
move.w   #32,(a0)   ;the  :=
```

Here we have assumed, as we did with record variables, that we do not yet know where **ai** is or how to find its address; so we have assumed that register **a2** can be set to the base of the array using some kind of operation similar to the **lea** instruction. This may indeed be a **lea** instruction, however it will not always be so. We shall be better placed to determine how to find this base address when we look at procedures and variable allocation within them.

As with scalar expressions, it is our responsibility to ensure that the expressions that we use to access array elements are within the bounds of the array itself: it is meaningless to access the 100th element of an array that only has 30 elements. In principle, checking for array bounds is the same as range checking for scalar expressions: to check that the value of the index expression is within the range of indices of the array we compare the index value against the minimum and maximum values permitted for the index:

```
lea      ai, a2
move.w   x, d0
sub.w    #1, d0        ; array starts at 1
blt      array_bounds_error
cmp      #9, d0        ; array bounds: [1..10]
bgt      array_bounds_error
muls.w   #2, d0        ; convert to offset
add.l    a2, d0        ; add in offset
move.l   d0, a0
move.w   #32, (a0)     ; the :=
```

We can use another of the 68000's addressing modes, the *address register indirect with index* addressing mode to optimise array access. The index addressing mode combines the use of an address register (which points to the base of the array), a second register (to provide the index) *and* a displacement.

An operand using this mode is written: **Off(a$_x$, r$_y$.s)** or **(Off, a$_x$, r$_y$.s)** where **a$_x$** is the address register, **r$_y$** is the index register which can be either an address register or more typically a data register, **s** is the size of the index (.**w** for word length or .**l** for long word length) and **Off** is a displacement or offset in the range -128..127.

The size specifier determines how much of the index register is to be used for the index size. In our case, since **ai** occupies less than 64 Kbytes, the indices into **ai** are integer or word length and so our index variables are also word length.

Using the indexed addressing mode we can shorten the sequence of instructions above by eliminating one **add** and one **move**:

```
lea      ai, a2
move.w   x, d0
sub.w    #1, d0        ; array starts at 1
blt      array_bounds_error
cmp      #9, d0
bgt      array_bounds_error
muls.w   #2, d0
move.w   #32, 0(a2, d0.w)
```

We can further reduce the instructions by making use of the displacement to take into account the fact that the first index of the array is 1 not 0. If we use a negative offset (-2) for the final move we can eliminate the subtraction from the index calculation. This is only possible if the maximum offset is in the range -128..127 bytes, otherwise we shall still have to perform an explicit subtraction. We can also replace the multiplication by 2 by an **add** which is a much cheaper operation:

```
lea      ai, a2
move.w   x, d0
cmp      #1, d0
blt      array_bounds_error
cmp      #9, d0
bgt      array_bounds_error
add.w    d0, d0
move.w   #32, -2(a2, d0.w)
```

We can compute the initial or base offset for the general case by calculating the size of the 'array' fragment from the first index to 0. This will be a negative amount if the first index is positive and positive if the first index is negative. The base offset can be expressed as the value of the expression:

-(1st index*size of array element)

If we had an array whose first index was negative, as in:

```
cha:array[-10..10]   of   char;
```

then the offset is found by multiplying the first index (which is -10) by the size of an element (which is 1 byte) and negating it, giving us an offset of 10 bytes – implying that the offset required to access an element of this array is 10. Only arrays whose first index is 0 use the address of the array without offsets to access elements in it.

The 68020 and 68030 offer a further enhancement to the indexed addressing mode: it is possible to *scale* the index. The scale factor is the number by which the index is *multiplied* before use in the address computation. The scale factor can be 1, 2, 4 or 8, corresponding to arrays whose elements are byte sized, word sized, long word or double long word sized. In our case, **ai** is an array of words, and so we can use a scale factor of 2. (The 68020/68030 also allows displacements to be 16 bit as opposed to just 8 bit on the 68000.)

If we also use the more advanced double comparison instruction **cmp2** available on the 68020/68030 then we get the sequence:

```
        lea       ai, a2
        move.w    x, d0
        cmp2      ai_bnds, d0
        bcs       array_bounds_error
        move.w    #32, -2 (a2, d0.w*2)
        ...  ...

ai_bnds:
        dc.w      1                    ;lower  bound  of  ai
        dc.w      10                   ;upper  bound
```

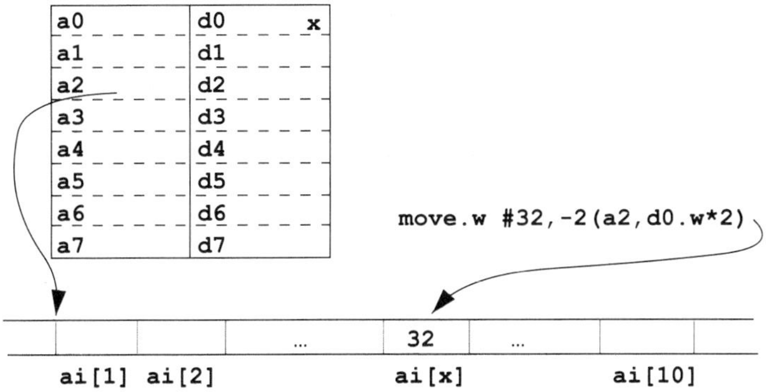

Figure 5.5 *Assigning an element of an array*

5.2.1 Arrays of records

Apart from simple vectors, like **ai**, we can also have arrays of records such as:

```
foobarray=array[1..10]  of  foobar;
...
fba:foobarray;
```

Since the size of each element of **fba** is 10 bytes, we cannot avoid the use of an explicit multiplication when we need to compute the offsets of elements within the array: the scale factor of the 68020's indexed addressing mode cannot help us. So if we had to implement an assignment statement which stored into the xth element of **fba** such as the assignment:

```
fba[x].bar.a:=y;
```

we should have to use an instruction sequence like:

```
with     foobar
move.w   x,d0
cmp.w    #1,d0 ;check  lower  bound
blt      array_bounds_error
cmp.w    #10,d0      ;check  upper  bound
bgt      array_bounds_error
mulu.w   #length,d0
lea      fba,a2
move.w   y,bar.a-length(a2,d0.w)
endwith
```

In the last **move** instruction, the expression **bar.a-length** refers to the initial base offset (which is -1 * length of a **foobar** record) but then we *add* an offset to address the field **bar.a** within the **foobar** record.

The most expensive operation here is the multiplication of the index by 10 which is the length of a **foobarray** entry. Earlier, in Chapter 2, we saw that it is possible, given that we know the multiplier involved in the calculation, to transform the multiplication into a series of 'shifts and adds'. In this case, the size of each entry in the array is 10, therefore we can perform a multiplication by ten by performing the simpler calculation:

$$x<<1+x<<3$$

We need only four 68000 instructions to implement this (assuming that **x** is already in **d0**):

```
lsl.w    #1,d0 ;x<<1
move.w   d0,d1
lsl.w    #2,d0 ;x<<(2+1)
add.w    d1,d0
```

The **lsl** instruction performs a logical shift to the left of a given number of bits. On average, the 68020 these four instructions execute in 12 cycles, compared to 29 cycles for the **mulu** instruction.

5.2.2 Arrays of arrays

In Pascal it is possible to have 2-dimensional (or even n-dimensional) matrices; for example, the declaration:

```
bi:array[0..20,1..10]of  integer;
```

declares a 2-dimensional array of integers. As with a 1-dimensional array, or vector, the array **bi** is laid out in memory as consecutive integer cells.

In this case however it must first be mapped into a 1-dimensional vector since memory itself is 1-dimensional:

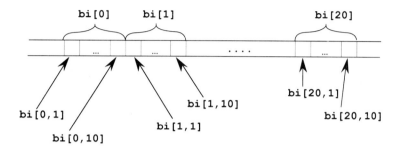

Figure 5.6 *The layout of a 2-dimensional array*

Each row of the 2-dimensional array/matrix is laid out as a normal vector; the vector of rows is then laid out contiguously. We can reduce any n-dimensional array into a single dimensional vector in the same way: lay out the various n-1 dimensional components of the array in a contiguous sequence. This is repeated recursively until you reach the 0th dimension: the individual elements of the array.

Accessing an entry in a 2-D matrix involves two multiplications: the first is by the size of an individual row in the matrix, which computes where the required row is relative to the base of the array, and the second is needed to access the required element in the row. So the Pascal assignment:

> **bi[x,y]:=z;**

is mapped to the sequence of 680x0 instructions:

```
move.w  x,d0    ;first  row  offset
mulu.w  #10*2,d0   ;could  expand  this
move.w  y,d1    ;next  column  offset
mulu.w  #2,d1   ;*  size  of  integer
add.w   d1,d0   ;complete  offset
lea     bi,a0   ;where  is  bi?
move.w  z,-2(a0,d0.w)
```

In this case the advanced versions of the indexed addressing mode (with the scale factor built in) on the 68020/68030 can only help marginally with the final index: it cannot remove the first multiplication. With higher-dimensional arrays it is even more important that the multiplications involved be as fast as is possible.

The multiplications involved in accessing a higher dimensional array can be avoided by using an alternative method for laying out arrays. If we take the case of a 2-dimensional array, we can observe that each row is a vector. Instead of simply laying out the rows of the array contiguously as we did above, we can have a vector of pointers to the base of each row.

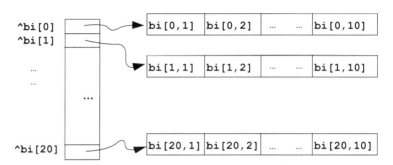

Figure 5.7 *A 2-dimensional array as a vector of vectors*

In order to access an element of this array, we look up the row address vector to get the address of the appropriate row, and then access the element within that row as we would for a normal vector. This is a matter of following pointers rather than computing offsets, which is potentially much faster.

The code for our previous assignment becomes the simpler sequence:

```
lea     bi,a0   ;where  is  bi?
move.w  x,d0    ;first  row  offset
asl.w   #2,d0   ;pointers  are  4  bytes
move.l  0(a0,d0.w),a0  ;get  row  address
move.w  y,d1    ;next  column  offset
asl.w   #1,d1   ;* size  of  integer
move.w  z,-2(a0,d0.w)     ;store  z
```

We are using here the **asl** (arithmetic shift left) instruction to implement a multiplication by four and by two. The first is needed because a pointer occupies four bytes, and the vector of row addresses is in effect a vector of pointers. Using the scale factors available on the 68020/68030 we can eliminate the left shifts:

```
lea     bi,a0   ;where  is  bi?
move.w  x,d0    ;first  row  offset
move.l  0(a0,d0.w*4),a0  ;get  row  address
move.w  y,d1    ;next  column  offset
move.w  z,-2(a0,d0.w*2)     ;store  z
```

This instruction sequence is typically twice as fast as the original sequence (assuming that one of the multiplications is actually replaced by a left shift). For this reason, this form of addressing higher dimensional arrays is used as standard by many 'C' compilers.

We can also use the same technique for implementing 3-dimensional arrays, or higher dimensional arrays:

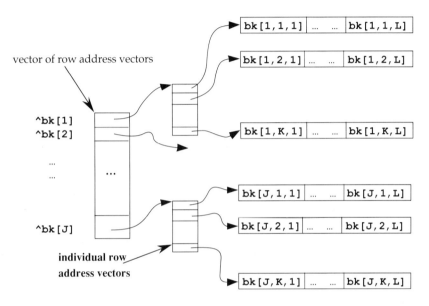

Figure 5.8 *Structure of* `array[1..J,1..K,1..L] of integer`

However, this technique for representing matrices does have an extra cost: for each row in the matrix there is an overhead consisting of a pointer to it. Similarly, for each plane in a 3-dimensional matrix, there is a pointer to it. For certain shapes of arrays (such as those which have many short rows) the memory overhead of row address vectors may be greater than the memory required for the array itself. Furthermore, the vector must be initialized when an array is created. This is itself an expensive operation.

5.2.3 Exercises

1. Given the following type and variable declarations:

```
jamjar=record
      jam:integer;   {16  bit  integers}
      jar:array[1..10]  of  ^jamjar;
      end;
......
jjp:^array[1..5]  of  jamjar;
jjn:^jamjar;
```

Write down the sequence of 680x0 instructions which is needed to implement the assignment statement:

```
jjp^[x].jar[y]:=jjn;
```

assuming that **x** and **y** are 16 bit integers. You should ensure that the array index variables, **x** and **y**, do not exceed the bounds of the various arrays involved.

2. Although on many occasions breaking up the multiplication into adds and shifts results in faster code, this is not always so. Assuming that the **add** and a **lsl** instruction take 3 cycles each, and that the general purpose multiply instruction takes 29 cycles for *any* value of operands, under what circumstances is it better to use the **mulu** instruction?

3. In the 'row address vector' method of representing higher dimensional arrays, there is an overhead of creating the row address vector each time the array variable is initialised. This could become a problem where the array is declared in a local procedure which is called often or even recursively. A normal contiguous array would not have this initialisation overhead.
    We can eliminate both the initialisation overhead, and most of the space overhead for each higher dimensional array variable, by creating a single standard vector of row offsets rather than row addresses. This vector is constant and could be kept with the program code: perhaps associated with the code for the program in which the array type is declared. It would contain *offsets* to the rows in an array; these rows are themselves laid out contiguously as a normal array.
    Show how an array of this type can be accessed, and show the instruction sequence needed to implement the assignment:

```
bi[x,y]:=bi[y,x];
```

using this strategy.

Advanced Pascal data structures

In this chapter we look at two related concepts in the representation of Pascal data: packed structures and sets. When the programmer indicates a *packed data structure*, be it an array or a record, then we must make every effort to use the fewest possible number of bits to represent the data structures. Packed data objects are important for two quite separate reasons: space efficiency and external interfacing.

Sets are used in Pascal where bit strings are used in other programming languages. Their implementation closely resembles the implementation of packed arrays of boolean.

6.1 Packed data structures

In many applications there tend to be a few data structures which are much more numerous and important than others. For example, in an accounting system there may be thousands of entries relating to various accounting events; each event would have an associated date component. A small change in the size that is needed to represent a date could have a significant effect on the maximum number of audit entries that the accounting system can handle.

On the other hand, since a packed structure will often *not* fit within convenient addressing boundaries, access to packed structures can be more complex and time-consuming than for a normally structured data object. Taken to excess – if *all* data objects were packed, for example – this can markedly reduce the overall performance of any application.

Another important justification for packed objects is access to external – i.e. non-Pascal generated – data. In a real-world computer system it is unlikely that a Pascal compiler can have the luxury of being the sole programming system used. Much more likely is the possibility of many languages being used, each for their intended class of applications – 'C',

Cobol, Fortran and even LISP or Prolog! Moreover, it is somewhat unlikely that other languages will structure their data objects in an identical way to Pascal.

A further important source of non-Pascal generated data is from physical input and output. I/O devices are quite likely to generate data which is not in a standard Pascal format. For example, a credit card reader, which is used to read the magnetic stripe on the back of credit cards, will read and write data which concerns a particular credit card. This data is highly compressed due to the fact that only a limited number of bits are available on the magnetic stripe.

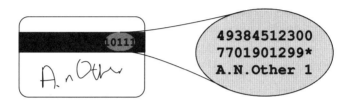

In this multi-lingual context it is important for a Pascal program to be able to access data structures generated under different language systems. The only 'safe' way of being able to guarantee access to other structures relies on a minimality assumption: if a programmer can predict *exactly* the number of bits a given Pascal data structure will occupy then it is possible to design them to match the characteristics of a data object from another language.

It must also be said that perhaps not too many Pascal compilers completely minimize the number of bits in a packed structure. For example, it would be reasonable to assume that a typical compiler will allocate 32 bits to pointers even though that 'wastes' 8 bits on a 68000 since it only needs 24 bits for an address.

Perhaps the most common packed structure that a Pascal programmer is likely to encounter regularly is the **string** which can be described with the declaration:

```
string=packed  array[0..255]  of  char;
```

or sometimes a different formulation is used:

```
string=packed  record
          length:byte;
          c:packed  array[1..255]  of  char;
       end;
```

Notice that in the second definition of **string** we had to indicate that *both* the whole record *and* the array of characters within it is to be packed.

If we had not said that **c** was packed then each entry in the array would probably have taken a 16 bit word on the 68000 and the whole record would have been nearly twice the size! (In fact the outer **packed** declaration would have been meaningless.)

A typical example of a packed structure with more than one field packed into a word is:

```
date_format=(american,british,other);   {2 bits}
month=(january,february,......,december);   {4 bits}

p_date  =  packed  record
    valid:boolean;          {1 bit}
    d_f:date_format;        {2 bits}
    mon:month;              {4 bits}
    day:1..31;              {5 bits}
    year:0..2100;           {12 bits}
end;                        {24 bits}
... ...
date:p_date;                {long word}
```

If we declare a variable in our program of type **p_date**, then we will devote a long word to the variable, even though only 24 bits of the variable are used. The remaining 8 bits are unused:

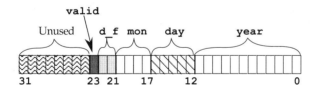

Figure 6.1 *The layout of a packed record*

However, if we had a packed array of **p_date**s then each record would be packed regardless of word boundaries: there would be no unused bits. (This also makes access to fields within the array even more complicated!)

In this example we have assumed that the packed record is packed from the right – from the least significant bit. This is a purely arbitrary decision, we might just as well pack the fields from the left or most significant bit. In any case the exact format of a packed record is not defined by the Pascal standard – each installation may have a different method. This variation is something that the Pascal programmer needs to be aware of when using packed data for applications involving access to non-Pascal data structures.

Recall that in a normal – unpacked – record each field rests on an appropriate addressing boundary of the machine. In a packed record the fields do not rest on byte boundaries; indeed a field might be spread *over* a byte or word boundary. For example, the **day** field (which occupies bits 12 through 16) straddles a byte boundary within the record. The lack of a regular addressing discipline means that we have to use more exotic methods for accessing and updating fields in a packed record.

Suppose that we had to change the day of the month in our **date** variable, we might do so with an assignment such as:

$$\texttt{date.day:=date.day+1;}$$

In order for us to be able to perform this assignment we have to extract the relevant bit field from the long word, increment its value, and replace the field into the variable – without altering any of the other fields in the record.

In order to extract the **day** field from the whole **date** record, we first of all 'mask off' all the other fields of the long word of the record by using an **and** instruction:

```
move.l    date, d0
and.l     #$1F000, d0
```

The number **$1F000** we used here is obtained from the bit pattern which has a 1 in every bit which belongs to the **day** field, and a 0 elsewhere. Where there is a 0 in the mask number the **and** instruction will clear the corresponding bit in **d0**, and where there is a 1 in the mask the original bit pattern will be preserved. This masking of unwanted bit patterns relies on the equations:

$$\mathbf{B} \wedge 0 = 0$$

$$\mathbf{B} \wedge 1 = \mathbf{B}$$

where **B** represents a bit from the data record.

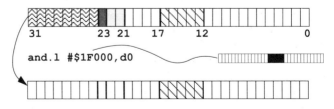

Figure 6.2 *Masking off unwanted data*

Having masked off the other fields, we now convert the **day** field into a normal number by shifting it to the right so that it is moved to the least significant position. This is so that we can perform normal arithmetic on the number in the **day** field.

```
lsr.l    #8,d0
lsr.l    #4,d0
add.w    #1,d0
cmp.w    #32,d0       ;range  error?
bge      range_error_yyy
```

The **lsr** instruction implements a logical shift to the right. The left hand bits are filled with 0 as the pattern is shifted to the right, and the last bit which is shifted off the right hand end of the register is collected in the **c** flag in the condition codes register. We have seen the **lsl** instruction which has the effect of multiplying a number by 2 for every bit shifted; the **lsr** instruction can be used to divide a positive number by 2 for every bit shifted. The **lsr** instruction is complemented by the **asr** instruction which preserves the sign of the number as it is shifted.

The maximum number of bits that can be specified as immediate data to the **lsl**/**lsr** instructions is 8: hence in order to shift by 12 bits we have to use two instructions and break the 12 bit shift into two shifts.

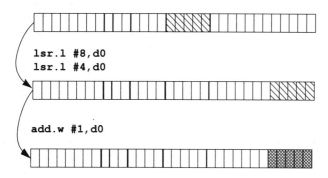

Figure 6.3 *Perform arithmetic on extracted field*

After the arithmetic operation we shift the answer back to the correct position in the long word for the **day** field with a logical left shift:

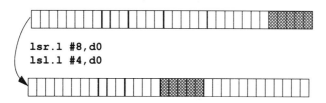

Figure 6.4 *Re-align data for packing into record*

Normally we would also have to use the **day** mask again on the result of the calculation, to make sure that no overflow in the calculation could contaminate the other fields. In this case the mask operation is not necessary since we abort the calculation and report an error if there is an overflow on the arithmetic.

Having performed the calculation on the **day** field we have to re-insert it into the original pattern for the record. We do this by first removing the existing **day** field from the **date** variable, with another **and** instruction:

```
move.l   date,d1
and.l    #$FFFE0FFF,d1
```

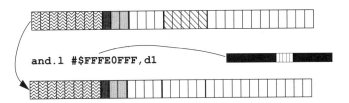

Figure 6.5 *Remove old field value from record*

Note that **$FFFE0FFF** is the complement of the mask we used for **day**: each bit in the mask is changed from a 0 to a 1 and vice-versa. Finally, we **or** the two patterns from the new **day** field and the rest of the **date** record, to get the final result and replace the new bit pattern into the **date** variable:

```
or.l     d0,d1        ;mix in new field value
move.l   d1,date       ;replace new record
```

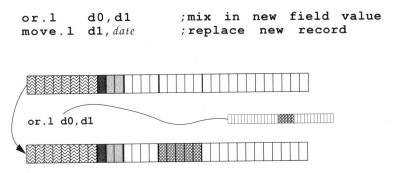

Figure 6.6 *Insert new data into packed record*

This assignment to the **day** field requires 13 instructions on the 68000 to perform; this should be compared to 5 instructions for an equivalent assignment if **date** were an unpacked record:

```
move.w    date.day,d0
add.w     #1,d0
cmp.w     #32,d0
bge       range_error_yyy
move.w    d0,date.day
```

Furthermore, the packed version executes approximately three times as slowly as the unpacked one. Clearly, accessing and updating packed records can be a lot more expensive than their unpacked equivalents.

The 68020/68030 processors have a number of special instructions which make access to bit fields within packed records somewhat easier. The main instructions we need here are the bit field extract instructions (**bfextu** and **bfexts** for unsigned and signed extraction respectively) and the bit field insert instruction (**bfins**). The first instruction extracts a string of bits of a given length from a source long word and places the result in a data register. So, our first group of instructions can be replaced by:

bfexts *date*{15:5},d0

which extracts the **day** field, and shifts it into position for an arithmetic operation, into the data register **d0**. The number **15** referred to in the instruction is the *bit* offset from the address **date** (counting from the left) where the **day** field starts, and **5** is the width of the field (5 bits). Both the offset and the width components of this instruction can be specified in a data register. If the offset is specified explicitly, as an immediate operand, then the offset is the range **0..31**, otherwise, if the offset is in a data register, then the offset can be up to ±2,147,483,647 bits! The maximum field size, whether specified in a data register or as part of the instruction, is 32 bits.

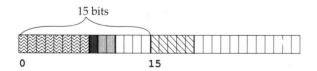

The complete assignment sequence is the same length as the unpacked assignment, though it uses different, more expensive, instructions:

```
bfexts    date{15:5},d0
add.w     #1,d0
cmp.w     #32,d0
bge       range_error_yyy
bfins     d0,date{15:5}
```

The **bfins** instruction puts the low order 5 bits from **d0** into the appropriate part of the **date** record.

6.2 Representing sets

A Pascal set is a different kind of data value than a simple scalar or array. A variable of type '**set of integer**' for example, has values which are *sub-sets* of the integers – the set [1,34,100] could be a value of such a variable.   Expressions and assignments over sets usually involve operations such as *element insertion* and *set intersection* rather than addition and multiplication which are typical expressions over integers.

Many Pascal compilers do not allow the programmer to have a variable of such a large type as a **set of integer**: usually the compiler imposes a limit on the number of elements in the base type of a set variable; this in turn allows the compiler to use an efficient representation for set variables.   The limit on the size of a set is not defined by the Pascal standard but we often see limits such as 32 and 256.   The limit of 32 is 'defensible' on the grounds that a long word can hold 32 bits and therefore sets of up to 32 elements are easy to implement.   On the other hand it can be argued that a set limit of at least 256 allows the programmer to construct a **set of char** which can be an extremely convenient data type.

There is no good reason why, for example, a declaration of the form:

```
i_set:set  of  0..1023;
```

should not be accepted by every Pascal compiler.

A set can be represented, in memory, as a (possibly packed) array of booleans: each index in the boolean array corresponds to an element in the base set. So, the **i_set** declaration might be *implemented* as though it were:

```
i_array:packed  array[0..1023]  of  boolean;
```

Given a particular value of the variable **i_set**, an element **I** in the range 0..1023 might be said to be '**in i_set**' if the corresponding array entry **i_array[I]** is **true**.

6.2.1 Set membership and element insertion

Perhaps the most basic operation on a set variable is to insert an element into the set held by it. We would do this with a Pascal assignment statement such as:

```
i_set:=i_set+[I];
```

If we interpret **i_set** as an array of booleans, then this element insertion is 'equivalent' to the assignment:

```
i_array[I]:=true;
```

Since we would want to use a packed structure to represent the set/array and since this set, at least, is too large to fit into a single long word (1024 bits needs 128 bytes), we have to be able to compute which bit in the array of 128 bytes is required to be switched on as a result of this assignment. This involves finding the appropriate byte and the appropriate bit within that byte.

To compute the appropriate byte offset within the array we divide **I** by 8 which is the number of set elements we can represent in a byte. The quotient of this division gives us the offset of the byte within the array, and the remainder gives us the position of a bit *within* the byte that corresponds to the element.

Since 8 is 2^3, we can divide the index by 8 very easily by right shifting the index by 3 bits. We can also, as a separate operation, take the remainder by masking off all except the lower 3 bits of the index. These two operations give us the offset of the byte in which the bit representing element **I** is held, and the bit position within that byte which represents **I** itself. All this requires just four 68000 instructions:

```
move.w  I,d0
lsr.w   #3,d0      ;index  ÷  8
move.w  I,d1
and.w   #7,d1      ;remainder  by  8
...
```

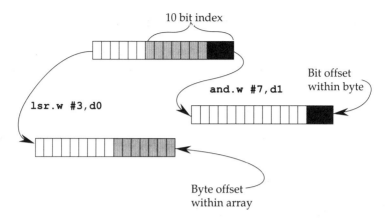

Figure 6.7 *Byte and bit offset from element index*

We use the number 7 in the mask to extract the bit offset due to the fact that 7, being of the form 2^n-1, has all 1's in its binary expansion: in fact $7 \equiv 0111B$. Once we have calculated the byte offset we can insert the element by turning on the required bit in the relevant byte. We do this using the **bset** instruction:

```
...
lea     i_set,a0      ;base of set
bset    d1,0(a0,d0.w)  ;turn on element
```

The **bset** instruction *sets* the bit indicated by its source in the memory byte indicated by its destination. In this case, the bit position to set is indicated by the contents of **d1**. If the destination were a data register then any of the 32 bits in the data register can be set by this instruction, however in the case of a memory address only bits within a single byte can be set. Notice that we have once again used the address register indirect with indexing addressing mode, this time to address the required byte in our packed array.

If we had wanted to *delete* the element **[I]** from the set then instead of setting the bit we would have cleared it with a **bclr** instruction:

```
...
lea     i_set,a0      ;base of set
bclr    d1,0(a0.d0.w)
```

We can also *test* to see if an element is in the set in a similar manner; except that instead of setting or clearing the bit we test it, using the **btst** instruction. This instruction sets the **z** flag in the condition codes register (leaving the other flags alone) according to the value of the bit that is tested:

```
...
lea      i_set,a0      ;base of set
btst     d1,0(a0,d0.w)
```

The **z** flag is set by the **btst** instruction if the bit tested is zero, i.e. if the element is not present in the set. If the element *is* present in the set then **z** will be cleared.

Having tested for the existence of an element, the next step depends on what context the test occurs in. If we wanted to set a boolean variable to **true** if the element **I** is in **i_set**, which we might do with a Pascal assignment like:

```
bool_var:=I in i_set;
```

then we have to convert the state of the flags, in particular the **z** flag, into a truth value which can be stored in a Pascal boolean variable. The 68000 has a special instruction: **sne** which sets the lowest byte of a data register to all 1's if the **z** flag is cleared, and to all 0's if not (in fact, there is a whole class of instructions of the form **s**$_{cc}$ where cc is one of the conditions such as **eq**, **lt** etc. which convert conditions into truth values). We can use the **sne** instruction to move the state of the **z** flag to a data register, and then to a Pascal variable; however, we must first reformat the 68000's notion of **true** to be consistent with Pascal's notion of **true**.

In Pascal, the **boolean** type is an *enumerated* type:

```
boolean=(false,true);
```

Under the normal convention for enumerated types, **false** is a constant with ordinality 0, and **true** is a constant with ordinality 1. Normally a value of an enumerated type is represented by its ordinality; and so, **false** is represented by 0, and **true** is represented by 1.

To convert the result of the **sne** instruction, which sets the whole byte to 1's or 0's, into a boolean, we must follow it by a suitable **and** instruction to mask off all but the least bit. This gives us the means of assigning the boolean variable:

```
...
sne      d0       ;state of Z flag
and.b    #1,d0    ;extract all but 1
move.b   d0,bool_var
```

The other context in which a set membership test often occurs is in the condition part of a conditional statement (i.e. **if-then-else**). In this case the state of the **z** flag is sufficient to guide the rest of the execution. The use of conditions to control execution is explored in Chapter 7.

6.2.2 Set intersection, union and difference

Other common operations on set variables include the formation of set unions, intersections and differences. These operations, which involve manipulations of the sets as a whole, are somewhat similar to assignments involving complete arrays, since they typically have to be processed piece-meal: byte by byte or long word by long word.

A typical Pascal statement to form the union of two sets **i_set** and **j_set** (say) would be written as:

```
j_set:=i_set+j_set;
```

We can compute the union of two sets represented as packed arrays of booleans by using the **or** instruction to union groups of bits together. We can see this clearly in the case of the union of two simple sets (**i_s** and **j_s**) each of which has up to 16 elements:

$$i\_s \quad = \quad [1,4,6]$$

$$j\_s \quad = \quad [2,4]$$

then the union of these sets is **[1,2,4,6]**:

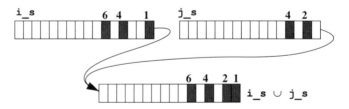

Figure 6.8 *Bitwise* **or** *as set union*

This union can be formed using the bitwise **or** instruction:

```
move.w   i_s,d0
or.w     d0,j_s
```

The extra work needed to union the larger sets with 1024 elements involves **or**ring each of the 32 long words/128 bytes of the sets in turn; typically we would perform this using a loop:

```
        move.w  #31,d0      ;32 long words to do
        lea     i_set,a0
        lea     j_set,a1
@1      move.l  (a0)+,d1
        or.l    d1,(a1)+    ;union 32 bits
        dbra    d0,@1
```

Recall that the **dbra** instruction will decrement the data register, and loop round to the label until the data register becomes **-1**. That is why the loop counter is set to one less than the number of iterations needed.

If we had wanted to perform a set intersection it would be essentially the same as set union, except that instead of **or**ring the bit patterns of the two sets together we **and** them:

```
        move.w  #31,d0
        lea     i_set,a0
        lea     j_set,a1
@1      move.l  (a0)+,d1
        and.l   d1,(a1)+    ;intersection
        dbra    d0,@1
```

and set difference is also similar, except that in this case there is no single bit-wise manipulation corresponding to set difference. However we can observe that set difference can be re-expressed in terms of intersection and complement:

$$A - B \quad \equiv \quad A \cap -B$$

where **-B** is the complement of **B**. Thus we can implement the set difference of **j_set** and **i_set** as:

```
        move.w  #31,d0
        lea     i_set,a0
        lea     j_set,a1
@1      move.l  (a0)+,d1
        not.l   d1          ;~i_set
        and.l   d1,(a1)+
        dbra    d0,@1
```

6.2.3 Exercises

1. Show how to use the **bfset** instruction (which sets all the bits in a
    bit field to 1's) to implement set element insertion more succinctly
    than using **bset**. The **bfset** instruction (which is not available on
    the 68000) is similar in format to the **bfins** instruction except that it
    has only one operand.

2. Show how to implement, in 68000 instructions, the Pascal
    assignment:

    ```
    bool_var:=i_set<=j_set;
    ```

    where **<=** means sub-set and **i_set** and **j_set** are sets of sub-range
    type: **0..1023**. Note that there is no direct 68000 instruction to
    perform sub-set test, but it can be re-expressed as a combination of
    intersection and equality.

3. Assuming that the variables **x** and **y** are integers and **z** is of type:

    ```
            z:set   of   0..1023;
    ```

    show the sequence of 68000 instructions needed to implement the
    assignment:

    ```
            z:=z+[x*(y+1)];
    ```

    you may assume that address register **a1** contains the base address of
    the set variable **z**.
      Ensure that the value of the variable **z** is faithfully represented in
    the machine.

CHAPTER SEVEN

Representing Pascal control

The process of constructing a program involves specifying not simply the data that is to be manipulated but also the actions to be performed over the data objects. We have seen that Pascal has a highly developed suite of mechanisms which can be used to specify data structures and expressions. It is now our intention to see how the control aspect of a Pascal program is mapped onto the computer.

The program control primitives define the combinations of actions which are legal in the language. They are chosen at least as carefully as the primitives for specifying data – based on experience of trying to build large programs.

Pascal has a simple collection of basic statement types; one of which – the assignment statement – we have already looked at in some detail. The other basic statement types are the conditional (**if-then-else**), the various loop statements: **for, while** and **repeat**, the **case** selection statement and the **goto** statement.

Together with these simple statements are the methods for grouping statements together into larger units. Of primary interest to us are the procedure/function definitions – with their corresponding call statements – and the compound statement. The procedure declaration is used, in Pascal, both as a way of grouping statements together *and* as a way of specifying the scope of variables; other languages, notably 'C' and Algol, separate out these aspects of procedures and blocks. It is when we see how procedures are implemented that we can finally see how to map variables to their proper place in the machine.

However, it should be pointed out that the most fundamental feature of programming in Pascal – the *single locus of control* or 'moving finger' which moves about the program text and which indicates which statement is being executed at any given time – is reflected at a very deep level in the machine: namely the program counter or PC. The program counter points to the currently executing instruction – which, we presume, is part of a sequence derived as a result of mapping Pascal statements to the assembler instructions.

Obviously this moving finger jumps around the program a great deal during execution but the *default action* on the completion of an instruction is to execute the next one in memory. This default is reflected in the most common and fundamental statement operator in Pascal: the ';' statement separator, which has the equivalent meaning of continuing execution with the following statements.

7.1 Simple Pascal control structures

As we noted above, Pascal has a range of simple control structures or methods of combining statements together. These are mainly derived from the structured programming methodology and correspond to segments of flow charts each of which have a single entry point and a single exit point.

7.1.1 Conditional `if then else`

The most basic type of control statement, after assignment, is the conditional statement. There are two forms of the conditional statement which have the corresponding syntaxes:

```
        if <test> then <S>
```
and
```
        if <test> then <S1> else <S2>
```

Whichever branch is taken – the **then** branch or the **else** branch – execution (normally) continues with the statement following the conditional. When a conditional statement is executed as 680x0 instructions the test or predicate part is evaluated first. The result of the test is usually to set some flags in the condition codes register in order to represent some condition; whereupon we can use a conditional branch instruction (b_{cc}) to select the **then** block of instructions or the **else** block.

We can describe the general structure of a sequence of 680x0 instructions which implements a conditional statement as:

```
                <compute test and set codes>
                b_cc      @ 0              ;select   branch
                <then instructions>
                bra       @ 1              ;exit     conditional
        @ 0     <else instructions>
        @ 1     ... ...                    ;continue
```

Normally, the test in a conditional involves accessing one or more variables or values and performing a comparison. The result of the comparison is reflected in the state of the flags in the condition codes register. The conditional branch instruction used selects the *sense* of the comparison based on the test in the Pascal program. So, we might, for example, wish to test a list of integers to see that the first element is greater than 20:

```
if  fbp<>nil  then
    if  fbp^.foo>20  then
       <s1>
    else
       <s2>
```

Here we have a nested conditional statement: the outer one controlling the inner conditional statement which is executed only if the **fbp** pointer is valid (not equal to **nil** at least). The inner conditional also has an **else** clause which results in **<s2>** being executed if the first list element is less than or equal to 20. This complete conditional statement can be mapped to the sequence of 680x0 instructions:

```
      move.l  fbp,a0
      cmp.l   #nil,a0     ;outer  test
      beq     @0
      move.w  foo(a0),d0  ;inner  test
      cmp.w   #20,d0      ;>20?
      ble     @1
      <s1>                ;then  branch
      bra     @0
@1    <s2>                ;else  branch
@0    ... ...             ;continue
```

The first **cmp** instruction is actually a **cmpa** instruction, which is a comparison instruction specialized to comparing against address registers. However, most assemblers allow the programmer to use the **cmp** mnemonic, and substitute **cmpa** for it, when the destination addressing mode is address register direct.

We should, at this point, look a little more closely at the conditional branch instruction, of which we have already seen some examples. The instruction:

```
cmp.w   #20,d0
```

compares the lower half of **d0** with the literal number **20**. It does this by subtracting 20 from the lower half of **d0**, *without* updating it. If **d0** was greater than 20 then the condition codes would be set by the **cmp** instruction so that a subsequent **bgt** instruction would take the branch given by its label. In this case we only want to execute the **else** statement (**<s2>**) if **d0** (which contains **fbp^.foo**) is less than or equal to 20. We can specify this using the same comparison followed by a **ble** instruction:

```
cmp.w    #20,d0
ble      @1
```

which will branch to **@1** if **d0** is less than or equal to 20. Altogether, there are 16 versions of the branch conditional instruction – corresponding to the 16 testable states of the condition codes register identified in Chapter 3.

The label operand of the **ble** instruction is an example of the *program counter relative addressing mode*. If the gap – in bytes – between the start of this instruction and the label **@1** was 10 bytes (say) then we could equally have written:

```
ble      *+10
```

where '***+10**' means 'add 10 to the program counter'. In order to take the branch – i.e. to go to the program instructions at **@1** – all that is required is to add 10 to the program counter. This is true no matter *where in memory* the two instructions – the branch and the target – are located, so long as they are 10 bytes apart. This, in effect, means that the program fragment is *position independent*; and that in turn means that we can change its position, i.e. move the program, dynamically without changing its meaning.

Having said that the **bra** instruction uses program counter relative addressing, we should also point out that this is the *only* addressing mode that **bra** can use: therefore it is slightly disingenuous to suggest that it has an addressing mode at all!

The 680x0 has good support for constructing position independent programs. So much so, that at least one operating system – the Apple Macintosh OS – *requires* that all programs are position independent. This is because the Macintosh OS does not guarantee where a particular program will be loaded into memory, which in turn allows a simplification of the hardware requirements for a Macintosh computer.

If a program *could* rely on being located in a fixed place in the computer's memory, then, in order to allow more than one program in the memory at a time, a hardware mapping unit – called a memory management unit – must be used to map logical addresses within an executing program to physical addresses in the machine; since it is certain that two co-resident programs *will* be in different places in the memory! It must also be said that enforcing a position independent discipline incurs a small overhead in the performance of an application.

The program counter relative addressing mode is available for other instructions, including **move** instructions. This allows us to have an instruction such as:

```
move.w  *+30,d0
```

for example, which will load the word located 30 bytes from the start of this **move** instruction into **d0**. Some assemblers will always use program counter relative addressing when the programmer uses a symbolic label and the label can be determined to be in the program, as in the instruction:

```
move.w  v_loc,d0
```

where **v_loc** is declared using a define storage directive:

```
v_loc ds.w    1
```

Conjunctions and disjunctions

The test predicate in a Pascal conditional statement can be quite complex; in particular the condition can involve conjunctions and disjunctions. In standard Pascal, if we have a conditional test of the form:

```
if   (fbp<>nil)and(fbp^.foo<20)   then
```

both of the arms of the conjunction may be evaluated; in much the same way as they would be had the test been written as:

```
bool_var1  :=  fbp<>nil;
bool_var2  :=  fbp^.foo<20;
bool_var  :=  bool_var1  and  bool_var2;
if  bool_var  then
```

To implement this form of conditional test we have to be able to remember the boolean values of the arms of the conjunction and explicitly 'and' them together. Recall that we can use the s_{cc} instructions (such as **slt** and **sge**) to extract conditions from the condition codes register. We use a **sne** instruction now to store the result of comparing **fbp** and **nil** prior to comparing **fbp^.foo** and **20**:

```
        move.l   fbp,a0
        cmp.l    #nil,a0     ;fbp<>nil?
        sne      d1          ;d1:=fbp<>nil
        move.w   foo(a0),d0
        cmp.w    #20,d0      ;fbp^.foo<20?
        slt      d0          ;d0:=fbp^.foo<20
        and.b    d0,d1       ;  ... and ...
        beq      @0          ;false->else
        <s1>
        bra      @1
@0      <s2>
@1      ... ...              ;continue
```

This definition of conjunction – and its corresponding version for
disjunction – can lead to a number of seemingly unnecessary run-time
errors since, as in this case, the *validity* of the second arm of the
conjunction may depend on the truth of the first. For example, if **fbp** was
equal to **nil** then it makes no sense to evaluate **fbp^.foo<20** since
trying to should result in a run-time error. In Pascal we would get an
error even though the conjunction is false anyway from the first conjunct.

The original Pascal standard required that both tests be performed and
the programmer had to make sure that all tests were valid. This is a
frequent cause for frustration, especially amongst new Pascal
programmers. The ISO standard is vaguer: it permits a compiler to test
both arms of conjunctions and disjunctions fully, but does not enforce it.

Some Pascal compilers implement a second form of conjunction called
the 'conditional conjunction'. In a conditional conjunction (and the
corresponding conditional disjunction) the right hand arm is only
evaluated if the left hand evaluates to **true** (**false** in the case of
disjunction), otherwise the conditional conjunction is **false**. Our
example test on the list element **fbp^** would be written:

```
if  (fbp<>nil)&&(fbp^.foo<20)   then
    <s1>
else
    <s2>
```

where **&&** indicates the conditional conjunction. Such a statement can be
expressed in standard Pascal as the nested conditional statement:

```
if  fbp<>nil  then
    if  fbp^.foo<20  then
        <s1>
    else
        <s2>
else
    <s2>
```

although in practice the **else** statement **<s2>** would not be expanded twice. We could also use | | to indicate conditional disjunction.

The conditional forms of conjunctions and disjunction are much kinder to programmers and lead to fewer run-time errors than the standard forms. This is because it is natural for the programmer to write tests which are themselves conditionally valid. We can implement the conditional conjunction with a series of conditional branches:

```
        move.l  fbp,a0
        cmp.l   #nil,a0     ;fbp = nil?
        beq     @0          ;skip out if nil
        move.w  foo(a0),d0  ;fbp is valid now
        cmp.w   #20,d0      ;fbp^.foo<20?
        bge     @0          ;skip out again
        <s1>                ;then case
        bra     @1
@0      <s2>                ;else case
@1      ... ...
```

While this form of conjunction is not available in all Pascal compilers, it *is* available as standard in some other programming languages, including 'C'.

7.1.2 Loop control statements

There are three types of loop control statements in Pascal – the **while** loop, the **repeat** loop and the **for** loop. A relatively simple processor like the 680x0 does not have direct support for the **while** and **repeat** loop structures (although there is some support for the **for** loop) so we have to build them with simpler instructions.

The repeat loop
The simplest type of loop statement in Pascal is the **repeat** statement. The body of this loop is always executed at least once, and the condition is used to decide if the loop should be re-entered. A skeleton of a **repeat** loop's construction:

```
        repeat
           <Statement>
        until  <Test>;
```

becomes, in 680x0 instructions, the structure:

```
@0      <Statement>          ;execute  statement
        <Test>               ;evaluate  test
        bcc     @0           ;loop  around?
```

So, we might have a simple **repeat** loop such as:

```
repeat
    i:=i+1
until  ai[i]>10;
```

which we can implement with the instruction sequence:

```
@ 0      add.w    #1,i         ;i:=i+1
         lea      ai,a0        ;test  ai[i]
         move.w   i,d0
         add.w    d0,d0        ;68000  version
         move.w   -2(a0,d0.w),d0 ;ai[]  start
         cmp.w    #10,d0       ;ai[i]≤10?
         ble      @ 0
```

The code that we have generated to implement this loop is not especially efficient since we are having to re-compute an array access for every test, whereas in fact, we know that in each iteration of the loop the array element being tested is actually the next one along.

If could take advantage of this fact, then a much more efficient loop code can be constructed which simply moves a pointer along the array:

```
         lea      ai,a0        ;point  to  first  ai[i]
         move.w   i,d0
         lea      -2(a0,d0.w),a0
@ 0      add.w    #1,i         ;i:=i+1
         move.w   (a0)+,d0     ;pick  up  next  element
         cmp.w    #10,d0       ;ai[i]≤10?
         ble      @ 0
```

It requires a very sophisticated compiler to generate this kind of sequence of instructions from the Pascal original. Furthermore, it is not all that clear how the knowledgeable Pascal programmer could write the loop so that a normal compiler could generate this code since the basic action of incrementing a pointer is not legal in Pascal. Later on, in Section 7.2, we look at some loop optimization techniques that a programmer or a compiler might employ.

The while loop
A **while** loop, which has the general form:

```
while  <test>  do  <Statement>
```

can be implemented with the structure of 680x0 instructions:

```
@0      <test>
        bcc       @1              ;exit from loop?
        <Statement>
        bra       @0              ;loop round
@1      ... ...                   ;continue
```

where **<test>** is implemented in the same way that we implement the conditional tests in conditional statements. The body of the loop – represented by **<Statement>** – is executed only if and while the condition holds. The only normal exit from this code is for the test to succeed and for the conditional branch to be taken to the continuation instruction.

As this loop is constructed, there is always at least one branch instruction in the loop body; with possibly a conditional branch out of the loop. We can save one of these instructions by organizing the code in a similar way to a **repeat** loop; but with an initial branch around the body to the code for the test:

```
        bra       @0              ;jump to test
@1      <Statement>
@0      <test>
        bcc       @1              ;exit from loop?
        ... ...                   ;continue
```

Such a saving may be important if the body of the loop only consists of a few instructions and the loop is executed frequently. We might have a **while** loop such as:

```
while ai[i]<ai[j]  do
    i:=i+1;
```

in which case we can implement this loop using the sequence of 680x0 instructions:

```
        bra       @1              ;initial  jump

@0      add.w     #1,i            ;increment  i
@1      lea       ai,a0           ;where is ai?
        move.w    i,d0            ;pick up ai[i]
        add.w     d0,d0           ;68000  version
        move.w    -2(a0,d0.w),d1
        move.w    j,d0            ;68020  version
        cmp.w     -2(a0,d0.w*2),d1
        bgt       @0              ;exit?
        ... ...
```

7.1.3 The `for` loop

A `for` loop is, in principle, similar to a **while** loop with a fixed type of conditional test and an extra *control variable* associated with it.

The existence of the `for` loop's control variable is usually taken as a hint to the compiler that it should be located in a data register – although it is not essential to do so. The general framework of a `for` loop such as:

```
for  <cont>:=<start>  to  <limit>  do
    <statement>;
```

can be realized in the structure of 680x0 instructions:

```
            move.w   start, control
            bra      @1              ;jump to test

    @ 0     Statement
            add.w    #1, control     ;increment control

    @ 1     control>limit?
            bcc      @0
            ... ...
```

In practice, `for` loops are often used in array processing; *any* operation (other than assignment) to a whole array requires a `for` loop to specify an iteration over the elements of the array, as in this example of summing two vectors:

```
for  i:=1  to  10  do
    ai[i]:=ai[i]+bi[i];
```

which we can implement in the 68000 sequence:

```
            move.w  #1,d7           ;we  assume  d7≡i
            bra     @1              ;jump  to  test
    @ 0     lea     ai, a0          ;ai [......
            lea     bi, a1          ;bi [......
            move.w  d7,d0           ;offset  into  ai/bi
            add.w   d0,d0
            move.w  -2(a1,d0.w),d1
            add.w   d1,-2(a0,d0.w)  ;ai[i]:=......
            add.w   #1,d7           ;increment  control
    @ 1     cmp.w   #10,d7          ;i>10?
            ble     @0
            ... ...                 ;continue
```

Of course a **for** loop need not have fixed bounds: either or both the initial value and the limit values can be specified through expressions (although it is undefined – in standard Pascal – what is meant if the expression governing the limit value *changes* in value during the body of the **for** loop). A more complex loop, to transpose a square matrix, might be:

```
for i:=1 to 10 do
    for j:=i+1 to 10 do
    begin
        e:=m[i,j];
        m[i,j]:=m[j,i];
        m[j,i]:=e;
    end;
```

Although in practice programmers may tend to prefer **for** loops which are incrementing, it is possible to have a *decrementing* loop in Pascal. Such a loop would be written using the **downto** keyword as in:

```
for j:=10 downto i+1 do
    begin
        e:=m[i,j];
        m[i,j]:=m[j,i];
        m[j,i]:=e;
    end;
```

The implementation of a decrementing loop is much the same as for an incrementing loop, except that we decrement the control variable and exit when it is less than the limit. This **for** loop has the implementation:

```
        move.w  #10,d6       ;assume j≡d6
        bra     @1
@0      lea     m,a0    ;m[......
        move.w  d6,d0
        mulu.w  #10,d0       ;each row has 10 els
        add.w   i,d0         ;column
        add.w   d0,d0        ;multiply by 2
        move.w  -22(a0,d0.w),d1   ;e:=......
        move.w  i,d2         ;other offset
        mulu.w  #10,d2
        add.w   d6,d2
        add.w   d2,d2
        move.w  -22(a0,d2.w),-22(a0,d0.w)
        move.w  d1,-22(a0,d2.w)   ;m[i,j]:= e
        sub.w   #1,d6        ;downto step
@1      move.w  i,d0         ;test limit
        add.w   #1,d0
        cmp.w   d0,d6        ;i+1<j?
        bge     @0           ;if so then exit
```

For certain kinds of decrementing loop, where the terminator is 0, the 680x0 has a special instruction – **dbra** – which combines the decrement of a control variable (which must be located in a data register) and the branch around the loop. The **dbra** has two operands: the data register and the label which is specified using the program counter relative addressing mode. It decrements the lower half of the data register and if it becomes -1 (i.e. if it was 0 to start with) then execution 'falls through' to the next instruction, otherwise the branch to the label is taken. So, if we had the **for** loop:

```
for j:=i+1 downto 0 do
    ai[j]:=ai[j]+k;
```

then we could implement it with the 68020 sequence:

```
        move.w  i,d7         ; j≡d7
        add.w   #1,d7        ; i+1
        blt     @1           ; early exit if j<0
@0      lea     ai,a0        ; ai[......
        move.w  k,d0
        add.w   d0,-2(a0,d7.w*2)   ; 68020
        dbra    d7,@0
@1      ......               ; continue
```

Notice that, in standard Pascal, the control variable may be undefined at the end of a **for** loop. This allows us to omit updating **i** with the final value of the control register **d7**.

The **dbra** instruction is a special case of the **db$_{cc}$** instruction, where $_{cc}$ can be any of the testable conditions. The condition $_{cc}$ is tested first, and if it is true then the loop will terminate and execution continues with the next instruction. Otherwise, **db$_{cc}$** acts like **dbra**: the control register is decremented and if it does not become equal to -1 the branch to the label is taken (presumably to the start of the loop body).

We can use a **db$_{cc}$** instruction to implement a string comparison in Pascal. Recall that a string is actually a **packed array of char** in Pascal, so a control expression of the form:

```
    if A<"foobar" then  ...
```

(where **A** is a variable of the appropriate type) could be compiled to:

```
        move.w  #6,d0
        lea     A,a0          ;address of A string
        lea     @0,a1         ;address of "foobar"
        bra.s   @1            ;branch to loop test

@0      dc.b    "foobar"

@1      cmp.b   (a0)+,(a1)+;compare bytes
        dbge    @1            ;continue looping end
        bge     @else         ;A is not < "foobar"
        ...                   ;then part of code
```

Apart from string comparison, Pascal does not often afford us an opportunity to use the general form of the **db_{cc}** instruction; but, if we could extend the **for** loop to add a **while** clause (as is seen in Simula 67 and 'C' for example) then we might have a statement like:

```
for j:=i downto 0 while ai[j]>k do
    ai[j]:=k;
```

and we could then use the **dbge** instruction to implement the loop controlling branch:

```
        move.w  i,d7          ;use d7 as loop variable
        blt     @2            ;j already <0?
        lea     ai,a0         ;keep pointer to ai
        bra     @1            ;branch to the loop test

@0      move.w  k,0(a0,d7.w*2)  ;loop body: ai[j]:=k
@1      move.w  0(a0,d7.w*2),d0
        cmp.w   k,d0          ;ai[j]≤k?
        dbge    d7,@0
@2      ... ...               ;d7 is invalid
```

The **dbge** instruction first of all tests the **ge** condition. If it is true – i.e. if the condition codes register matches it – then execution continues with the following instruction and the loop terminates. If the condition is false then the **dbge** instruction is equivalent to a **dbra** instruction: it decrements the loop counter register and branches to the label if it was not 0.

Because of the complexity of this instruction, in particular because we cannot predict the state of the loop control register, we have to assume that it is *invalid* after the completion of the loop: the programmer cannot rely on its value.

In practice it may be quite rare for a Pascal compiler to generate such instructions from a **for** loop in the program since most programmers write their **for** loops in increasing order rather than decreasing order. However, an important use for the **db$_{cc}$** instructions is to implement the 'hidden loops' generated automatically by the compiler to implement whole array or record assignments or string comparisons – in such a situation the compiler 'knows' the whole loop and it is easy to arrange it to make best use of the **db$_{cc}$** instructions.

7.1.4 Case statements

A Pascal **case** statement is used as a way of specifying a multi-way branch: it is often used when the different possible values of an expression can determine one of several actions to take. A classic example of this might be in a 'calculator' program which reads in expressions and evaluates them, by reading in a character and performing a case analysis on the character:

```
case ch of
   '0'..'9':        { read a digit }
   '+':             { add two numbers }
   '-':             { subtract  ......}
   ... ...
   'Q':             { stop }
end;
```

Such a case statement is logically equivalent to a nested **if-then-else** structure:

```
if ch in ['0'..'9'] then  ... else
if ch = '+' then  ... else
if ch = '-' then  ... else
... ...
if ch = 'Q' then  ... else
   {report an error}
```

While it is possible that some compilers might generate instructions equivalent to a nested conditional for a **case** statement (this might be especially true if there are only few cases) on the whole we would expect a compiler to optimise the selection so that at least each alternative could be reached with the same effort.

One common way of achieving this is to build – in the instruction stream – a **case** *selection table* of addresses of the sections of code which correspond to the alternative branches. This table is then indexed, using the value of the **case** expression, in the same way that an array is indexed, but instead of retrieving data the address of the appropriate section of code corresponding to the selected case is found.

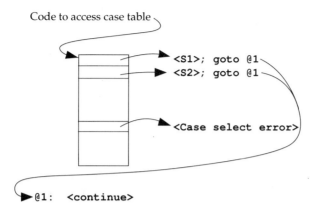

Figure 7.1 *Structure of a case selection table*

The main code for a case statement consists of computing the value of the expression and using this value to index the table. The table would normally consist of offsets to instructions rather than addresses:

```
        <compute exp>,d0              ;case exp. into d0
        cmp.w   #mincase,d0   ;min>label?
        blt     error_case_select
        cmp.w   #maxcase,d0   ;label>max?
        bgt     error_case_select
        add.w   d0,d0         ;index
        move.w  @0(d0.w),d0   ;get offset
        jmp     @0(d0.w)
@0      dc.w    @1-@0         ;offset to @1
        dc.w    @2-@0         ;offset to @2
        ......
        dc.w    error_case_select-@0
        ......
@1      <S1>                  ;1st statement
        bra     @99           ;exit case
@2      <S2>                  ;2nd statement
        bra     @99           ;exit case
        ......
@99     ......                ;continue
```

We have used a new instruction and a new addressing mode in this sequence of instructions. The instruction:

```
        move.w  @0(d0.w),d0   ;get offset
```

uses the *program counter indirect with indexing* addressing mode. This is similar to the other indexed addressing modes except that here we are using the program counter instead of an address register. In effect the program counter is used as the base address of an array from which we make an indexed access. The offset, in this case, is used to allow for the gap between the table and the start of the **move** instruction.

On the 68000 (as opposed to the 68020/68030) the offset must be in the range -127..127, so the table of offsets to labels must be close by. As with the normal indexing modes, there is a version of this addressing mode on the 68020/68030 which allows a scale factor to be used with the index.

We have also seen a new type of jump instruction:

```
jmp      @0(d0.w)
```

which is also using the program counter indexed addressing mode with an offset to @0. The **jmp** instruction is similar to the **bra** instruction except that the normal addressing modes are available to specify the target address – except for the register direct and immediate modes. This means, for example, that we can specify a jump to the contents of an address register:

```
jmp      (a0)
```

which jumps to the program whose address is in **a0**. This instruction will be used again when we look at the structure of code which implements Pascal procedures.

Notice that the addressing mode used in the **jmp** instruction is not to be confused with the 'address register indirect with displacement' addressing mode which would be written

```
jmp      0(an)
```

If an address register is to be used as an index, then the form:

```
jmp      *+0(ax.w)
```

is to be preferred.

The third new aspect of the code fragment for **case** selection is the use of *label subtraction* in the definition of the offsets in the table. A directive such as:

```
dc.w     @2-@0         ;offset to @2
```

causes the assembler to store in the word the difference between the addresses @2 and @0. Provided that both @2 and @0 don't move relative to each other, this difference is a fixed number which the assembler can determine even without knowing where they are in absolute terms.

An alternative method to implement a **case** selection table which is sometimes useful is to build the table from instructions – in particular **jmp** instructions – rather than label offsets. On the 680x0 certain forms of the **jmp** instruction occupy exactly four bytes; we can use this fact to build a 'jump table':

```
@ 0        jmp        @ 1
           jmp        @ 2
           ... ...
           jmp        error_case_select
```

and we index into the correct **jmp** instruction as though we were accessing a table of long words:

```
      compute    exp, d0        ; case   expression
      cmp.w      #mincase,d0    ; label<min?
      blt        error_case_select
      cmp.w      #maxcase,d0    ; max<label?
      bgt        error_case_select
      jmp        @0(d0.w*4)     ; 68020  only
```

The 'indexed jump' selects one of the **jmp** instructions to execute, executes it, which then causes a jump to the instructions for the selected case. If we are prepared to risk the possibility that an expression might be out of range, and not do the bounds check, then the index selection becomes quite short:

```
      compute    exp, d0
      jmp        @0(d0.w*4)    ; 68020  only
```

which is somewhat faster than a series of **if-then-else** statements.

In general, case labels in a **case** statement are not complete: there will be holes in the range of labels between the minimum label and the maximum label for which there is no case defined. For each of these holes in the table we insert a jump to the error reporting routine (or an offset to it in the case of a table of offsets). If there are too many holes in the range then it may not be worth constructing a table and an **if-then-else** construction might be more economical. Alternatively, if the case labels split into disjoint segments which are far apart then an **if-then-else** form might be used to select from two or more tables; each of which implements a segment of the case statement.

7.1.5 Exercises

1. Show the instructions needed to implement the fragment of Pascal control statements:

```
while  i>j  do
begin
   if  2*i  =  j  ||  j>10  then
      ai[i]:=j
   else
        ai[j]:=i;
   i:=i-1;
end;
```

2. The sea-brigade of the Pascal standard block has decreed that there should be an extension to the language: the conditional expression. An example of the use of this expression might be:

```
i:=  if  i<j  then  j  else  i;
```

Sketch out how you would compile such an expression, and give the exact instructions for the statement:

```
while  ai[if  i<j  then  i  else  j]<10  do
      i:=ai[i];
```

7.2 Coding for performance

Once of the explicit motivations for writing programs in assembler is to gain an efficiency advantage. Although modern compilers often generate very good code (i.e. sequences of instructions which are nearly optimal in their use of resources) it is still the case that a human programmer can often generate faster code sequences than can an automatic compiler.

There are a number of reasons for this – a human programmer often has a better grasp of the intentions behind a particular fragment of code and can therefore use this additional knowledge to produce a more specialized translation. A good example of this would be represented in the case of a multiplication by a power of 2: we know that if we are going to multiply by a power of 2 we can use a left shift operation instead of a general purpose multiplication instruction. A compiler could only perform this substitution if, in each multiplication, the multiplier was known.

Another reason why automatic compilers may not be so efficient is that it is hard for a compiler to have a global grasp of the program. Typically a compiler will translate sections of programs on a piece meal basis – each structural component of the Pascal original would be matched with a corresponding section of generated instructions. This leads to a fragmentary style of code generation.

We can see the cost of this in many loops, particularly when combined with arrays. For example, the loop:

```
for i:= S to E do
    fab[i].foo := fab[i].foo+jab[i].foo;
```

where **fab** and **jab** are **foobarray**s, would often be implemented in a fairly literal manner:

```
         move.w  S,d7             ;d7≡i
         bra     @2               ;go to end of the loop
@1       lea     jab,a0
         move.w  d7,d0
         asl.w   #1,d0
         move.w  d0,d1
         asl.w   #2,d0
         add.w   d1,d0            ;i*10
         move.w  foo-length(a0,d0.w),d2   ;jab[i].foo

         lea     fab,a0
         move.w  d7,d0
         asl.w   #1,d0
         move.w  d0,d1
         asl.w   #2,d0
         add.w   d1,d0            ;i*10
         add.w   d2,foo-length(a0,d0.w)

         add.w   #1,d7            ;increment control var

@2       cmp.w   E,d7
         ble     @1               ;end of loop?
```

A single pass through this loop involves executing 17 instructions. This code sequence has several deficiencies which are obvious to a human programmer. First of all, the offset into the **fab** and **jab** arrays are computed twice, even though that is not necessary. Eliminating this would save 5 instructions from the loop.

However, more radical savings are possible from this program. Consider the successive values of the offsets into **fab** and **jab** arrays in successive iterations of the loop. The first access is to the elements

$$\texttt{fab[S]} \qquad \text{and} \qquad \texttt{jab[S]}$$

The next iteration of the loop will involve accessing the elements:

$$\texttt{fab[S+1]} \qquad \text{and} \qquad \texttt{jab[S+1]}$$

In general, in subsequent iterations of the loop, we know that we will be accessing `fab[i+1]` and `jab[i+1]` respectively. If we already have the addresses of `fab[i]` and `jab[i]` then computing the addresses of `fab[i+1]` and `jab[i+1]` is trivial: we simply add the length of a **foobar** record to each address. If we can do that instead of recalculating the offset each time then we could save many instructions.

So, a more efficient way of implementing the loop is to establish two extra pointer variables (**a2** and **a3** say) which will step through the **fab** and **jab** arrays as the loop progresses. We initialise these variables by setting them to the first accessed elements. The reformulated loop is:

```
        move.w  S,d7

        move.w  d7,d0
        asl.w   #1,d0
        move.w  d0,d1
        asl.w   #2,d0
        add.w   d1,d0       ;S*10

        lea     fab,a0
        lea     -length(a0,d0.w),a2   ;a2≡fab[S]

        lea     jab,a0
        lea     -length(a0,d0.w),a3   ;a3≡jab[S]

        bra     @2

@1      move.w  foo(a3),d0  ;jab[i]
        add.w   d0,foo(a2)  ;fab[i]:=  ...  +  ...

        lea     length(a2),a2   ;a2≡fab[i+1]
        lea     length(a3),a3   ;a3≡jab[i+1]

        add.w   #1,d7

@2      cmp.w   E,d7
        ble     @1
```

In this version of the loop, only seven instructions are executed in each iteration (although more are executed during the loop set up).

Furthermore, the instructions are also cheaper (there is no indexed addressing for example). In all, the body will execute 100% faster than the original.

This kind of manipulation of programs is called *strength reduction*. Strength reduction relies on being able to determine the relationship between successive iterations of loops and substituting 'recurrence relationship' code for the original.

While some compilers do regularly employ strength reduction techniques they are quite expensive in compiler time, and problematic to implement correctly (i.e. without changing the meaning of the original in some subtle way). On the other hand, it is an obvious technique to the assembler programmer and it becomes second nature to program in this way directly.

Some languages – most notably 'C' – have taken a different approach to the problem of strength reduction. Instead of relying on the compiler, 'C' provides sufficient hooks to allow programmers to implement it themselves. A 'C' equivalent of the strength reduced program would be:

```
fp  =  &fab[i];
jp  =  &jab[i];

for  (i=S;  i<=E;  i++)
    fp++  ->  foo  +=  jp++  ->  foo;
```

It is precisely because it is so easy to code like this in 'C' that it is a popular language with many programmers. The drawback of providing these hooks is that they are easily abused, and it is unfortunately easy to make undetected mistakes. In this case, for example, it would be very hard to ensure that the array accesses represented by the statement

```
fp++  ->  foo  +=  jp++  ->  foo;
```

are within bounds.

CHAPTER EIGHT

The Pascal procedure

Procedures and functions are used in most programming languages as a means of structuring programs on a larger scale than individual statements. A procedure allows logically related groups of actions to be given a name and to be invoked in a single step. Procedures are especially important in Pascal as they are also used to establish the scoping of variables.

So, as we come to examine procedures (and functions) we look at a number of issues such as how arguments are passed to procedures, how variables are allocated and referenced, how a lexically scoped recursive language like Pascal can be supported and how the machine registers are 'conserved' in the environment of multiple procedures. We shall also see that the 680x0 is particularly well suited to the implementation of Pascal's procedures with its special mechanisms to support variable allocation and parameter passing.

The most fundamental requirement of an implementation scheme for procedures is the ability to call a procedure and subsequently return to where we called it from once the procedure has completed. Since Pascal allows procedures to be called recursively, any procedure calling mechanism for Pascal must also be able to separate multiple invocations of the same procedure.

The 680x0 has a 'procedure call' instruction – **jsr** – which allows for this. A call to a Pascal procedure with no parameters:

```
procedure  proc;
begin
   ......
end;
      ...
      proc;
```

can be implemented with a simple **jsr** instruction:

```
proc    ... ...             ;body of proc
        rts

        ... ...
        jsr     proc    ;call proc
```

The effect of the **jsr** instruction is to push the return address (i.e. the address of the instruction which follows the **jsr** instruction) onto the system stack, and then cause a jump to the program address specified by the operand of the **jsr**:

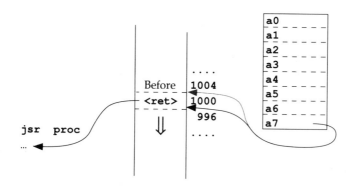

Figure 8.1 *The system stack after a* **jsr** *instruction*

<ret> is the return address left on the stack by the **jsr** instruction – it is the address of the instruction which follows the **jsr**.

At the end of the instruction sequence which implements the called procedure **proc** we insert a **rts** (return from subroutine) instruction. This 'undoes' the effect of the **jsr** instruction: it 'pops off' the address from the system stack and puts it into the program counter; i.e. continues execution from the point after the call.

This simple mechanism allows us to have an arbitrary depth of procedure calls – including recursive calls – since we are using a memory stack to keep track of which procedure calls are in force and where to return to for each separate invocation.

Although a primary function of the system stack is to keep track of which procedures have been called, and from where, it is not the only role that it plays (we have already seen that it is used in the evaluation of expressions, for example). As programmers, it is our responsibility to ensure that the system stack is balanced – that after executing a return to a calling procedure, the stack is returned to the same height/place as before the **jsr** instruction. It is a rather common error for assembler programmers in particular to fail to ensure this simple condition; this leads, at times, to some spectacular behaviour from our programs.

8.1 Parameters and local variables

In practice there are few procedures which have neither arguments nor local variables. Since a procedure can have either or both and since we have to be able to separate out the various invocations of a procedure, our concern with parameter passing is to ensure that we have a *consistent* mechanism – bearing in mind that a Pascal procedure can be recursive.

It is rather unlikely that a compiler can have access to both a procedure definition *and* all of its calls simultaneously. For example, a procedure which has been prepared for insertion into a library will be compiled quite apart from any potential calls to it. This means that when we compile a procedure we cannot rely on knowledge about calls to it, and similarly we cannot necessarily 'know' how a procedure is defined when we compile calls to it.

For this reason, a major concern in handling procedures with parameters, is to have a consistent and predictable mechanism for passing and accessing parameters to procedures.

So, we achieve this by using a standard parameter passing convention for *all* procedures; even if this may lead to some slight inefficiencies for some procedures. Such a convention consists of arranging for the parameters of a call to be put into a specific place where the procedure can access them during its execution. We explore two choices for locating parameters: the system stack and the machine registers, but first we shall look at the stack method.

In Pascal, there are fundamentally two classes of parameter that can be passed to a procedure: scalar and non-scalar; and there are two ways that a parameter can be specified: call-by-value and call-by-reference. For example, with a procedure template such as:

```
procedure   qs(fab:foobarray;
             f:integer;var  t:integer);
```

and with a call statement such as:

```
qs(fab,i+1,j);
```

we can see the some of the possible combinations of parameter types – **fab** is a non-scalar passed by value, **f** is a scalar also passed by value and **t** is a scalar is passed by reference.

The semantics of call-by-value are such that we have to compute the value of any scalar expression such as **i+1** that appear in the call statement before entering the procedure. If we use the system stack to pass parameters then all that we need to do is evaluate the expression – for

example by using the techniques described in Chapter 4 – and leave its
value on the stack:

```
move.w   i, d0
add.w    #1, d0        ; i+1
move.w   d0, -(a7)
```

If a scalar parameter is to be passed by reference, i.e. if it is a **var** parameter
as in the case of **t** above, then it must also be the case that the argument to
the call is a variable reference. (The address of an expression such as **i+1**
has no particular meaning.)   We pass a **var** parameter by leaving the
address of the variable on the stack rather than its *value*:

```
lea      j, a0          ; j  is  a  var  parameter
move.l   a0, -(a7)
```

The 680x0 has a shorthand for this construction – the **pea** (push effective
address) instruction:

```
pea      j
```

The **pea** instruction pushes the address specified by its operand onto the
system stack as opposed to the value of the operand. Of course, for us to be
able to use **pea** here, it must have been the case that we could specify
where the variable **j** is via a standard addressing mode. For example, it
may be that **j** was a field in the **j_r** variable which is a **j_rec** record
(say), in which case to pass the **j** parameter we would have:

```
lea      j_r, a0        ; where  j_r  is
pea      j_rec.j(a0)
```

where **j_rec.j** is the offset of the **j** field in the **j_r** record variable.
    If a non-scalar is passed as a **var** parameter then a pointer to it is passed
in the same way that we would for a scalar **var** parameter. On the other
hand if a non-scalar object is passed by value to a procedure then it must
be copied in order to prevent any assignment to the non-scalar affecting
the original.
    Before we can copy a non-scalar, we must find space for it somewhere.
This space – which is usually on the system stack – could be allocated
either during the parameter passing sequence or it can be copied later by
the called procedure. Given the possibility that the non-scalar may be very
large (an array for example), it would be advantageous to avoid
unnecessary copying. In particular it may be that, for example, we can
determine that the non-scalar is never updated by the called procedure. If
this were true, then copying the structure would be wasted effort.

For this reason then, and because it simplifies variable allocation, we always pass a pointer to a non-scalar even if the parameter is a value parameter. If the compiler (which, you will recall, is us) recognizes that a copy of a non-scalar is needed, then a copy is constructed during the initial entry into the procedure rather than during the call sequence. Another way to interpret this is that it is as though we *had* declared the parameter as a **var** parameter but included a local copy of it too:

```
procedure  qs(var  fab1:foobarray;
       f:integer;var  t:integer);
var  fab:foobarray;    { local copy of parameter }
begin
   fab:=fab1;          { copy fab1 into local var}
   ... ...
```

All the parameters, whether they are **var** or value parameters, are pushed onto the system stack just before the call to the procedure. The calling sequence for the complete call:

```
qs(fa,i+1,j);
```

involves, in order, pushing the address of **fa**, computing and pushing **i+1**, pushing the address of **j** and then entering the **qs** procedure's instructions:

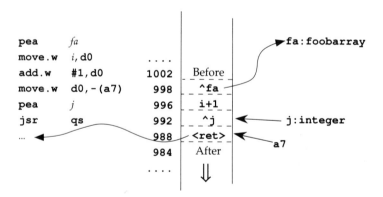

Figure 8.2 *Parameters on the system stack*

Accessing parameters in a procedure body
The observant reader will notice that the parameters of the call are laid out on the system stack in much the same way as a record – except that instead of being addressed by a Pascal pointer variable, it is addressed by the system

stack pointer **a7**, and there is another field automatically generated by the machine: the return address.

If we could rely on **a7** being predictable (which in fact we can't) during the execution of **qs**, then we could access the parameters of **qs** by using *offsets from* **a7**. For example, the **fab** parameter is located at **10(a7)**; and this allows us to identify and access **fab** from within the procedure. Given an expression in **qs** that involved accessing an element of **fab** such as:

······**fab[f].foo**······

we can generate the exact instructions needed to access this element:

```
move.l  10(a7),a0   ;fab[…
move.w  8(a7),d0    ;f…
mulu    #10,d0
with    foobar      ;foo  &  length  in  scope
move.w  foo-length(a0,d0.w),d1
endwith            ,
```

instead of the somewhat under-specified:

```
lea     fab,a0  ;fab[…
move.w  f,d0    ;f…
mulu    #10,d0
with    foobar      ;foo  &  length  in  scope
move.w  foo-length(a0,d0.w),d1
endwith
```

which we have used so far. We might also, as assembler programmers, prefer to use symbolic names – **qs.fab** and **qs.f** – as offsets, instead of the magic numbers 10 and 8 respectively.

Recall that if a parameter is passed as a **var** parameter then its address is passed rather than its value; this complicates access to the value of such a parameter. For example, in the expression:

…**f+t**…

the variable **f** is passed by value, so to access it requires a simple **move** instruction:

```
move.w  qs.f(a7),······
```

However, the **t** parameter is a **var** parameter; this implies that to access its value we must first access its address and then access its value:

```
move.l  qs.t(a7),a0
move.w  (a0),······
```

This would be normal for a non-scalar variable, which is always accessed via its address, but we have not seen it for scalar variables.

One problem with our technique for accessing parameters through offsets to the system stack is that we cannot always predict where it is going to be, relative to its position at the start of the procedure. Furthermore, this method does not allow for access to the parameters of a procedure from sub-procedures which are defined *within* its scope – it may not be possible to access the parameters of an outer procedure since we cannot predict how many other procedures have been invoked. We can solve this problem, and also see how to allocate local variables, by using another 680x0 mechanism – the **link** and **unlk** instructions.

8.1.1 Local variables

In general, a procedure is likely to have local variables which will also need to be allocated space. We do this on entry to the procedure since we need to create a separate allocation of the local variables for each invocation of the procedure in order to separate out the different calls: each time a procedure is called it starts out with 'fresh' variables. We already allocate space for parameters on the system stack – during the pre-amble to the procedure call – so it seems reasonable to allocate space for variables on the system stack also.

The 680x0 has a mechanism which can be used to implement this quite neatly: the function of the **link** instruction is to reserve space on the system stack and to leave an address register pointing at the reserved area. A **link** instruction which reserves 16 bytes, addressed by **a6**, would be:

```
link    a6,#-16
```

This instruction performs three actions to reserve the 16 bytes: the current value of the address register – **a6** – is pushed onto the system stack, the stack pointer – **a7** – is then moved to **a6**, and finally 16 is subtracted from **a7**. This last step ensures that there are 16 bytes on the stack which will not be overwritten should there be a subsequent stack push. The instruction semantics is to *add* the amount to the system stack pointer, which is why we specify a *negative* amount to add!

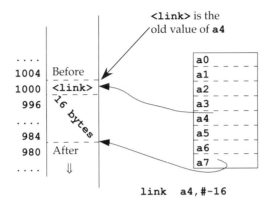

<link> is the
old value of **a4**

link   a4,#-16

Figure 8.3 *Allocating space using a* `link` *instruction*

We can express the effect of a `link` instruction in terms of other, simpler, instructions:

```
move.l  a6,-(a7)   ;save old link register
move.l  a7,a6      ;establish new link
add.l   #-16,a7    ;reserve 16 bytes
```

The fact that the 'free space' is below **a6** – which does not directly point to the allocated block – is largely immaterial: we simply use a negative offset from **a6** when we wish to refer to a location within the free space. The amount of space that we need to allocate is found by counting the space needed for each of the local variables and adding to it any space needed for local copies of non-scalar parameters which have been passed by value. In the case of **qs**, the full declaration of the procedure may look like:

```
procedure   qs(fab:foobarray;
        f:integer;var   t:integer);
var  i,j:integer;
begin
    ......
```

in which case we need four bytes for the local variables **i** and **j**, and 100 bytes for the copy of **fab** (assuming that it is an array of 10 **foobar** records, each of which is 10 bytes long):

```
qs      link    a6,#-104
```

After the `link` instruction has been executed, and after copying non-scalars which have been passed by value, we have a complete stack frame in which we can execute the newly entered procedure:

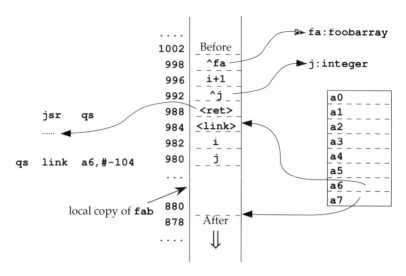

Figure 8.4 *Copying non-scalar parameters on the stack*

We can view the set of local variables as being part of a record: the difference between this record and a normal data record is that the offsets are negative, but we can assign symbolic names to them all the same:

```
qs.i   equ      -2
qs.j   equ      -4
qs.fab          equ    -104
```

In an assembler which allows record definitions, this might be done via the declaration:

```
qs     record decr   ;negative  offsets
i      ds.w   1
j      ds.w   1
fab    ds.b   100    ;100  bytes  for  copy
       endr
```

If we need to assign a local variable within the body of the procedure we now know where it is:

```
i:=i+j;
```

becomes

```
move.w qs.j(a6),d0
add.w  d0,qs.i(a6)
```

In fact, we can also use the link register to gain access to the parameters of the call: whilst a negative offset is needed to access a local variable, an appropriate positive offset will access the parameters of the call. The long words at the link register (offset 0) and immediately above (offset 4) are occupied by the previous link address and the return address respectively, but above that – from offset 8 upwards – are the parameters of the call.

The link register is fixed, and therefore offsets from it are valid, throughout the execution of the procedure body; unlike the system stack pointer which can vary considerably. This applies even if there are procedures which are called from within the body: provided that the link register is preserved across a call. (This is why the **link** instruction saves the old link register.)

So, we can now completely determine where all local variables and parameters to a procedure are located: they are accessed via offsets to a link register which is established on entry to the procedure. In particular, we can now completely specify all our assembler instructions.

8.1.2 The procedure epilogue

The 'epilogue' of a procedure must now perform other duties apart from simply returning to the caller. The allocated space must be 'returned' to the stack, the parameters which have been pushed onto the stack must be cleared off and only then can execution continue with the caller.

The complement of the **link** instruction is **unlk**. This instruction resets the system stack to its state to just before the link: the old value of the link register is restored and the system stack is cleared of all allocated space. In fact, the instruction

```
unlk    a6
```

is equivalent to the two instructions:

```
move.l a6,a7       ;release  reserved  space
move.l (a7)+,a6    ;restore  link  register
```

The fact that the **link** instruction preserves the old link value, and the **unlk** restores it, allows us to support local variables and parameters within recursive procedures. A new invocation of the same procedure will re-use **a6** to access its own locals and parameters; when the recursive call is completed the **unlk** instruction restores the previous environment so that access can be made to *its* locals and parameters. We can re-use the link register again in this way because we never need, in a recursive call, access to the local variables for both the recursive calls at the same time.

Having cleared the local variables with the **unlk** instruction, it remains to clear the parameters from the stack and to return to the caller. After the local variables have been de-allocated a typical stack frame still has the return address 'on top of' the parameters:

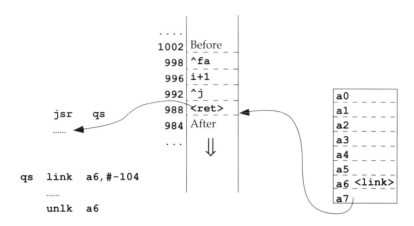

Figure 8.5 *Stack after an* **unlk** *instruction*

There are two possible ways to clear the parameters: we can immediately execute a **rts** instruction (since the top of the stack now contains the return address left by the **jsr** instruction), and let the caller remove the arguments that it has stacked; or we can remove them *before* returning to the caller.

The first method can be done using a stack adjustment after the **jsr** instruction:

```
jsr    qs
add.l  #10,a7      ;adjust  stack
```

We 'drop' parameters from the stack simply by adding a number to the **a7** register!

The disadvantage of this approach is that the stack adjustment must be replicated for each call and this means that compiled programs are larger; but perhaps more seriously it makes certain optimizations harder – in particular tail recursion is not possible. Tail recursion occurs when the last statement in a procedure body (or function body) is a call to another procedure. In such a situation we can normally reclaim the space occupied by the calling procedure before entering the new call — this means that certain programs will only use a bounded amount of space on the stack. Tail recursion is an important optimization, especially for symbolic languages.

In order for us to clear the stack *before* the return we have to perform some shuffling:

```
move.l  (a7)+,a0   ;return  address
add.l   #10,a7     ;drop  parameters
jmp     (a0)
```

Notice that we have, in effect, split the sub-routine return operation into two parts and inserted the stack adjustment into the middle. Although this sequence of instructions is longer than the first one, it executes in the same amount of time on the 68000: demonstrating that **rts** is a relatively expensive operation.

The 68010/68020/68030 processors have an instruction which simplifies the stack adjustment somewhat. The **rtd** instruction combines the effect of a sub-routine return with the corresponding stack adjustment; we can return and clean up the parameters from the **qs** program with the single instruction:

```
rtd     #10
```

8.1.3 A complete Pascal procedure

We are now in a position to see how a complete Pascal procedure can be implemented as a series of 680x0 instructions. Recall that in the introduction we promised that we would be able to translate the Pascal procedure:

```
procedure  swap(var  i,j:integer);
var  k:integer;
begin
   k:=i;
   i:=j;
   j:=k;
end;
```

This procedure has two **var** parameters: i and j, and one local variable **k** which occupies two bytes. If we use the register **a6** as our link register, we can access the local variable **k** with the negative offset -2, and the two **var** parameters **i** and **j** have positive offsets of 8 and 12 respectively.

The assignment

```
k:=i;
```

involves accessing the variable **i**, via a single indirection because it is a **var** parameter, and the local variable **k**. We can therefore implement this assignment with two instructions:

```
move.l  12(a6),a0  ;a0 = ^i
move.w  (a0),-2(a6);k := i
```

The complete **swap** procedure becomes:

```
swap   link    a6,#-2      ;allocate  k
       move.l  12(a6),a0
       move.w  (a0),-2(a6);k:=i
       move.l  8(a6),a1
       move.w  (a1),(a0)   ;i:=j
       move.w  -2(a6),(a1);j:=k
       unlk    a6          ;deallocate  k
       rtd     #8          ;clean  up  and  return
```

In our mapping of this program we have assumed that the compiler is clever enough to detect that the address registers **a0** and **a1** only need to be loaded once with the addresses of the variable **i** and **j** respectively.

8.2 Nested, scoped and global

Pascal allows procedures and functions to be locally scoped: i.e. a procedure can be declared to be local to or within the scope of another one. In fact the whole program can be viewed as a large procedure whose outer context is the operating system.

A procedure can access variables, parameters and procedures which are either defined within its scope or are part of the context in which the procedure itself is embedded. This can mean, for example, that a variable reference in a procedure body can be local, from an enclosing scope, or even a variable defined at the program scope level: i.e. a global variable. In general, a particular procedure may have access variables from several scopes. That in turn means that our scheme for accessing variables must be elaborated slightly.

We can do this quite simply by using a different address register as the link register for each scope or lexical level. For example, we might say that all the global variables in the program are accessed via address register **a6**, then all first level procedures defined at the global level use **a5**. This allows a first level procedure simultaneous access to its own variables – via **a5** – and to the global variables – via **a6**. Similarly a second level procedure – one which is defined locally to a first level procedure – might use **a4** for its local variables and parameters whilst maintaining access to outer scope variables through **a5** and **a6**. Thus a second level procedure can access its own variables, those of its enclosing procedure and the global variables.

In practice we might not have such complete freedom to choose link registers. For example, the Macintosh O/S requires that register **a5** is used for global variables. We can still use **a6** for the 1st level, and **a4** for the 2nd level and so on. The exact order or register usage is not important so long as the compiler is consistent.

We can use the same address register for all of the procedures at a given lexical level because although a procedure can access variables in outer procedures, under the scoping rules it cannot access variables at the same or higher lexical scope. Similarly, recursion can be safely implemented because a recursive call is simply a call to a procedure at the same lexical level as the caller!

In the Pascal program below we need to support three lexical levels, the program level and two inner levels:

```
program  pr;
var   a:integer;          {lexical  level  0}

    procedure   r;        {lexical  level  1}
    begin
       a:=2;
    end;

    procedure   p;        {lexical  level  1}
    var   b:integer;

        procedure  q;     {lexical  level  2}
        var   c:integer;
        begin
           r;
           c:=a+b;
        end;
    begin{p}
       q;
    end;

begin{main  program}
   a:=3;
   p;
end.
```

which we can do using **a6** for the globals, **a5** for the variables within the level 1 procedures **p** and **r**, and **a4** for procedure **q** which is at lexical level 2. Notice that the global variables are allocated using a **link** instruction; just as we do for the other procedures. This allows us to consider that the operating system can call our program just as though it were another procedure!

```
r       link    a5,#0        ;no vars,  level 1
        move.w  #2,pr.a(a6)  ;a:=2;
        unlk    a5
        rts


p.b     equ     -2           ;b in p
p       link    a5,#-2       ;level 1
        jsr     q            ;call q
        unlk    a5
        rts


q.c     equ     -2           ;c in q
q       link    a4,#-2       ;level 2
        jsr     r            ;call L1 pr
        move.w  pr.a(a6),d0  ;a
        add.w   p.b(a5),d0   ;a+b
        move.w  d0,q.c(a4)   ;c:=a+b
        unlk    a4
        rts



;  main program

pr.a    equ     -2
pr      link    a6,#-2       ;global var
        move.w  #3,pr.a(a6)  ;a:=3;
        jsr     p
        unlk    a6
        rts                  ;to O/S......
```

There are 8 address registers which, in principle, can all be used as link
registers; however, **a7** is already in use as the system stack pointer, and if
we wish to be able to implement indirect access to variables then we need
at least one, and preferably two, address registers for use in intermediate
calculations. This leaves 5 address registers that we can potentially use,
and that in turn means that we can support procedures up to five lexical
levels deep. This should support all practical examples of Pascal programs;
however if a deeper level is necessary then we can re-use some of the
registers and provide extra links to the missing lexical levels.

8.2.1 Registers and register allocation

So far, we have seen that we can allocate variables to locations on the
system stack. An assembler programmer would probably not use memory
– system stack or otherwise – for all the variables in the program; instead a
typical programmer would try to put the most important variables in
registers. This would be to gain the extra performance that registers give

over memory (after all, one of the motivations for using an assembler is to gain increased speed).

Some compilers also attempt to use the registers for holding program variables as opposed to using them as pointers to memory locations which themselves contain the variables. Typically, reflecting the different capabilities of the two register banks on the 680x0, we might use data registers to hold numeric or character values and address registers to hold pointer variables.

Obviously, the scope for using registers to hold variables is limited by the fact that there are only a fixed number of registers and the compiler must use some of them to support other necessary features. However, we do not need all 16 registers to support Pascal and and so some can be used to hold users' variables.

If some of the registers are to be used to hold variables, then we must ensure that their validity is maintained; if a procedure calls another one then any variables which are in registers must either be preserved by the calling procedure, so that they can be restored when the procedure returns, or the callee can save any registers that *it* uses and restore them before returning.

In either case, the likelihood is that several registers will need to be saved and restored on either side of a call. The 680x0 has an instruction – the **movem** move multiple instruction – which simplifies the process of saving and restoring groups of registers. This instruction has two forms, the first is used when saving registers and the second when restoring.

In order to save all the data registers except **d3**, and address registers **a2** and **a4,** on the system stack we would use:

```
movem.l   d0-d2/d4-d7/a2/a4,-(a7)
```

The specification of the registers to be **movem**ed allows any or all of the data and address registers to be saved in a single instruction. The same registers can be restored from the system stack using the instruction:

```
movem.l   (a7)+,d0-d2/d4-d7/a2/a4
```

The decision as to whether a given variable is allocated on the system stack, or in a register, depends on the complexity of access to it – whether the variable in question can be accessed from an inner scope or not – and the use to which it is put.

As we observed earlier, a compiler might make an effort to put integer variables into a data register if the variable is used as the control variable in a **for** loop. A pointer variable might be allocated into an address register if it is used frequently in pointer manipulations.

There are many competing uses for the registers – link registers, control variables, **with** statements, user variables and intermediate values in expressions. The use to which the registers are put depends on a balance chosen by the compiler writer. In many situations it is possible that all the requirements can be met without compromise.

For example, provided that they are preserved prior to their use, the address registers which are needed to support higher lexical levels can be made available to the lower lexical level procedures for use in **with** statements.

8.2.2 Exercises

1. Given the Pascal program below, show the complete sequence of 680x0 instructions that would implement the program. You may assume that address registers **a4** through **a6** are available as link registers, although you should indicate which you intend to use for a given lexical level:

```
program  telephone_sort;
{ sorts a list of telephone directory entries on the extension number }
const
    number_of_entries  =  30;
    max_array  =  number_of_entries  +  1;
    max_length  =  30;
type
    entry  =  record
                extn_no:  integer;
                name:packed  array[1..max_length]  of
                      char;
          end;
    dir  =  array[0..max_array]  of  entry;
var
    count:  integer;
    directory:  dir;
```

```
procedure  quicksort(var  d:dir;  first,last:
integer);
var
   middle:  integer;

   procedure  split(var  greater:  integer);
   var
      less,  ref_val:  integer;

      procedure  swap(i,  j:  integer);
      var
         temp:  entry;
      begin
         temp:=d[i];  d[i]:=d[j];
         d[j]:=temp;
      end;

   begin  {split}
      less  :=  first;
      greater  :=  last + 1;
      ref_val  :=  d[less].extn_no;
      repeat
         repeat
            less := less + 1;
         until(d[less].extn_no>=ref_val);
         repeat
            greater := greater - 1;
         until
            d[greater].extn_no<=ref_val;
         if less < greater then
            swap(less,  greater);
      until (less >= greater);
      swap(first,  greater);
   end;{split}


begin  {quicksort}
   if first < last then
      begin
         split(middle);
         quicksort(d,first,middle-1);
         quicksort(d,middle+1,last);
      end;
end;  {quicksort}
```

```
begin{main}
   directory[0].extn_no  :=  -1;
   directory[max_array].extn_no  :=  MAXINT;
   for  count  :=  1  to  number_of_entries  do
       with  directory[count]  do
           readln(extn_no,name);

   quicksort(directory,1,number_of_entries);

   for  count  :=  1  to  number_of_entries  do
       with  directory[count]  do
           writeln(extn_no  :  8,  '       ',name);
end.{main}
```

Using a suitable program development system, attempt to assemble, run and test your program.

2. Translate your answer to Question 6 in Exercise 2.2.4 into the appropriate sequence of 680x0 instructions.

3. Using a language of your choice, implement a Pascal compiler using the techniques outlined in this book.

8.3 Functions

In Pascal, functions can be viewed as being procedures with an extra argument which is represented as the result variable. A function call is implemented in the same way as a procedure call except that it always takes place in the context of an expression evaluation:

```
i:=max(j,k)+1;
```

The extra, hidden, parameter to the function call is filled in when the function variable is assigned in the body of the function:

```
function  max(i,j:integer):integer;
begin
   if  i<j  then
       max:=j        {assign  result  var}
   else
       max:=i;       {here  too}
end{max};
```

We can incorporate the hidden argument by passing an initially blank value on to the stack as the 'first' parameter:

```
move.w  #0,-(a7)      ;result  ...
move.w  p.j(a6),-(a7)  ;j of context p
move.w  q.k(a5),-(a7)  ;k of context q
jsr     max            ;call max
... ...
```

On entry to the function the space for the result is above the normal arguments to the function on the stack:

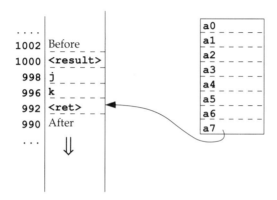

Figure 8.6 *Parameters to a function call on the stack*

When the function **max** has returned, the result of the function will be left on the stack, although the arguments **j** and **k** will have been cleared. This allows us to use the value of the function in an expression in the normal way:

```
... ...
jsr     max            ;call max
move.w  (a7)+,d0
add.w   #1,d0          ;max()+1
move.w  d0,p.i(a6);i:=......
```

The body of a function is compiled in exactly the same way as a procedure body, except that whenever an assignment to the function variable is indicated, then the 'hidden' space above the arguments to the call is assigned:

```
move.w  8(a5),12(a5)   ;max:=j
```

Apart from that, we allocate local variables on the stack in the same way as we do for procedures. The complete **max** function can be implemented as the sequence of instructions:

```
max.i equ      10            ;parameter  i
max.j equ      8             ;parameter  j
maxrx equ      12            ;result  parameter

max     link   a5,#0         ;no  locals.
        move.w max.i(a5),d0  ;i<j?
        cmp.w  max.j(a5),d0
        bge    @0
        move.w max.j(a5),maxrx(a5)   ;max:=j
        bra    @1
@0      move.w max.i(a5),maxrx(a5)   ;max:=i
@1      unlk   a5
        rtd    #4            ;clear  i  &  j
```

Notice that even if there are no local variables we still use a **link** instruction – with an allocation of zero bytes – to establish a convenient pointer to the parameters of the procedure or function.

This scheme of implementing function calls fits in very well with our method for implementing expressions using the system stack for intermediate results. A function call simply leaves its result on the stack as its contribution to the value of the expression.

However, we can also combine function calls with a register based scheme for expression evaluation provided that we preserve the intermediate registers prior to making the call, and restore them afterwards. In this kind of system, we would also use a data register – **d0** (say) – to return the value of the function, rather than using the stack.

8.4 The `goto` statement

The **goto** statement is almost redundant in Pascal; its function is largely replaced by the structured control statements such as **while** loops and **if-then-else** conditionals. However, there are a number of situations where a **goto** can be much more expressive and economical than the standard control structures; a classic example of this is in the early exit of a loop:

```
while  fbp^.foo<10  do
begin
    ......
    fbp:=fbp^.next;
    if  fbp=nil  then  goto  10;
end;
10:    ......
```

For simple situations like this, the **goto** statement is easily mapped to a **jmp** instruction:

```
        bra      @1
@0      ......
        move.l   p.fbp(a6),a0   ;fbp  in  scope  p
        move.l   next(a0),a0
        move.l   a0,p.fbp(a6)
        cmp.l    #nil,a0        ;fbp=nil?
        beq      @10            ;goto 10

@1      move.l   p.fbp(a6),a0   ;fbp^.foo<10?
        cmp.w    #10,foo(a0)
        blt      @0

@10     ......
```

Complications can arise, however, when the **goto** statement results in a transfer *out* of a procedure. This can occur when we jump from a nested procedure to a label in an outer scope, as in this example:

```
procedure  a;
label  10;

    procedure  b;
    begin
        ...
        goto  10;
        ...
    end;

begin
    a;
    ...
10:...
end;
```

In such a circumstance, we have to be careful to restore the system stack and various link registers to their correct state appropriate to the outer scope. A simple **jmp** instruction from a procedure to a point in the calling procedure potentially leaves the stack in a disordered state. Without adjustment the stack would still reflect the position *within* the called procedure – it would be unbalanced. However we can readjust the stack to take into account the **goto**.

Since the target label must be in an outer scope to the procedure with the **goto** statement it must also be the case that the link register for that lexical level is still in force, similarly for the lexical levels which are below it. It is not permissible, in Pascal, for a **goto** statement to exit to a procedure at the same or higher lexical level. We could take advantage of this and simply do nothing – we could ignore the space allocated on the stack.

When the 'target' procedure finally exits, it will execute an **unlk** instruction to clean up the stack in the normal way. This also has the effect of cleaning up the stack from the **goto** procedure as well; and it does not really matter that the stack was unbalanced: it becomes rebalanced after the **unlk** instruction.

However, it may still be important to clean up immediately after a **goto** because we cannot predict *when* the target procedure will finally exit; and until it does the stack will have some garbage on it. If the target procedure *never* exits, then this garbage is never reclaimed. Repeated occurrences of this could lead into problems of overflowing the system stack. We should therefore clean up after a **goto** by readjusting the system stack to eliminate the garbage.

The appropriate adjustment to the system stack would be to set it, at the point of the label, to the value it would normally have at the label *had there been no call or subsequent* **goto**. Generally, this involves setting the system stack to the same value as it had after the local variables were allocated – with a **link** instruction – at the beginning of the procedure.

So, a label in a procedure may not be simply a point within the program, but it may be translated into code which adjusts the stack. This code could also be executed for a normal 'flow through' the label not as a result of a **goto**. In this case the adjustment should have no effect. We can perform the adjustment using the **lea** instruction:

```
@10    lea      -locals(ax),a7
```

where **ax** is the appropriate link register, and **locals** represents the amount of space required for the local variables in the target procedure; i.e. it is the value used in the procedure's initial **link** instruction.

Notice that if a register saving scheme is in place then we must also make sure that we restore any registers that were saved prior to actually executing the jump. For example, if the end sequence of a procedure contained the sequence

```
movem.l         (a7)+,d3-d5/a2-a4
rts
```

then a **goto** out of this procedure would also have to restore these registers:

```
movem.l         (a7)+,d3-d5/a2-a4
jmp       label
```

Apart from the data registers, it is vital that any frame registers that may have been used are restored prior to the jump. This includes the local variables allocated by the exiting procedure.

In the case of a jump out of more than one lexical level it is often impossible to predict which frame registers have been used and need to be restored. In this case it becomes necessary to force the execution of the exit sequences of the procedures that the **goto** is passing through before jumping to the appropriate label in the target procedure. This can be done by patching return addresses on the stack, but this is a complex operation. In general, using a **goto** to exit a procedure is not to be recommended, and some languages (such as 'C') do not permit non-local **goto**s.

CHAPTER NINE

Symbolic programming languages

The symbolic programming languages – such as LISP and Prolog – tend to be quite different to the 'literal' programming languages such as Pascal. The difference arises primarily from the different motivations in the designs of the languages. Pascal is a relatively rigid type of language with very precise and tight rules about the legal data and program structures. On the other hand symbolic languages like Prolog, and especially LISP, are much 'looser' programming languages.

There is less discipline in the use of data and control in LISP and Prolog, which in turn frees the programmer from many detailed constraints. Symbolic languages are also much higher level and richer than Pascal. A typical LISP language system has literally thousands of library functions available to the programmer. The aim of such language systems is to take more care of the programmer and allow for greater productivity in the programming process.

On the other hand, the extra discipline imposed by writing programs in Pascal means that it is easier for the compiler to generate faster and more compact code from Pascal programs than it is possible from LISP and Prolog programs. Programs written in Pascal are often correspondingly faster than their equivalents in symbolic languages.

9.1 Recursive data structures

The differences between the symbolic languages and the engineering languages are reflected both in the data structuring features and in the control features. The dominant hallmark of symbolic languages is the liberal use of recursion: both data structures and control structures are recursively defined.

Symbolic languages are typically 'pointer free'. Instead of using pointers as addresses to records or arrays these languages use *recursive data structures*. A recursive data structure is defined in terms of itself. For

154

example, a Pascal list of integers would normally be defined using a type
declaration similar to:

```
i_list=record
       i:integer;
       next:^i_list;
     end;
```

The declaration of the component **next** within **i_list** is as a *pointer* to
another **i_list** record. The scalar property of Pascal pointers allows us
to predict exactly the size of an individual **i_list** record, even though
we might not be able to predict the size of a whole list.

Because Pascal has the separate notions of variable and pointers to
variables, *access* to a variable is written differently depending on whether
it is through a pointer or directly. If we want to check that the **next** entry
in a list is less than 20 (say) then we write:

```
if  ip^.next^.i<20  then   ...
```

The distinction between records and pointers to records disappears in a
language with recursive data structures; instead, pointers are handled
automatically. If Pascal were to have recursive data structures (which it
doesn't) then the above declaration might be:

```
i_list=record
       i:integer;
       next:i_list;          {  recursive  reference}
     end;
```

Our test on the first list element would now be expressed as:

```
if  ip.next.i<20  then   ...
```

which is the exact expression we might use if there were no pointers
involved in the original **i_list** data structures.

The **i_list** data structure is recursive since it seems to include itself in
its own definition. If we implemented the record according to the normal
rules for allocating space for records, a single **i_list** record would
occupy an infinite amount of space. In a language which supports
recursive data structures the **next** sub-record would be implemented by a
pointer to it; although this pointer would be *transparent* – it would be
invisible to the programmer. By using a pointer, as would be explicitly
necessary in a legal Pascal structure, the record becomes finite in size.

The fact that there are pointers in the expression above is hidden from
the programmer. Instead, the pointers involved in the implementation of
recursive data structures must be handled automatically by the language
system. Recursive data structures are a more high-level way of describing

data objects since the programmer does not need to be concerned with the fiddly details of using pointers.

Since pointers are no longer explicit in a system with recursive data structures, it follows that the programmer has less control over them. In Pascal, when we assign a record variable **ip** (say) to another record variable **jp** (say), we can choose whether to change the *pointer* to the record or the *contents* of the record itself:

```
ip := jp;           { pointer assignment }
```

versus

```
ip^ := jp^;          { record assignment }
```

In a language with recursive data types we cannot easily manipulate pointers – so the first statement is not part of the language – and the second statement is usually implemented as though it were the first; i.e. record assignment is performed in terms of pointer assignment.

If we don't maintain a distinction between pointers and records, and in particular if record assignment is implemented using pointer assignment, then the programmer also loses control over which individual data objects are in use and which are not. For example, when the **jp** variable 'goes out of scope', we cannot free the space used by the record addressed by **jp** because **ip** may still be referring to it. It is very difficult to predict just when the structure pointed at by **jp** can finally be reclaimed.

Typically a *garbage collector* is needed to clear up discarded data objects. This can lead to greater overheads both in execution time and in the memory needed for representing data objects.

9.2 LISP data structures

LISP was invented in 1957 by John McCarthy and his fellow workers in order to be able to implement *artificial intelligence*. It was obvious to them that FORTRAN was not a powerful enough programming language to make it practical to use for such an advanced objective. Many of the attributes of LISP arise from the basic requirement of being able to support the complex algorithms used to model intelligent behaviour.

Like FORTRAN, LISP represented a significant step in the use of mathematical concepts – in this case the notion of an abstract function – in the design of a programming language. In terms of the techniques invented to represent data, LISP was a great achievement and it has become an important vehicle for much of the artificial intelligence work carried out since that time. LISP is also a very powerful applications language. LISP is undoubtedly the simplest and most popular symbolic language in common usage.

Fundamentally, LISP has just two data types: the *atom* and the *list pair*. The LISP atom concept is more general than the Pascal notion of constants. As well as numeric constants, a LISP program can also have uninterpreted symbols as constants. This means that we can have, as a data item in our program, a symbol such as **fred**. This symbol need not be the name of anything – it needn't stand for a number or character as would be necessary in Pascal. Logically, an atom is simply an uninterpreted symbol: it always stands for itself.

Some examples of LISP atoms are:

123.4 fred   **nil**   **'john doe'**

LISP also has a method for combining data: the dotted pair or **CONS** pair. A **CONS** pair is simply a combination of two LISP objects (each of which might be a dotted pair also). We write the dotted pair of **A** and **B** as:

(A . B)

where **A** is referred to as the **CAR** of the pair and **B** is the **CDR**. The terms **CAR** and **CDR** are used for historical reasons: the earliest implementations of LISP were on the IBM 709 computer. This machine had two registers called the **C**urrent **A**ddress **R**egister and the **C**urrent **D**ecrement **R**egister. A frequent operation in LISP is to build the two components of the **CONS** pair; so they were typically loaded into the **A**ddress register and **D**ecrement register prior to building the pair in one step.

Where the **CDR** of a dotted pair is another dotted pair then we can use an alternative notation: the list notation. This is similar to the dotted pair except that instead of writing:

(A . (B . C))

we can write:

(A B . C)

There is a special case where the 'last' element is the special atom **()** or **nil** or ***nil*** – depending on the version of LISP. In this case the final dot is omitted, this allows us to write lists in a natural way:

(1 2 3 4 5)

instead of

(1 . (2 . (3 . (4 . (5 . nil)))))

There is no restriction on the form of the individual elements of a list: they can be other lists for example. This is heavily used in LISP applications and it often leads to deeply nested list structures with many levels of parentheses:

```
((a  .  1)  (b  c  d)  ((e  23.3)  f))
```

Note that the fractional number **23.3** is differentiated from a dotted pair by the absence of spaces around the dot.

This notation for describing data structures is called the *S-expression* notation. The S-expression notation is a fully recursive language for describing tree-like data objects. It is quite possible to program in LISP without any understanding of how S-expressions are implemented. The language of S-expressions is sufficient as a tool for 'thinking' about data. This is the second great achievement underlying the LISP language.

LISP programs are also valid data objects which are written as lists:

```
(defun  app  (x  y)
        (cond   ((nilp  x)  y)
                (T  (cons  (car  x)
                           (app  (cdr  x)  y)))))
```

The fact that LISP programs are also S-expressions is simultaneously a source of frustration and pleasure for LISP programmers. Frustration because the restricted form of the syntax often leads to deeply nested structures with a correspondingly large number of parentheses. On the other hand, the fact that programs are data makes some very powerful programming techniques possible.

9.2.1 Representing S-expressions

As we have noted, we cannot directly represent a recursive data structure such as a S-expression using a record. Instead, we have to represent the S-expression using a collection of records with pointers linking them together to represent its structure.

We can visualise this collection of records and pointers more easily by using so-called *box diagrams*. Each dotted pair is represented by a box with two compartments: the **CAR** and the **CDR**:

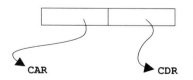

Figure 9.1 *A box diagram of a LISP dotted pair*

The lines coming out of the box indicate pointers to the **CAR** and **CDR** of the dotted pair. We can represent an atom as another kind of box:

"frederick the great"

Figure 9.2 *A box diagram of a LISP atom*

Each box corresponds to a record in the memory of the computer and each pointer is represented by the address of the box pointed at. Box diagrams can easily become quite complicated:

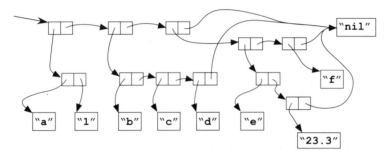

Figure 9.3 *Box diagram of* ((a . 1) (b c d) ((e 23.3) f))

The box corresponding to the **nil** atom tends to have a large number of references. To simplify our later box diagrams we will use the special box ⊠ to denote pointers to **nil** as in Figure 9.4:

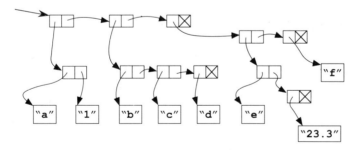

Figure 9.4 *Box diagram of* ((a . 1) (b c d) ((e 23.3) f))

A principal requirement of any data structure used to represent S-expressions is the ability to distinguish the two main cases – atom and dotted pair. One way of differentiating them is to include a *tag* with every S-expression's record which indicates what kind of structure it is. We could do this with the equivalent of the Pascal declaration:

```
tg=(atom,dotted);
...
s_exp=record
   case tag:tg of
      atom:......                  { see below for atoms }
      dotted:(car,cdr:^s_exp);
   end;
```

This scheme, which is fundamentally that used in early LISP systems, is called the *tagged record* representation, since each S-expression record has its type embedded in it. The other method, the tagged pointer architecture, associates with *each pointer* the type of object that it is pointing at. So, under this scheme, pointers are formed into cells, each consisting of a pointer and a tag, and a dotted pair is an array of cells:

```
cell=record
   case tag:tg of
      atom:......
      dotted:(ptr:^pair);
   end;
...
pair=array[car..cdr]of  cell;
```

This representation, which is the basis of many modern LISP and Prolog systems, is used because it reduces the overheads for some common types of atoms: notably integers. Some LISP systems have additional methods for structuring data: vectors for example, and the tagged pointer scheme makes this easier.

9.2.2 Representing LISP atoms

Paradoxically, the data structures needed to represent atoms are much more complex than those used for lists. This is because we need to remember much more about a LISP atom than we do about a Pascal constant. For example, the print name of an atom (the sequence of letters that are used to identify it) must be preserved by the LISP language system because it is a requirement that S-expressions can be printed as well as read in. There is no such requirement in Pascal, and so the Pascal compiler can 'forget' the names of constants declared by the programmer. (Of course, a Pascal symbolic debugger might choose to remember constants in order to aid the programmer.)

Furthermore, in LISP, atoms may have a number of *properties* associated with them – for example the program 'text' of a function is associated with the atom corresponding to its name. By accessing this text (which is represented using an S-expression) the programmer can inspect and modify the definition of functions in the system. This allows function definitions to be edited and the functions to be redefined which is also a fundamental requirement of any LISP system.

An atom can have other properties associated with it such as which module the symbol was defined in, a current 'value' and so on. LISP has a general mechanism which allows programmers to associate *any* kind of property with a LISP atom. All this means that the structure needed to represent an atom can be itself a complex example of an S-expression:

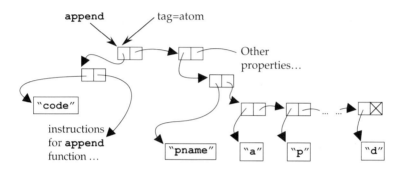

Figure 9.5 *The* append *atom structure*

Notice that the structure for an atom itself uses dotted pairs extensively. The distinguishing feature of an atom structure and a normal S-expression is that the **tag** field of the 'top-most' record is set to **atom** rather than **dotted**. Below this top-level dotted pair the structure of an atom is a normal S-expression albeit in a particular format. Standard access functions which operate over S-expressions also operate over the internal structure of an atom.

Another feature of the atom structure is that the print name of an atom can be arbitrarily long, since it is represented by a list of characters. (This would have been a relief for FORTRAN programmers in the 1950's used to identifiers being restricted to only 6 significant letters.) It is important to be able to 'hold' all of the characters that make up a name since we need to be able to read, print and re-read any S-expression. Unless all the letters in a print name are remembered there would be a risk of two atoms printing the same way, and hence being confused when the S-expression is re-read.

Symbol dictionary

Finally, especially given the complexity of an atom's structure, we make some effort to *share* the memory occupied by it. In particular, *all* references to an atom, in all S-expressions, are resolved to a single copy of the atom's structure in memory. This includes references from within programs and from within the system stack. This is done using a special symbol dictionary – traditionally called the OBLIST – which is used to keep track of all the atoms in the system.

Whenever an atom is read in, the dictionary is searched for one of the same name, and only if the atom is not already in the dictionary is a new atom structure created; otherwise a reference to the pre-existing atom structure is used. This ensures that all occurrences of atoms in S-expressions 'point' to the same object in memory and there is the added bonus that, once an atom has been read in, comparing with it another can be achieved by comparing addresses only. This is in contrast with Pascal strings where each occurrence of a string would be represented by a separate copy of the characters in the string and string comparison is implemented as a loop which compares the individual characters of the strings.

Having a unique location for each atom in turn means that certain crucial operations – such as finding the definition of a program – can be efficiently implemented.

9.2.3 Numeric atoms

In principle, the structure of an atom applies as much to numbers as it does to symbols. However, most LISP systems distinguish internally numeric atoms from other types in order to allow more efficient arithmetic manipulations. If we apply some restrictions to numeric atoms, such as not permitting them to have properties, we can simplify their representation considerably:

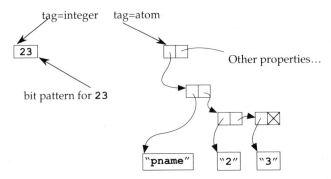

Figure 9.6 *Alternative representations of '23'*

Other possible special cases of atoms which would benefit from specialised representations include floating point numbers, single character symbols and 'special' system pointers (such as `nil`).

Big nums in LISP

Given that computers are often perceived to be almost wholly concerned with numbers and numeric calculations, it is perhaps a little ironic that very few programming languages implement arbitrary precision arithmetic. They often don't even allow the programmer to implement arbitrary size numbers. This is in spite of the fact that most processors give quite good support for multiple precision arithmetic. One exception to this is LISP which has 'big nums'.

A big num is a large number – one that cannot fit into a single machine register. So, in terms of computers, big nums are not scalar although mathematically they are. Big nums can be quite large: in certain mathematical theorem proving and algebra packages, implemented in LISP, a 'small' big num might have 80 decimal digits in it, whereas large big nums are measured in 'screen-fulls' and may have thousands of digits in them. Clearly arithmetic on such numbers is not as straightforward as 32 bit arithmetic, and therefore may well be slower; however, slower is better than not at all.

We need to consider two aspects of the representation and manipulation of big nums: the data structures needed to represent a number with an arbitrary number of digits (binary or otherwise) and the algorithms needed to perform arithmetic. We shall see that the latter tend to be reminiscent of long-hand arithmetic.

The simplest structure for a big num is a list of all the digits that make up the number:

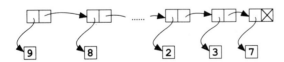

Figure 9.7 *98,537,195,986,590,732,017,237 as a list of digits*

However, this could be quite expensive in space: each dotted pair (and so each digit in the big num) occupies 10 bytes (say); whereas a single byte can hold the equivalent of over two decimal digits: a big num represented in this way would be 20-25 times as expensive as a regular number. More economically, we can split the binary expansion of the number into 32 bit chunks:

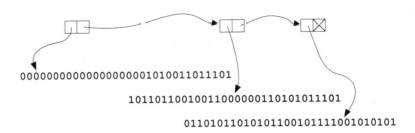

00000000000000000000001010011011101

10110110010011000000110101011101

011010110101011001011110010101

Figure 9.8 *98,537,195,986,590,732,017,237 in bit strings*

This representation is only 2-3 times larger than the space needed to represent the pure bit string itself.

If we are to perform arithmetic on such numbers then we have to do it on a piece-meal basis also – preferably in 32 bit chunks. This means that we need to see how multi-word arithmetic can be done in a fixed word machine.

Suppose that we were to add the numbers 120 and 150 in 8 bit arithmetic. The 680x0 processor allows us to do so, using the **add.b** instruction:

```
move.b  #120,d0
add.b   #150,d0
```

The result of this addition is 14 (since $\lfloor 270 \rfloor_{256}=14$), but the processor also sets the carry flag to 1 to indicate that the result overflowed the ability of 8 bits to represent the result. It is also true that the binary expansion of 270 consists of a leading 1 (the carry bit) followed by the binary expansion of 14:

$$270 \quad = 1*2^8+0*2^7+0*2^6+0*2^5+0*2^4+1*2^3+1*2^2+1*2^1+0*2^0$$

$$14 \quad = \quad 0*2^7+0*2^6+0*2^5+0*2^4+1*2^3+1*2^2+1*2^1+0*2^0$$

We can use this fact to implement multi-precision arithmetic. Suppose that we wanted to perform the calculation 1000+2000 in a system which only allowed 8 bit arithmetic. The numbers 1000 and 2000 are 0000001111101000B and 0000011111010000B in binary respectively, which, split into 8 bit 'chunks' form the numbers:

$$1000 \quad = 00000011B*256 + 11101000B = 3*256 + \mathbf{232}$$

$$2000 \quad = 00000111B*256 + 11010000B = 7*256 + \mathbf{208}$$

If we wish to add 1000 and 2000 we can do this in chunks also:

$$1000+2000 \qquad = 3*256 + \mathbf{232} + 7*256 + \mathbf{208}$$

$$= (3+7)*256 + (\mathbf{232+208})$$

If we add the numbers corresponding to the lower halves in 8 bit arithmetic we get 184 with the Carry flag set since $|232+208 = 440|_{256}=184$. This means that the sum can also be expressed as:

$$= (\mathbf{3+7+1})*256+\mathbf{184}$$

$$= \mathbf{11}*256+\mathbf{184}$$

We can perform this kind of multi-precision arithmetic just as easily on the 680x0. The e**X**tend flag is used on the 680x0 in preference to the Carry flag to implement multi-precision arithmetic. The e**X**tend flag is generated in a similar way to the Carry flag, but it may also be used as input to some specialized arithmetic instructions.

The normal **add** instruction only adds two integers, it will *generate* a valid Carry (and e**X**tend) flag but it does not use it for input. The **addx** instruction on the other hand is an *extended* addition – it adds its operands in the same way as **add**, except that it also adds in the e**X**tend flag as well as generating the next one. So, we could have added 1000 and 2000 in 8 bit chunks on the 680x0 using the instructions:

```
move.b  #232,d0    ;lower  half  of  1000
add.b   #208,d0    ;lower  half  of  2000
move.b  #3,d1      ;upper  half  of  1000
move.b  #7,d2      ;upper  half  of  2000
addx.b  d2,d1      ;d1=3+7+X=11
```

The result is held in the registers **d1** and **d0**, and corresponds to the final answer of 11*256+184=3000. The **addx** instruction, unlike the **add** instruction, requires that *both* its operands be in data registers, or they can both be address register indirect with pre-decrement operands. The same applies to the analogous instruction **subx**.

Clearly we would not normally go to the trouble of performing 16 bit arithmetic in this way since the 680x0 has perfectly adequate 16 and 32 bit addition instructions. However, we have to use techniques like these to add 70 bit numbers or 2000 bit numbers. The big num algorithms for addition, subtraction and multiplication etc. do precisely this, for numbers represented as lists of 32 bit chunks. These algorithms will also have to take care of factors such as aligning the lists of chunks together, and performing mixed arithmetic between normal numbers and big nums.

9.2.4 CONS pairs, heaps and collecting garbage

One rather common and fundamental expression found in LISP programs involves the **CONS** function. The value of a **cons** expression:

```
(cons  a  b)
```

is a dotted pair, whose **car** is the value of **a** and whose **cdr** is the value of **b**. Thus, assuming that there is no conflict with side effects, we have the equivalence:

$$(car \ (cons \ a \ b)) \ \equiv \ a$$

and

$$(cdr \ (cons \ a \ b)) \ \equiv \ b$$

To implement **cons** requires us to create a new dotted pair which is represented, as we have seen, by a record structure. The space for this record has to be found dynamically since the **cons** structure is the result of a dynamic evaluation. All the space which is used for creating dotted pairs is found from a *heap*. The heap forms a central data structure which is as important to LISP as the system stack is to Pascal (although it, too, is important to LISP). The organization of heaps is a critical issue to the implementer of LISP systems – an error here can cause great problems which are often hard to to detect.

One simple method of organizing a heap involves allocated a region in the memory and linking all the unused records into a *free list*. We can take advantage of the fact that each dotted pair must have room for two pointers: one for the **car** field and one for the **cdr** field. Since these fields are by definition unused for records in the free list, we can use one of them to build the free list itself. Also, since all S-expressions have the same size record structure, we do not have to search for a block of the correct size: the first block in the free list is guaranteed to be the correct size for the **cons** pair.

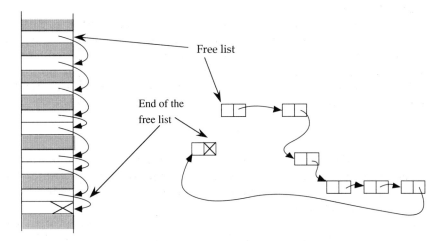

Figure 9.9 *The free-list of unused list pairs*

A typical LISP program might, on average, 'consume' one dotted pair from the free list *every other* expression/statement which is executed. Clearly, since it is a frequently accessed data structure, it would a good idea to reserve a register **a6** (say) to point to the head of the free list.

To implement a **cons** expression involves extracting a dotted pair record from the free list, updating **a6** to point to the remainder of the free list and filling in the **car** and **cdr** fields of the new record (the **tag** field of each record in the free-list would normally already be pre-set to **dotted**):

```
cmp.l   #nil,a6          ;end of free list?
beq     garbage_collect
move.l  a6,a0            ;get pair
move.l  cdr(a6),a6       ;step over
move.l  (a7)+,cdr(a0)    ;fill in
move.l  (a7)+,car(a0)    ;from stack
move.l  a0,-(a7)         ;return pair
```

The free list will become empty – at regular intervals – when all the pairs in the heap have been allocated. At this point we have two choices – we can try to increase the size of the heap or we can invoke a *garbage collector*. Since no physical computer has an infinite capacity, at some point the first option becomes impossible, in which case we must investigate collecting the S-expressions which are no longer in use.

Garbage collection

As we noted above, in a language with recursive data types, it is difficult for the programmer to keep track of which structures are in use at any one time. Although it is clear from the text of a LISP program when *new* **cons** pairs are created, it is less obvious when a **cons** pair is no longer needed. Sometimes it is obvious, as can be seen in the (rather tautologous) expression:

```
(car (cons a b))
```

After evaluating the **car**, the newly generated **cons** pair can be discarded. However, most **cons** pairs have a longer, unpredictable, lifetime than this. It is theoretically impossible to automatically *predict* when a given **cons** pair will become garbage.

In any case it is tedious to have to do so, and if the system can automatically keep track of which data objects are in use, and which are not, then this removes a burden from the programmer. It is the task of the garbage collector to clear up those data objects which have been created but which are no longer in use.

There are many possible schemes for garbage collection, but they are all based on the principle of identifying those objects which are still in use (the mark phase) and removing the rest (the collect phase). Some garbage collection systems have additional constraints over and above the basic one of collecting all the unused space – for instance a real time garbage collector is required to be as fast as possible (with the possibility of not necessarily collecting all the space at once for example); other systems are required to execute in minimal space and yet other garbage collectors have to be able to deal with objects of different sizes. We will look at one simple scheme – stop, mark and collect. We stop when we run out of records in the free list, mark the objects which are in use and collect the rest into the free list.

The mark phase of a garbage collector examines all of the data objects – S-expressions in our case – that are in use and sets a special **marked** flag on them. This **marked** flag appears as a boolean field in the S-expression record:

```
s_exp=record
   marked:boolean;     {true if S-exp is in use}
   case tag:tg of
       atom:......
       dotted:(car,cdr:^s_exp);
   end;
```

The collect phase involves trawling over the *whole* of the space allocated to the heap and collecting up – into the free list – all those records which are *not* in use (i.e. not marked during the mark phase). The collect phase usually also un-marks those records which are in use.

There are many marking algorithms, many of which attempt to run in the least possible amount of space. (Recall that the garbage collector is only called when we have run out of space, therefore it is reasonable to assume that there is not much space for the garbage collector itself to run in.) However, the basic marking algorithm is quite simple: if we have a pointer to a structure which we know is in use, then either it is already marked, in which case we do nothing, or we mark it and we recursively mark the **car** and **cdr** fields:

```
procedure   mark(m:^s_exp);
begin
    if  not  m^.marked  then
    begin
        m^.marked:=true;
        mark(m^.car);
        mark(m^.cdr);
    end;
end;
```

Notice that we must mark a dotted pair before marking the **car** and **cdr** fields to prevent looping in the case that a structure is circular, which frequently happens in a LISP system.

There are only a few places from which ultimately *all* the structures in use can be reached. If a given S-expression is not referenced from either the currently executing LISP program (in which case the reference would originate from a value on the expression stack) or from the atom dictionary (which leads in turn to the defined LISP functions) then it is not possible to access the S-expression and therefore it must be garbage. Thus, it is relatively simple for the LISP system to ensure that the **mark** procedure can access all of the objects in use.

The collect phase of the garbage collector involves going through the heap space and examining *every* record in it. It is at this point that we can appreciate some of the beauty of LISP data structures: since every S-expression is ultimately built from the same dotted pair record it is a simple matter for the collector to recognize valid from invalid data, simply from the **mark** flag:

```
procedure  collect;
var  p:^s_exp;
begin
   p:=start_of_heap;          {trawl  the  heap  }
   repeat
      if  not  p^.marked  then    {in  use?  }
      begin
         p^.cdr:=free_list;     {put  in  free  list}
         free_list:=p;
      end;
      p^.marked:=false;        {clear  mark  flag}
      p:=succ(p);              {go  to  next  S-exp}
   until  p=end_of_heap;
end;
```

This pseudo-Pascal procedure sketches out the main aspects of the collection phase of the garbage collector. If the collect phase fails to find any garbage, then the evaluation of the LISP program must terminate and return some kind of error condition to the user.

9.3 Executing LISP programs

Functions are tied in to LISP at a rather deeper level than in Pascal. Whereas in Pascal, functions and procedures are seen as ways of collecting together sets of simpler statements, in LISP a program is better seen as a composition of functions.

One of the fundamental differences between LISP and Pascal that explains many of the surface differences is that LISP is its own *meta-language*. In a meta-language, program structures can be represented and manipulated as data objects and in the same context these data structures can be executed as normal *object-level* programs. So, LISP programs are also examples of LISP data structures and many LISP programs represent, manipulate and execute other LISP programs.

The fact that LISP is its own meta-language brings great power to the language – for example, it is relatively easy to extend LISP by adding extra syntactic forms which are themselves implemented as normal LISP programs. However, it also means that it is harder to *implement* LISP as efficiently as we can implement Pascal, because we can make fewer assumptions about the exact nature of a LISP program.

Because of the complexity of implementing LISP, early LISP systems were nearly always based on interpreters: a LISP program was not compiled in the same way that we have seen that Pascal programs are compiled; instead a special interpreter program was used which interpreted S-expressions to produce values. LISP compilers are relatively modern, and although nowadays few LISP systems are *not* compiler based, they also contain – as a library function – an interpreter for LISP programs.

LISP execution can be seen as a two-phase activity: expression evaluation and function application. Evaluating expressions is the primary way in which we initiate a LISP execution and function application is the method used to help expression evaluation.

There are, in fact, three types of expression in LISP: function and primitive operator application, **prog**ram sequences and special forms, which include conditional expressions.

9.3.1 Evaluating and accessing S-expressions

For the most part, the same techniques that we explored in Pascal expressions also apply to evaluating LISP expressions. In LISP we have a richer collection of expressions – not just arithmetic expressions but also expressions involving accessing and building S-expressions.

S-expressions are accessed through the special access functions **CAR** and **CDR**. The value of the *expression*

> **(car x)**

is the S-expression contained in the **car** field of the S-expression identified by the variable **x**, and

> **(cdr x)**

refers to the **cdr** field of **x**. Since, by Pascal standards, all S-expressions are non-scalar, all LISP variables contain addresses of values rather than values directly. The address contained in a variable is usually of an object which is in the heap. This means that accessing the value of a variable – such as **x** here – involves at least one memory indirection. The **cdr** expression, for example, is compiled into code which picks up **x**'s contents, checks that the address contained refers to a dotted pair and then accesses the cdr field of that pair:

```
move.l   x, a0            ;x is an address
cmp.b    #dotted,tag(a0)  ;pair?
bne      cdr_error        ;illegal  access
move.l   cdr(a0),...      ;cdr is a pointer
```

Lists are dominant in a LISP system and accessing list structures is always performed using the **car** and **cdr** access functions. To simplify accessing structures, particularly when the sequence of **car**s and **cdr**s is known already (such as when the programmer wants to access the third element of a list) LISP has a suite of path access functions, based on **car** and **cdr**. For example, the expression

(caddr x)

is equivalent to the expression

(car (cdr (cdr x)))

It specifies a path along a S-expression tree:

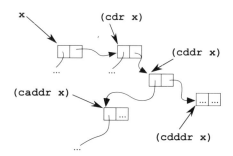

Figure 9.10 *Paths along x*

An added advantage of path access functions is that it is easier to compile expressions involving them more efficiently. The **caddr** expression is implemented with a sequence such as:

```
move.l  x,a0                    ; x
cmp.b   #dotted,tag(a0)         ;dotted  pair?
bne     cdr_error
move.l  cdr(a0),a0             ; (cdr  x)
cmp.b   #dotted,tag(a0)         ;dotted  pair?
bne     cdr_error
move.l  cdr(a0),a0             ; (cddr  x)
cmp.b   #dotted,tag(a0)         ;dotted  pair?
bne     cdr_error
move.l  car(a0),...            ; (caddr  x)
```

This might be compared with the analogous Pascal expression to access the second integer along in a list of integers:

x^.next^.next^.i

with its corresponding expansion into 680x0 instructions:

```
move.l   x, a0
cmp.l    #nil,a0
beq      nil_error
move.l   next(a0),a0     ;x^.next...
cmp.l    #nil,a0
beq      nil_error
move.l   next(a0),a0     ;...next^.next
cmp.l    #nil,a0
beq      nil_error
move.l   i(a0),...       ;next^.i...
```

Although these expressions are based on completely different language paradigms, the code sequences are remarkably similar.

9.3.2 Function application

A LISP function application, such as in the expression:

(append X Y)

is implemented in a similar way to a Pascal function call. We have to place the arguments of the function **X** and **Y** in a standard place, which is usually the system stack, and invoke the **append** function via a **jsr**. The call sequence for this call would be something like:

```
move.l   X, - (a7)
move.l   Y, - (a7)
jsr      append
```

Notice that we do not pass a hidden 'space' parameter for the result of the function as we did for Pascal functions. This is because there is no possibility of a LISP function assigning its value before returning to the caller: in Pascal, a function's value is set by assigning the function variable which could be any time within the execution of the function. When a LISP function returns, the values on the stack are replaced by the value of the function which is the value of the outermost expression in the LISP function's body.

LISP has only one mode for passing arguments to a function: we pass the value of the argument. However, since all values in LISP are S-expressions, and since we can't pass an arbitrary S-expression in a fixed length register, we pass the *address* of the value of the argument rather than the value itself. So, in Pascal's terms, LISP is neither call-by-value nor call-by-reference, but something in between. It is possible, for example by using an S-expression overwriting primitive such as **replaca**, to change the value of an argument to a function.

LISP has traditionally always been an *incremental* programming language (which is another point of difference with Pascal). The effect of this is that functions can be defined and redefined, at will, during an interactive session with the LISP system. A LISP function can be (re-)defined *at any time*, including during and as a result of the execution of a LISP program itself.

Furthermore, it is quite likely that during program development some functions are not yet defined, and yet we can *still* start the execution of the LISP program. In contrast, a Pascal program cannot start executing until all of the referenced procedures and functions are defined and implemented at least to the extent of a stub being written. Of course, when we come to enter a LISP function we cannot proceed if it is not defined, but even then, some program development systems allow the programmer to furnish the missing definition on the spot.

Whilst being able to define and redefine a function interactively is undoubtedly a powerful facility for programmers, it has the effect that we cannot predict where the code for the **append** function (say) is going to be before we start executing a LISP program that calls it. In particular, when we compile any LISP function which calls **append**, we cannot insert the address of the instructions for **append** into the operand of the **jsr** instruction; instead we have to first of all check that there *is* a function to execute!

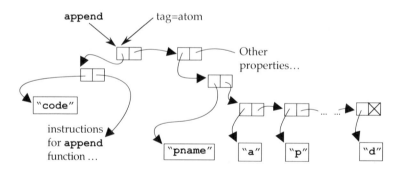

Figure 9.11 *Code properties of the* **append** *atom*

Although the address of the **append** function's code may not be fixed, we can fix the address of the **append** atom. Once an atom has been read into the system its address does not change; we can use this fact to locate the code of the **append** function. Recall that the structure of a LISP atom includes, as a property, the defining program for any function associated with the atom.

Given the address of the **append** atom, we can implement our entry into the **append** program by searching its property list for the code:

```
        move.l  append, a0
@ 0     move.l  car(a0),a1
        cmp.l   #code,car(a1)    ;code  property
        beq     @1               ;found  it!
        move.l  cdr(a0),a0
        cmp.l   #nil,a0          ;last  property?
        beq     un_defined       ;append  is  undefined
        bra     @0               ;try  next  property

@1      move.l  cdr(a1),a0       ;get  code
        jsr     (a0)             ;start  append  code
```

A more sophisticated approach, which avoids searching on every function call, is to associate a code sequence with *every* atom, and to reorganize the atom's structure so that this code is always at the top:

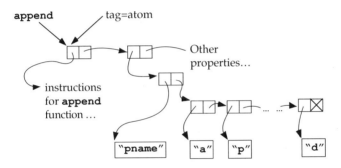

Figure 9.12 *Revised layout of code property of* `append`

Notice that if every atom has a code property in the same place, then we do not need to identify it explicitly; we can assert that the first entry in the atom structure is always the code for the atom:

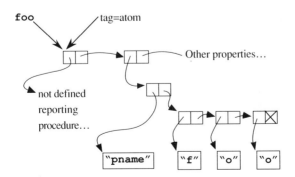

Figure 9.13 *Layout of an undefined function's atom*

If a given atom has no function associated with it, then it still has an address of valid code to execute – it is simply the address of a standard error reporting procedure.

With this structure for atoms, we are guaranteed that there is always *something* to execute, even if it is only an error procedure; and that, in turn, means that we don't need to check for valid code. Furthermore, by fixing the location of the defining code, we can eliminate the search through the atom's property list and use instead a simple indirection:

```
move.l   append, a0
move.l   car(a0),a0
jsr      (a0)
```

The indirection is essential, because we cannot be certain that **append** is not going to be redefined. Redefining a function is implemented by overwriting the **car** field in the top-level record in the structure of its name atom.

When a function returns, the arguments to the function will have been removed from the stack and the value of the function is left on the stack in their place. Thus, just as with Pascal functions, we can use the returned value either as the argument to yet another function application or we can use it in a primitive operation. For example, the expression:

```
(car  (append  X  Y))
```

would be implemented with a sequence such as:

```
move.l   X, - (a7)
move.l   Y, - (a7)
move.l   append, a0
move.l   car(a0),a0
jsr      (a0)          ; (append  X  Y)
move.l   (a7) +, a0
move.l   car(a0), ...  ; (car  (append  ...
```

Evaluating a function body
Once we have entered a function body then we have to consider the treatment of variables introduced by the function and the evaluation of the body proper. A LISP function is defined using a template such as:

```
(defun  function-name  parameters  body)
```

The list of atoms in *parameters* is the list of parameters to the function. (LISP has a separate mechanism – the **prog** feature – which can be used to introduce local variables.) The way that parameters are handled in LISP is quite different to a Pascal procedure's local variables and parameters. The *body* of the function template is the expression to evaluate on entry to the function and the value of this expression is also the value of the function.

LISP is a *dynamically scoped* language; in contrast to Pascal and other modern variants of LISP, such as SCHEME, which are *lexically scoped* languages. What this means is that, when a function is entered, the variables introduced by its template are 'in scope' – i.e. they can be referenced – for the whole of the *execution* of its body. In a lexically or statically scoped language, the variables can only be referenced by expressions which are *textually* within the function template itself.

For example, in the function **bar** below, the reference to the variable **X** would be illegal in a lexically scoped language since it is not declared (or bound) within the declaration of **bar** (there is a definition of **X** in **foo** though):

(defun foo (X Y) (bar Y))

(defun bar (Z) (times Z X))

In a dynamically scoped language, an expression such as:

(foo 2 3)

is implemented by applying **foo** to arguments **2** and **3**, this results in the call to **bar**:

(bar 3)

and *this* results in the call to **times**:

(times 3 X)

Since **bar** has been invoked within the dynamic scope of **foo**, the value of **X** which is available to **bar** is 2; so the expression that is to be evaluated is:

(times 3 2)

It is perfectly possible to construct programs which give one answer if a dynamic scoping assumption is made and another if lexical scoping is assumed.

This difference is crucial both to the programmer and to the implementation of variables in LISP. In particular, in a dynamically scoped language, we have to be able to refer to the names of the parameters of a function during the execution of the function body including any functions which are called within it. A variable reference in a function body cannot be implemented as an offset within a block of data allocated with a **link** instruction since we cannot determine the offset (or which link register) at the time that we compile a function.

The difference between lexically scoped variables and dynamically scoped variables was not properly understood when LISP was invented in 1957. Unfortunately, as often happens, many LISP programmers have exploited the features of dynamic scoping and are unwilling to change, hence even modern versions of LISP (such as Common LISP) must at least support it.

We can implement dynamic binding of variables to values using a technique called *shallow binding*. For each variable, we associate with its name (which is an atom) a property which contains the value of the variable.

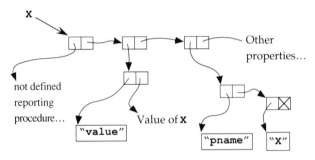

Figure 9.14 *Structure of a variable atom*

Since we are likely to refer to the value of an atom more frequently than we call its program, we can optimise access slightly by rearranging the atom structure so that the first two entries in the property list are always predefined (which also means that we do not need explicit property identifiers) and that the value is the first entry in the structure and the function code is the second:

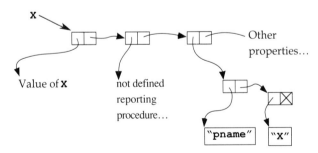

Figure 9.15 *Revised structure of a variable atom*

To take into account the fact that the atom's value is now at the top of its structure, the sequence to enter a function must have an additional **cdr** to step over the atom's value.

So, as we enter a function body, our first action is to assign the parameters to their new values; however, because a parameter atom may already have a value associated with it (from an outer execution scope), we must save its old value; which we can do by saving it onto the system stack when we assign the variable.

The prologue of a function steps through each argument, saving the old value of the parameter variable, and assigning it to its new value. The space used on the stack for the arguments of the function is used to keep the old value of the parameters while the function is executing:

```
move.l  X,a1                    ;assign  parameter  X
move.l  car(a1),a0
move.l  8(a7),car(a1)           ;get  parameter
move.l  a0,8(a7)                ;save  old  value
```

Notice that we can use the absolute addressing mode, in the 680x0 instruction which accesses **X**, to refer to the address of **X**'s atom structure. This is because the address of an atom is fixed once it has been entered into atom dictionary. The complete prologue sequence for **append** becomes:

```
move.l  Y,a1                    ;assign  parameter  Y
move.l  car(a1),a0
move.l  4(a7),car(a1)           ;get  parameter
move.l  a0,4(a7)                ;save  old  value  of  Y
move.l  X,a1                    ;assign  parameter  X
move.l  car(a1),a0
move.l  8(a7),car(a1)           ;get  parameter
move.l  a0,8(a7)                ;save  old  value  of  X
```

Accessing a parameter's value within the body of a function becomes an indirection through the atom address of the parameter:

```
move.l  X,a1
move.l  car(a1),...             ;value  of  X
```

Once we have set up the parameters to a function we execute the body proper. As we noted above, this consists of an expression which might be another function application, or it may be a **prog** sequence or a special form such as a **cond**itional expression.

9.3.3 Program sequences

Program sequences specify a list of expressions to be evaluated in sequence. At its most simple level, a **prog** expression has the structure:

$$(\textbf{prog} \quad (\textbf{var}_1 \quad ... \quad \textbf{var}_n)$$
$$\textbf{exp}_1$$
$$...$$
$$\textbf{exp}_m)$$

where **var$_1$** ... **var$_n$** are variables which are declared to be in scope during the execution of the **prog**, and **exp$_1$**, ... ,**exp$_m$** are the expressions to evaluate. Some of these expressions may be atoms, in which case they are not evaluated but are interpreted as labels.

The entry to a **prog** sequence is similar to the prologue for a function: we have to save the old values of the new variables – which we can do on the system stack. When we exit the expression these variables are restored using the values saved on the system stack.

Two special functions, **go** and **return** are used also within **prog** expressions. The **return** function evaluates its argument and that value becomes the value of the whole **prog** – thus causing it to exit also. The **go** function is the LISP equivalent of **goto**, it is used to jump to another point within the **prog** sequence: a label is indicated by an atom in the **prog** sequence as opposed to a normal function application. Jumps out of the current **prog** are not permitted in LISP, which considerably simplifies its implementation.

Clearly, implementing a **prog** sequence is not all that different to implementing a single expression. We evaluate the expressions in turn, pushing arguments to functions etc, and calling the indicated functions. However, since the values of the expressions are disregarded – by dropping the results from the stack as soon as the invoked functions return – it must be the case that they 'operate' by performing side-effects, such as assigning a value to a variable.

9.3.4 LISP conditional expressions

The **cond** expression is LISP's fundamental form of conditional expression. This has a similar role to the Pascal **if-then-else** statement; although instead of selecting one of two sets of statements to execute, the **cond** expression can select from a number of expressions. The basic form of **cond** is:

```
(cond    (Pred₁  Val₁)
         (Pred₂  Val₂)
         ... ...
         (Predₙ  Valₙ) )
```

Each pair of items (**Pred$_i$** **Val$_i$**) forms an arm of the conditional. The value of the **cond** expression is the value of the first of the expressions **Val$_i$** whose corresponding test expression **Pred$_i$** evaluates to true, which in LISP is any non-nil value.

The implementation of a **cond** expression in 680x0 instructions is similar to the implementation of a Pascal **if-then-else**. Each test predicate **Pred$_i$** is evaluated, and after it returns the returned value is compared against **nil**. If it is equal to **nil** then the next test is tried, otherwise the value expression is evaluated and the value of that is the value of the **cond** as a whole:

```
@ i      push args to Pred_i
         jsr     Pred_i           ;evaluate  test
         cmp.l   #nil,(a7)+       ;answer=nil?
         beq     @i+1             ;next  pair
         push args to Val_i
         jsr     Val_i            ;compute  val_i
         ... ... ...              ;exit  cond
@i+1     ... ...                  ;next  conditional
```

There are a number of primitive predicate functions, for example the **eq** function which compares two S-expressions for equality (strictly, **eq** tests for *pointer equality* rather than *structural equality*). Just as with ordinary function application, when the test part of a conditional arm is a primitive predicate the compiler may insert more specific instructions to evaluate such tests. For example, in the conditional arm:

```
(cond  ((eq  X  nil)   ......
```

We can implement the test for **X** being equal to **nil** quite cheaply:

```
move.l  X,a0
cmp.l   #nil,car(a0)
bne     ... ...
```

If none of the conditional arms of a **cond** expression succeeds then an error must be reported. However, a common LISP idiom is to make the predicate in the last conditional arm the atom **T** (i.e. true). This ensures that the last arm will be taken in the event of the previous conditional arms failing, and the fact that it is constant enables us to have a slightly better code sequence for the **cond** expression as a whole. In addition, some LISP systems use a different version of **cond** which is more like the Pascal **if-then-else** statement.

We can now see the complete set of instructions needed to implement the simple LISP function for **append** below:

```
(defun  append  (X  Y)
        (cond  ((eq  X  nil)  Y)
               (T  (cons       (car  X)
                        (append  (cdr  X)))))))
```

which in 680x0 instructions becomes:

```
append:
        move.l  Y,a1                ;assign  parameter  Y
        move.l  car(a1),a0
        move.l  4(a7),car(a1)       ;get  parameter
        move.l  a0,4(a7)            ;save  old  value  of  Y
        move.l  X,a1                ;assign  parameter  X
        move.l  car(a1),a0
        move.l  8(a7),car(a1)       ;get  parameter
        move.l  a0,8(a7)            ;save  old  value  of  X
        move.l  X,a1                ;X=nil?
        cmp.l   #nil,car(a1)
        bne     @1
        move.l  Y,a1                ;return  Y  as  val
        move.l  car(a1),-(a7)
        bra     @2                  ;go  to  epilogue

@1      move.l  X,a1                ;(car  X)
        move.l  car(a1),a1          ;value  of  X
        move.l  car(a1),-(a7)       ;save  (car  X)
        move.l  cdr(a1),-(a7)       ;(cdr  X)
        move.l  Y,a1                ;access  Y
        move.l  car(a1),-(a7)
        jsr     append              ;call  append
        cmp.l   #nil,a6             ;(cons  ......
        beq     garbage_collect
        move.l  a6,a0
        move.l  cdr(a6),a6          ;collect  pair
        move.l  (a7)+,cdr(a0)
        move.l  (a7)+,car(a0)
        move.l  a0,-(a7)            ;result  is  pair
@2      move.l  (a7)+,d0            ;result  off  stack
        move.l  (a7)+,a0            ;return  address
        move.l  Y,a1                ;undo  Y
        move.l  (a7)+,car(a1)
        move.l  X,a1                ;undo  X
        move.l  (a7)+,car(a1)
        move.l  d0,-(a7)            ;push  return  value
        jmp     (a0)                ;exit  append
```

Notice that we do not have to perform any indirections in order to perform a recursive call to **append**; instead we can use a **jsr** instruction to a fixed label. If the **append** function were to be deleted (just prior to its redefinition for example) then the recursive call would disappear also.

Prolog

Prolog's heritage is a combination of predicate logic and advanced grammars. A 'pure' Prolog program can be identified with a logical view as statements (axioms or clauses) which the programmer asserts to be true of the world. This is quite different to a Pascal program which is essentially a *machine* or *mechanism* which is constructed to behave in a certain way: the fact that the materials that make up a Pascal program are abstract entities in the memory of the computer does not detract from this basic view.

Execution in Prolog also has a logical perspective: the execution of a Prolog query is an attempt to *prove* that it follows from the true statements in the program. This mirrors, to some extent, the mathematical basis of LISP – a 'pure' LISP program consists of a set of function definitions and a LISP execution consists of evaluating an expression.

However important logic is, of equal importance to understanding Prolog's history is the language processing work carried out in the late 60's and early 70's – in particular the automatic compiler construction systems or compiler-compilers that were being designed then. Work on grammar formalisms led to systems which could use a suitable definition of a language to automatically parse examples of the language. It is also the case that language processing is one of Prolog's more natural application domains.

In 1971 the two worlds of logic and automatic parsing came together and invented (between them) Prolog: Robert Kowalski realized that predicate logic could be the basis of a programming language rather than simply a problem expression language and Alain Colmereaur extended and applied the algorithms used for automatic parsing to the problem of performing logical inferences. This pioneering work was then followed in 1975 by David Warren who developed the world's first Prolog compiler and made it a practical programming language.

10.1 Prolog data structures

Prolog is, like LISP, a language which has recursive data structures. In fact there is much in common between the two languages in terms of the mechanisms needed to support data; however Prolog's terms are more complex than LISP's S-expressions.

A Prolog term can be an *atom*, which has similar characteristics to a LISP atom, it can be a *variable* or it can be a *compound term*. Prolog atoms are written as sequences of letters or graphic characters; the first letter of an alphanumeric atom must be lower case:

```
fred        uPjohn        $&&       'a quoted atom'
```

The representation of a Prolog atom is much the same as for a LISP atom. However there is no tradition, in Prolog systems, for an atom to have associated properties in the way that a LISP atom can have. This means that a Prolog atom is somewhat simpler to implement than a LISP atom.

The 'new' data types in Prolog, compared to LISP, are the logical variable and the compound term. A variable is written in a similar manner to an alphanumeric atom except that the first character must be uppercase or underscore:

```
Var         X              _variable          _1
```

The compound terms are the Prolog equivalent of dotted pairs; except that we can construct arbitrary tuples not just pairs:

```
tree(left(nil),  label(X),  tree(right,20,X))
```

Prolog also has a list notation, which is analogous to LISP's list notation with a little more punctuation:

[1,2,3] which is equivalent to (1 2 3) in LISP

[X|Y] which is equivalent to (X . Y) in LISP.

Prolog lists are just special cases of compound terms whose name is '.'. We could assume that they were implemented in the same way as other compound structures, but in practice many Prolog systems optimize lists and use structures which are similar to LISP **cons** pairs to represent them.

The most interesting difference between Prolog and LISP data structures relates to the logical variable. Uniquely amongst programming languages, a Prolog variable is a true place holder: it stands for any – as yet unknown

– term and can be substituted for by any Prolog term. In particular, a Prolog variable *need not be instantiated*, ever. So, if we have a Prolog term such as:

```
foo(X,   a,   bar(X))
```

then this is a perfectly valid structure and we do not need to know more about **X**: it may remain unbound or uninstantiated. It is also possible to make two variables the same. A Prolog goal (which is analogous to the Pascal procedure call and the LISP function call) such as:

```
..., X=Y, ...
```

effectively *aliases* the variables **X** and **Y**, and so all occurrences of both variables are identified with each other. A subsequent goal might bind one of the variables, in which case they are both bound simultaneously. Aliased variables are very common in Prolog programs, although the number of times we make *explicit* use of aliasing is rare.

In order to be able to implement an arbitrary Prolog term as a structure in memory we have to use a mechanism similar to the LISP dotted pair; however in the case of Prolog, with its more complex terms, we no longer have the luxury of having the same size of record for each type of data.

A Prolog term is built from components which differ in size: variables, atoms and the different size compound terms. We can, however, use the tagged pointer style of representation to represent Prolog terms. A Prolog tagged pointer cell might be described using the Pascal declaration:

```
tags=(variable,atom,number,list,compound);

cell=record
   marked:boolean;              {for  garbage  collection}
   case tag:tags of
      atom:......               {atom  structure}
      number:(i:integer);
      variable,
      compound:(ptr:^cell);
   end;
```

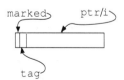

Figure 10.1 *Structure of a Prolog cell*

A cell is sufficient to capture a scalar such as an integer or atom, but a compound term is represented by *aggregating* arrays of cells together. So, for example, the compound term:

foo (... , ... , ...)

is represented by a sequence of four contiguous cells which respectively hold the *function symbol* (**foo**) and the three arguments. If they are scalar arguments then they will be held directly in the cells composing the array; if an argument is compound then the corresponding cell will effectively be a pointer to the sub-term's structure:

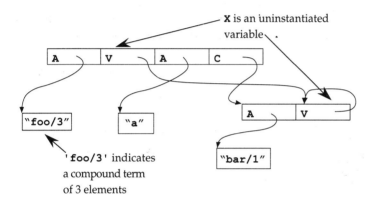

Figure 10.2 *Box diagram of* **foo(X, a, bar(X))**

An unbound variable – i.e. one which is still uninstantiated – is represented by the pointer in its cell pointing to itself.

The aggregations of cells which we use to represent terms are not normal arrays in the usual sense because we allow pointers 'into' the arrays, as in the case of the variable references above.

Although list pairs are logically another type of compound term, they are sufficiently common that a special form for them is justified. This is represented by a separate **list** tag value. A cell of 'type' **list** consists of a pointer to two adjacent cells: the first forming to the head (or **car**) of the list pair, and the second forming the tail (or **cdr**) of the list pair.

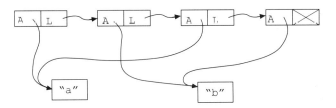

Figure 10.3 *Box diagram of Prolog term [a,b,a,b]*

Since *every* variable could be bound to another variable, or to another term, it is possible for 'binding chains' to develop. If, in our example term above, we allow **X** to become bound to a variable **Y**, we would implement this by changing the self reference in the **X** cell to point to **Y**:

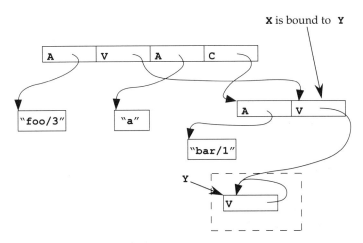

Figure 10.4 *Binding a variable to another variable*

At some later point **Y** may become bound to **gar(U)** in which case both **X** and **Y** become bound to **gar(U)**. Since it is impractical to physically replace each occurrence of **X** and **Y** by their new values, we implement this shared binding by relying on the variable-variable bindings that we made from **X** to **Y**, and then the binding from **Y** to **gar(U)**: we determine the value of **X** *indirectly* via a chain of variable links. The new picture for the term is:

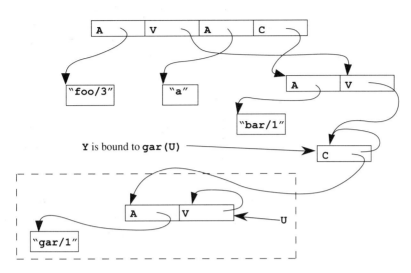

Figure 10.5 *Binding a shared variable to a term*

An immediate consequence of this scenario is that every time we access any term we must check for, and dereference, any variable-variable links. If we are looking for the value of the first argument of **foo** (say) which is **X**, then we must dereference first of all from the first cell in the **foo** compound term to the master location for **X**, and then to the location for **Y** and finally through **Y** onto the true value of **X** which is **gar(U)**.

The process which does this dereferencing is crucially important to the performance of a complete Prolog system even if most of the time not much dereferencing is done. A standard algorithm for dereferencing, based on the cell declaration above, could be expressed as the Pascal loop:

```
while  (p^.tag=variable)  and  (p^.ptr<>p)  do
   p:=p^.ptr;
```

which, in assembler, could be implemented relatively straightforwardly:

```
         move.l  p,a0
@1       cmp.b   #variable,tag(a0)
         bne     @2                  ;p  a  variable?
         cmp.l   ptr(a0),a0
         beq     @2                  ;self  reference?
         move.l  ptr(a0),a0          ;p:=p^.ptr
         bra     @1
@2       ... ...                     ;p  left  in  a0
```

Although Prolog terms are more complex than LISP S-expressions, the major difference between the languages lies in the way that data is accessed and manipulated in Prolog; in which, Prolog is quite different to most other programming languages. We have already seen that a LISP S-expression is accessed via the various *selector* functions: **car, cdr, cadr** etc. In Prolog a different mechanism based on *unification* is used.

10.1.1   Unification in Prolog

Unification is a form of pattern matching where both patterns to be matched may become instantiated. For example, in the clause head:

    foo(f(X,g(Y))):-......

the term **f(X,g(Y))** is a template which must match the corresponding term in a call to **foo**. The nature of this matching may be quite complex, involving variables in both the head and the call being instantiated. A typical call to **foo** might be:

      ...,foo(f(U,U)),...

In order for these templates to match we need to bind the variable **X** to the variable **U** – i.e. establish a variable link between them – and also to bind **U** to the term **g(Y)** with the result that both **X** and **U** become bound to the same term.

    Unification can be used for accessing data as well as constructing it; it is used to pass data *into* a procedure and to return results *out* of a procedure. In this case, the variable **X** which is local to the clause, is bound to a component of its incoming data and **U** which occurs in the call is bound to the term **g(Y)**. A further difference between Prolog unification and LISP selector functions is that unification can *fail*: a match between terms might not succeed as in:

      bar(A,g(G))   and   **bar(2,h(X))**

This unification fails because **g(G)** is not unifiable with **h(X)**. Failure in Prolog unification leads to the system *backtracking* and some earlier choice of rule is abandoned (together with all the consequent execution) and another rule is tried. We shall see that in order to be able to backtrack to try another alternative rule, we need to build a data structure in which to record sufficient information to allow the system to try the alternative. These records are called *choice points* to indicate that they represent a possible choice in the execution of the Prolog program.

    All this means that the support needed to support Prolog's data structures is somewhat more complex than Pascal's or LISP's data structures.

Compiling unification

Normally, a Prolog compiler arranges its data management by 'compiling' the terms in the head of a clause into a sequence of instructions whose function it is to unify the appropriate terms in the call.

For example, in the Prolog clause:

```
append([E|X], Y, [E|Z]) :- append(X, Y, Z).
```

the term **[E|X]** is compiled into instructions which check that the first argument of a call to **append** is a non-empty list. If it is, then the local variables **E** and **X** are bound to the head and tail – i.e. the **car** and the **cdr** – of the list pair.

The first step in this unification involves some instructions which make sure that the first argument of the **append** call can be coerced into a list pair:

```
        move.l   arg1,a0              ;access  1st  argument
@1      cmp.b    #variable,tag(a0)    ;dereference    it
        bne      @2
        cmp.l    ptr(a0),a0
        beq      @3
        move.l   ptr(a0),a0
        bra      @1
@2      cmp.b    #list,tag(a0)
        bne      fail                 ;not  a  dotted  pair
        ... ...                       ;we  know  its  a  pair
        bra      @4
@3      ... ...                       ;we  know  its  a  var
@4      ... ...                       ;continue  with  next
```

There are three possible situations that can arise here: the first argument may (after following variable links) already be a list pair, or it may be an unbound variable or it may a different kind of term altogether, in which case the unification fails.

If the term is a list pair then the required action is to assign the local variables **E** and **X** to the head and tail of the list; something which is easily accomplished by a series of **move**s.

The most complex case is when the term to be unified is an unbound variable; in this circumstance a new list pair must be created and bound to the variable. The space for this new list pair is allocated out of a heap (just as the LISP **cons** function found space for list pairs out of its heap). However, Prolog's heap is not organised in the same way as LISP's heap and a better term for it would be the *constructed term stack*. This stack is *not* normally structured around a free-list but instead a pointer to the next free location is maintained:

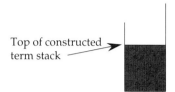

Top of constructed term stack

The reason for using a stack like this is that when the system backtracks a previous choice of clause which was made to solve a call is undone, and all of the terms which have been constructed since then are no longer needed and can be removed. This garbage can be removed by a simple adjustment of the top of the constructed term stack. This is a much simpler operation compared to a full mark and collect style garbage collection needed to clear up discarded S-expressions in LISP. It is still the case, however, that a garbage collector is needed to clear the constructed term stack, and this needs to be more sophisticated than a LISP garbage collector.

As with LISP's free-list, we would normally dedicate an address register (**a6** say) to point to the next free location in the constructed term stack, constructing a new list pair consists simply of incrementing the top of the stack and assigning the old top as the address of the list pair:

```
move.l  a6,ptr(a0)      ;bind  variable
move.b  #list,tag(a0)   ;list  pair
add.l   #2*cell,a6      ;adjust  c.t.s.
```

We also need to initialise the head and tail of the new list pair to unbound variables and to bind the local variables **E** and **X** to them, just as we would for an incoming list pair:

```
move.l  ptr(a0),a0
move.b  #variable,tag(a0)
move.l  a0,ptr(a0)      ;new  unbound
move.l  a0,ptr(E)       ;bind  E
move.b  #variable,tag(E)
lea     cell(a0),a0     ;next  cell
move.b  #variable,tag(a0)
move.l  a0,ptr(a0)      ;new  unbound
move.l  a0,ptr(X)       ;bind  X
move.b  #variable,tag(X)
```

Since we have bound a variable from outside the clause in this step – by assigning it to a list pair – we require a little further housekeeping. It may be that the variable that we are assigning is older than – i.e. created before – the most recent choice point. This is because the variable was in the call, and allowing for the possibility of variable-variable links, we cannot predict where the variable that was bound originated.

In the case that the newly bound variable *is* older, we must also record the fact that we have bound it. This allows the system to undo the binding – by clearing the variable to unbound – should this or a later unification fail. That in turn would allow a subsequent choice of clause, with its attendant unification, to result in the variable having a different value. This record of the variable being bound is maintained in a simple list of addresses, called the *trail*.

The complexity of Prolog's data management sometimes leads to a slower performance than the equivalent LISP or Pascal program. However, it is also the case that a Prolog program is somewhat more succinct and high-level than a LISP or Pascal program; and this allows the programmer to be more productive.

10.2 Controlling a Prolog execution

A Prolog execution is logically equivalent to a mathematical proof. One immediate consequence of this is that we have the notion of *success* and *failure* in terms of the success or failure to find a successful proof of a hypothesis or query. The 'proofs' and 'hypotheses' that we speak of are extremely simple – a Prolog system is not itself intelligent, it is merely a programming language based on mathematical notions of truth and proof.

We can illustrate Prolog's proof methods using the fallible greek syllogism which we can express using the set of Prolog clauses:

```
fallible(H):-human(H).                    R1

human(turing).                            R2
human(socrates).                          R3

greek(socrates).                          R4
```

together with the standard 'hypothesis' or top-level query to prove that there is a fallible greek:

```
:-fallible(X),greek(X).
```

A Prolog program 'solves' this problem by solving, in turn, the sub-queries:

```
fallible(X),...
```

and, for the same **X**:

> ..., `greek(X)`

In other words, after the goal `fallible(X)` has been called, and is successfully completed, then the next goal `greek(X)` is called. If it also succeeds, then the whole query terminates successfully.

In order to solve the first goal we attempt to *reduce* it into simpler sub-goals by using one of the clauses in the Prolog program – in this case the only clause that might work is the single `fallible` rule $R1$. To use a clause to reduce a goal we have to match (i.e. unify) the head clause with the goal.

This step also involves introducing any new local variables which are associated with the clause. In the case of unifying the head of $R1$ with the `fallible` goal we introduce the new variable `H`, and we bind it to the variable `X` from the goal. As a result of using the rule, the original problem is reduced to showing that there is a human greek:

> : - | `human(X)` | $R1$, `greek(X)`

The next step for the Prolog evaluator is to solve the newly introduced `human` goal. There are two clauses which can potentially be used to reduce it: $R2$ and $R3$ (both of which happen to be atomic facts with no sub-goals or pre-conditions associated with them).

In the face of a choice of clauses to apply, Prolog tries the first one but records the fact that there are one or more alternatives which will be tried, if necessary, later on. Apart from the recognizing the choice point, reducing the `human` goal using $R2$ is essentially the same as before: we are required to unify the goal:

> ..., `human(X)`, ...

with the head of $R2$:

> `human(turing):-`...

This time there are no local variables to introduce, though we do make a binding: we bind `X` to the atom `turing`. Since there are no preconditions in the $R2$ clause, there are no new sub-goals introduced in this step. Using an atomic fact is the main way that a goal is *eliminated* from an evaluation as opposed to being simply replaced by other sub-goals. The next goal to solve now is:

> :-`greek(turing)`.

As before, we try to solve this goal by finding a clause in the program which we can use to reduce it. The only clause for **greek** in the program is *R4*; attempting to use it involves unifying

> ..., **greek(turing)**, ...

with

> **greek(socrates) :-**...

But this is impossible – because **turing** and **socrates** do not match – and so the unification fails. At this point the Prolog system must go back to a previous point where there was a choice and try again. Prolog always goes back to the most recent choice point, as in when we selected the first of two **human** clauses. So, the Prolog system *backtracks*, undoing the effect of any steps subsequent to the choice point, and tries again.

Recall that, when we used *R2* to reduce the **human** goal, we bound **X** to **turing**. Since this binding was made *after* the choice point, i.e. after we selected the first rule for **human**, the binding to **X** must be undone, restoring it to unbound. Notice that, since we bound **H** in the head of the **fallible** rule to **X** in the goal *prior* to making the choice, the binding for **H** stands. If we had to backtrack again then this binding too would disappear.

In effect, after backtracking, we are back to trying to solve the query:

> :- $\boxed{\textbf{human(X)}}_{R1}$, **greek(X)**

but this time we cannot use the first clause for **human**. Instead we use the second; which results in binding **X** to **socrates** and the next query is:

> :-**greek(socrates)**

Since the second rule for **human** was also the last one we did not need to record a choice point this time, and if *this* new query were to fail then the whole top-level query would fail also. However, it does not fail because this goal matches with *R4*. After solving the **greek** sub-goal there are no further goals to solve. The 'answer' **socrates** may then be displayed as the proof that there is a fallible greek.

In practice, in a Prolog system, the real top-level query is one which is not seen by the programmer and it *never* terminates. This query invokes a special read-evaluate-print program whose function is to continually read a query from the terminal, evaluate it and print out an answer if it is true and print a message if not. After completing one query the loop carries on for more queries.

Although we have used the language of problems to be solved and methods for solving them (rules and reducing goals etc.) Prolog is *not* a problem solving system. Viewed as an problem solving strategy, Prolog's execution mechanism is rather inadequate. For example, it is quick to fall into endless loops which a better problem solver would avoid. However, viewed as a *programming* mechanism, and assuming that the programmer is fully aware of Prolog's procedures, it offers a powerful built-in search mechanism that allows a rather high-level style of programming. In particular, the pattern directed style of program invocation is a powerful and high-level paradigm for supporting programming.

Rules, in conjunction with a rule application mechanism, are commonly used in expert systems for example, where they fit quite naturally into the style of programming for cases. Each case that an expert system has to deal with can be expressed using a set of rules whose patterns express the situations that the rules can be applied to. Similarly, language processing based on grammars is also a natural application domain. The fragments of the grammar are rules which can be used to parse fragments of the language being processed.

10.2.1   The Prolog evaluation stack

As with Pascal and LISP, a Prolog system uses an evaluation stack to record the progress of an evaluation of a query. This stack is somewhat more complex than a Pascal stack and it has different entries in it corresponding to the various activities that we have seen above.

In order to record the entry of the evaluation into a sub-goal, we have a 'call record'. This record, like the call frame for a Pascal procedure, records the environment of the caller – the return address corresponds to the next goal to solve, and it also points to the caller's local variables. The call record also has an entry for the calling or 'parent' call record; this is necessary because, unlike Pascal, it is not always the case that the parent of a procedure call is immediately above the call record.

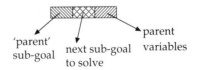

'parent'
sub-goal

next sub-goal
to solve

parent
variables

Figure 10.6 *Structure of a call record*

Arguments to a Prolog goal are not normally passed via the evaluation stack. Instead they are placed in a series of 'argument registers'. These are usually fixed global locations within the memory, although some Prolog compilers may use one or more 680x0 registers to hold Prolog arguments. Using argument registers to pass parameters is analogous to using 680x0 machine registers to pass parameters to a Pascal procedure. However, the principal role of an argument register is to hold the argument during unification. Once the unification is completed then the contents of the argument registers will have been 'read' and either recorded in local variables or matched against some structure in the head of the clause. In either case the contents of the argument registers are no longer needed. This is in contrast with Pascal arguments which can be accessed from any point within the body of the procedure, or even from within procedures declared locally to it.

As with the 680x0, a Prolog system usually has a fixed number of these argument registers, setting an upper limit on the number of arguments a goal may have. However, 32 seems to be a reasonable limit as there are few Prolog goals with more than 32 arguments.

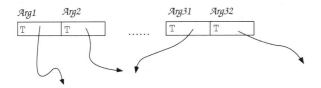

Figure 10.7 *Argument registers*

Each argument register is logically a cell with a tag and a value part; i.e. an argument register can 'hold' any term. If the argument register is an integer then the value part will be the integer, otherwise it will be a pointer to some other structure. The only restriction normally imposed is that an argument register cannot be an unbound variable: it must always point to a location within the evaluation stack proper or on the constructed term stack. An argument register containing an unbound variable is represented by a variable-variable link to an unbound cell on the evaluation stack or constructed term stack.

The local variables introduced by a clause when it is used to reduce a goal are also kept on the evaluation stack. As with Pascal, these variables are accessed via offsets from a base pointer, usually an address register; however, unlike Pascal, we are not able to use the simple **link** and **unlk** mechanism to allocate and deallocate space for them.

Each variable 'slot' is, like an argument register, a single cell and can hold any term. Some Prolog systems initialize variables as they are allocated to be unbound, others do not. Initializing variables reduces the performance (since the effort to initialize the variables might be redundant) but it makes implementing a garbage collector somewhat simpler.

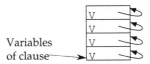

Figure 10.8 *Local variables introduced by a clause*

The third type of entry in the evaluation stack is the choice point record. This is used when there is a choice of clause in reducing a goal. In the choice point record are kept sufficient details to allow us to restore the evaluation stack to the state *just before* the choice point record is created. This allows us to backtrack and to make another choice as necessary.

The Prolog argument registers are also saved as part of the choice point record. The motivation for saving them is the same as saving registers in a Pascal procedure: they will be needed again to participate in another unification; furthermore, the arguments are *only* needed again in the event that the system backtracks.

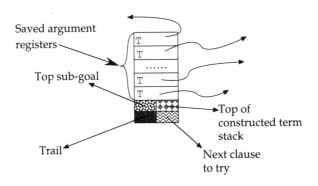

Figure 10.9 *Structure of a choice point*

The *trail* is used to record those variables which have been bound since a choice point is created. This is generally kept as a separate data structure to the main evaluation stack although logically it is part of the choice point record's function to record the bound variables.

It is not necessary to record *every* binding in the trail; we only need to record bindings to those variables which will *survive* a backtrack. When the system backtracks all the variables created after the choice point will automatically disappear – their creation will itself be undone – therefore it is not necessary to record the fact that such variables have been bound. We only need to create entries in the trail for variables which are *older* than the most recent choice point, and which therefore will still be present after backtracking albeit with possibly different values.

The final data structure is one we have already seen: the constructed term stack. Like the LISP heap this is used to record terms which have been dynamically created during a Prolog evaluation. However, we organize it like a stack to facilitate backtracking. The constructed term stack grows as new terms are created during unification, and shrinks as part of backtracking. One of the fields in the choice point record indicates the stack top at the point that the choice point is created.

Any terms created after the choice point are placed above this marker; and so, when the system backtracks all the terms above the marker can be discarded. This form of garbage collection is so powerful that it can remove the need for many, if not most, calls to the garbage collector – indeed early Prolog systems did not have a garbage collector. However, a real garbage collector is still needed for those programs which do not backtrack.

10.2.2   A sample evaluation

We can chart the progress of our fallible greek query in terms of the state of the evaluation stack system at various points. Initially, the stacks are empty, and the Prolog 'moving finger' indicates a point just before the first goal in the query:

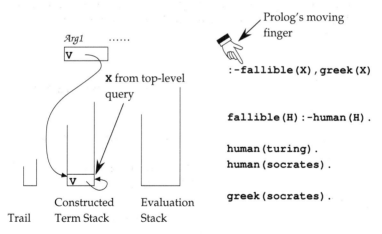

Figure 10.10 *Initial state of the Prolog stacks*

We have arbitrarily put the only variable so far in the system – **X** – in the constructed term stack (C.T.S.) for convenience. In practice, we cannot easily predict where this variable would be located.

The first step that the evaluator makes is to enter the **fallible** program. This involves setting the first argument register to point to **X** and to create a call record indicating that there is another goal to solve after the **human** goal:

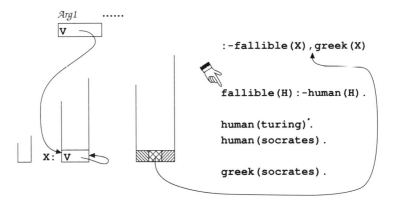

Figure 10.11 *Create a call record*

We now have to unify the head of the **fallible** clause with the goal. We must also create a new local variable – **H** – which is introduced as a result of using the **fallible** clause and which is allocated on the evaluation stack.

As a result of unifying the head and goal we bind **H** to the first argument register – which is itself bound to the top-level goal variable:

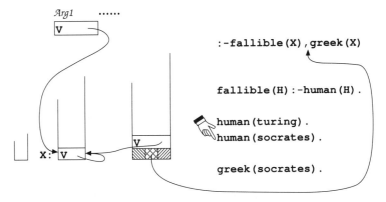

Figure 10.12 *Bind local variable to argument*

We now enter the **human** procedure. Since this is the last sub-goal in the rule for **fallible** we do not need to create a call record here; however, since there are two clauses for **human** we *do* need to create a choice point record (sometimes we might need both a call record and a choice point record). In the choice point record are recorded the current goal, a pointer to the constructed term stack, the trail and the previous choice point record. We also record the argument registers. To avoid overly cluttering up our diagram we only show some of these pointers emanating from the choice point record:

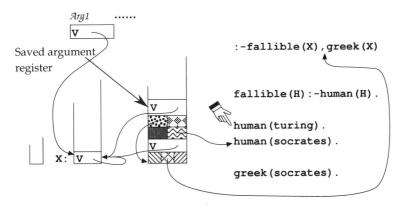

Figure 10.13 *A **human** choice point*

Having created a choice point, we unify the head of the **human** clause with the goal. This involves binding the goal variable **X** to the constant **turing**; and an entry is created in the trail because the goal variable is older than the choice point we have just created. After performing the unification the next step is to attempt to solve the **greek** goal:

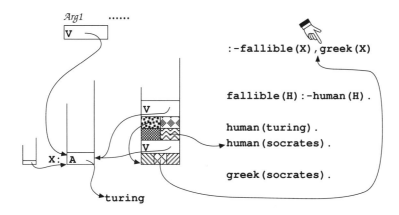

Figure 10.14 *First attempt at finding a **greek***

Solving the **greek** goal involves using the only clause there is for **greek**. As we enter the **greek** goal, the first argument register is loaded with the value of **X**, which is **turing**. In this case it happens that the first argument register has not changed much in value; however with deeper computations we would certainly expect the argument registers to be constantly changing:

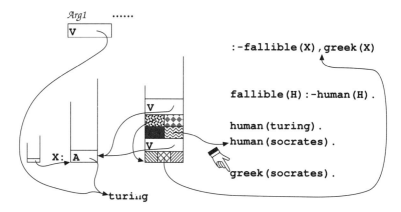

Figure 10.15 *Attempt a greek solution*

This unification attempt – in which we try to match **greek** and **turing** – fails, therefore we are required to backtrack. This involves clearing the most recent choice point, undoing any bindings done since it was created, and resetting the various argument registers. All of which leaves us with the stacks in the state:

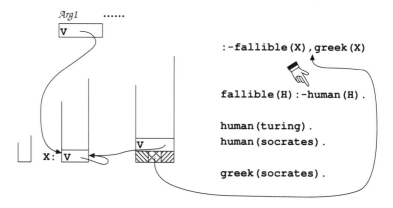

Figure 10.16 *Re-attempt to solve human*

We are back in the state where we needed to solve the **human** goal, although the first **human** clause has been tried, and therefore we must try the second one. We can now proceed to use the second **human** clause, which this time succeeds by binding **X** to the greek **socrates**:

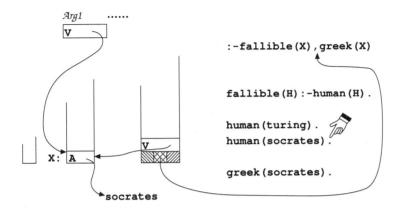

Figure 10.17 *Bind answer to* `socrates`

Notice that, since there is no choice point in the way, we did not need to create an entry in the trail when we bound **X** this time.

We can now move on to the final state, where the **greek** goal has been entered and completed – and **X** is bound to the compatible **socrates**. Since there are no more goals to solve, and there are no choice points 'protecting' the call record for **fallible**, most Prolog systems optimise the stack by removing the call record from the stack:

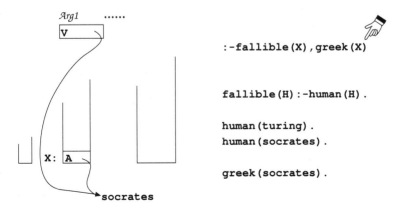

Figure 10.18 *The final state of the fallible greek stacks*

10.3 Using a virtual machine

Recall that a small Prolog fragment which represented a list pair needed a large number of 680x0 instructions to fully implement unification with it. It is clear that the 680x0 is not perfectly adapted to the execution of Prolog programs. This is not the case for Pascal, where we could justifiably argue that the 680x0 is an almost perfect Pascal machine. Unfortunately, when it comes to Prolog there is a large gap between the facilities offered by the 680x0 and the requirements of the language.

One consequence of this, is that compiled Prolog programs tend to be quite large: a compiled program may be 20-50 times larger compared to the original Prolog source. This should be compared with Pascal where it is not uncommon for a compiled Pascal program to be *smaller* than its source version.

In order to avoid having large bulky sequences of instructions to implement a Prolog program, we often use a *virtual machine* as a layer between the Prolog source and the underlying 680x0. A virtual machine is an abstract machine that is designed to be well suited to the execution of Prolog. A Prolog compiler would compile instructions for the virtual machine rather than the 680x0 directly and a special purpose *emulator* running on the 680x0 emulates the virtual machine instructions generated by the Prolog compiler.

The advantage of a virtual machine is that the compiler can 'target' a more suitable vehicle for the programming language than the raw machine; resulting in more compact compiled programs. Similar techniques have been used to implement systems for other languages: at least one early Pascal compiler was based on the use of the virtual machine concept: UCSD Pascal. In that case the motivation was portability as well as compactness of compiled programs.

There are a number of virtual machine designs suitable for Prolog; the most famous is the Warren Abstract Machine (WAM). In the WAM, instead of our long instruction sequence for unifying a list pair we have just three WAM instructions:

```
get_list        Arg1
unify_var       Arg4
unify_var       Arg1
```

where **Arg1** and **Arg4** refer to argument registers 1 and 4 respectively.

Of course, the emulator must still be able to implement these WAM instructions, and to do so will require essentially the same instructions that we saw above for unifying a list pair. We have gained a considerable space advantage because the operation 'unify against a list', for example, is implemented only once within the WAM emulator instead of for each list pair in the program. However, there is likely to be a performance penalty in using an emulator rather than compiling directly to 680x0 instructions.

One key overhead in the use of a virtual machine emulator is the interpretation and decoding of WAM instructions. One simple way of implementing such an instruction decoder could be realized in the pseudo-Pascal fragment:

```
repeat
   case pc^ of
      get_list:   ......
      ... ...
      unify_var:   ......
   end;
   pc:=pc+1;
until false;
```

We can use the same implementation technique which we saw in Chapter 7 for **case** statements to implement this fragment:

```
dcode  move.l  pc,a0
       move.w  (a0),d0          ;pc^
       cmp.w   #min_opcode,d0
       blt     case_error
       cmp.w   #max_opcode,d0
       bgt     case_error       ;WAM  opcode  legal?
       add.w   d0,d0
       move.w  @0(d0.w),d0
       jmp     @0(d0.w)
       ... ...
@0     dc.w    get_list-@0
       ...
       dc.w    unify_var-@0
get_list:
       ... ...                  ;implement  get_list
       bra     exit
       ... ...
exit   add.l   #1,pc            ;adjust  virtual  pc
       bra     dcode
```

The result is a code sequence which involves executing 9 instructions in order to simply start executing the 'real' code for an instruction; together with a further two instructions to increment the virtual program counter and to branch back to the decode cycle.

On the other hand, it may only require a small number of instructions to implement a given virtual machine instruction; the **unify_var Arg1** instruction, for example, can be implemented in just three instructions:

```
move.b  tag(T),tag(Arg1)
move.l  ptr(T),ptr(Arg1)
add.l   #cell,T
```

where T is an internal register to the WAM. The T register is used during unification as a pointer which follows the internal structure of lists and compound terms. Each **unify_** instruction leaves T pointing at the next argument of a compound term.

Thus, for three instructions which implement the 'meat' of the **unify_var** virtual machine instruction, we have 12 'overhead' instructions. It is quite important to try to optimize the implementation of the decode instruction loop: in general a *single* extra instruction in the decode loop can result in a performance degradation of 10-20%.

If we arrange the decoding of virtual machine instructions more carefully, then we can optimise the decoding of instructions considerably. For example, we can eliminate the error checking in the case statement code: all we need to ensure is that the Prolog compiler generates correct virtual machine instructions.

A further optimisation could be to use the scaled addressing modes available on the 68020 and 68030. This would allow us to eliminate an instruction from the decode cycle:

```
add.w   d0,d0
```

Furthermore, we can increment the virtual machine's program counter at the same time as accessing the opcode; and we could allocate an address register (**a4** say) to be the program counter. Together, these optimisations give the instruction decoding sequence of:

```
move.w  (a4)+,d0
move.w  @0(d0.w*2),d0
jmp     @0(d0.w)
```

which, together with a **jmp** instruction at the end of the 680x0 instructions used to implement each virtual machine instruction, gives us four 680x0 instructions to decode a virtual machine instruction.

We can improve this still further if, instead of using arbitrary numbers to represent virtual machine instructions, we use 680x0 addresses as the opcodes: a virtual machine opcode is also the address of the 680x0 instructions which implement it.   Each opcode now occupies 4 bytes instead of 2, which is still far short of the space needed for the instructions. This allows us to reduce the instruction decode and increment cycle to just two 680x0 instructions:

```
move.l   (a4)+,a0
jmp      (a0)
```

These instructions can be duplicated at the end of each implementation of a virtual machine instruction, eliminating a **jmp** to a central decode loop. The   complete   instructions   used   to   implement   the   **unify_var** instruction are now:

```
unify_var:
        move.l  (a4)+,a0       ;acquire Argn
        move.b  tag(a2),tag(a0);use a2 for T
        move.l  ptr(a2),ptr(a0)
        lea     cell(a2),a2     ;T is incremented
        move.l  (a4)+,a0       ;decode next ins.
        jmp     (a0)
```

In this regime, for this virtual machine instruction, the overhead for instruction decode is reduced from 300% to 25%.

The exercise that we have just gone through of optimising a crucial section of code, is a good example of one of the prime motivations for programming directly in assembler.   We have gained a considerable performance benefit which it is extremely unlikely that a Pascal compiler could generate – it simply requires too many assumptions which we, as programmers, could make but a compiler could not.

There are many other aspects which are related to the implementation of Prolog which we have not covered in this chapter.   To fully cover the techniques needed to implement a Prolog system would justify a book in its own right!   It has been our intention to outline some of the more interesting aspects of implementing Prolog rather than providing a complete guide to its implementation.

Addressing modes for the 680x0

An addressing mode is a specification of an operand to an instruction. It specifies how the operand of the instruction is to be computed. There are some ten addressing modes on the 68000 itself with a further eight or so on the 68020/68030. This means that in the specification of an instruction's operand there may be up to 18 ways of determining the kind of operand it is.

A.1   Register direct addressing

Register direct addressing refers to the operand being in one of the registers. There are two versions of register direct addressing – data register (written as d_n) and address register (written as a_n). If an operand is specified using either mode then the data to be manipulated, or the location for the result of the operation to be stored, is one of the registers. For example, the instruction

```
move.w  a0,d3
```

uses register direct addressing for both the source and destination operand. The effect of this instruction is to move the word length contents of address register **a0** to data register **d3**.

When a data register is addressed as a word length quantity, as in this case, only the lower half of the register is involved. So, for this instruction only the lower half of **d3** would be affected, and the upper half of the register remains intact. When a data register is addressed as a byte quantity then only the lowest quarter of the register takes part in the instruction.

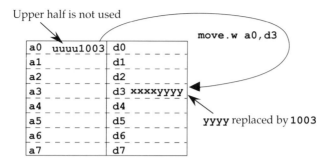

Figure A.1 *Register direct addressing*

In contrast to the situation with data registers, whenever an address register is the destination the *whole of the register* is always affected. If a word length quantity is moved into an address register then it is sign extended – the upper half of the address register is set to all 1s or all 0s depending on the value of the most significant bit of the lower word.

An address register cannot be manipulated as a byte quantity – only word and long word widths are available.

A.2   Immediate addressing

Immediate addressing is used when the operand value of an instruction is fixed. It is useful for putting constant values into registers or for comparing variable quantities against a known value.

In the instruction

```
cmp.b    #32,d0
```

the operand **#32** is the source operand and it is an immediate operand (indicated by the presence of the '**#**' character in front of the literal number). This instruction compares the lowest byte in register **d0** with 32, which also happens to be the code for an ASCII space character.

Immediate addressing only makes sense in the case of a source operand. Since the data is actually part of the instruction, using immediate addressing for the destination would amount to allowing program instructions to modify themselves. An ability for programs to modify themselves is important to have, on a theoretical level, but it is not obviously useful for an addressing mode.

A.3 Absolute addressing

In absolute addressing the operand of the instruction has built into it the *address* in memory of the data/operand. Either the source or the destination (or both in some cases) may be specified absolutely (written as the address without a preceding '**#**' character).

Absolute addressing is used when memory locations are referred to specifically, for example, a memory location might represent a specific variable or it may be necessary to jump to a specific program in a particular place in memory.

For example, the instruction

```
move.l  1000,d4
```

moves the long word at address **1000** into data register **d4** *overwriting the whole of its contents.*

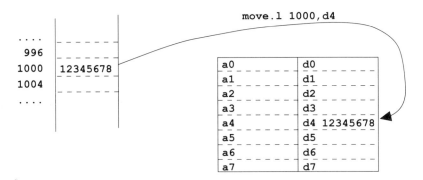

Figure A.2 *Absolute addressing*

Absolute addressing is also used for many program control instructions; for example, a **jmp** to a specific address is a case where the address of the operand (i.e. where to continue execution) is part of the instruction.

There are, in fact, two forms of absolute addressing: word and long word. These forms refer to the size of the address itself rather than the data object being addressed. The word form addresses the first 32K bytes and the last 32K bytes of the address space. This form is useful for low memory programs and variables. The long form can address any memory location in the address space. Normally the correct form of an absolute address is determined automatically by the assembler, however the programmer can specify it by suffixing a **.w** or **.l** in the address:

```
move.w  d0,1000.w  ;a word length address
move.w  d1,1234.l  ;a long address
```

A.4 Address register indirect

The address register indirect addressing mode which is written

(a_n)

uses an address register to specify the *address* of the operand. The specified register contains the address in memory of the data value for the instruction or where to place the result. In register direct addressing the data value to be manipulated is in a register whereas in register indirect addressing the register contains the address of the data.

Address register indirect is often used for pointer following – where the memory is loaded from some variable into an address register and then dereferenced and for storing into records via a pointer.

In the instruction

```
move.l  d0,(a6)
```

the long word value of **d0** (i.e. the whole of **d0**) is written out to the address referred to in register **a6**.

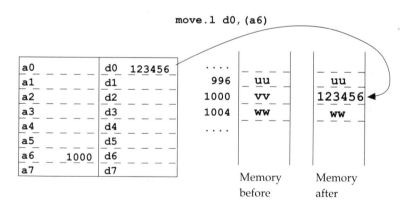

Figure A.3 *Address register indirect addressing*

A.5   Address register indirect with displacement

The address register indirect with displacement addressing mode, which is written as

$$O(a_n) \quad \text{or} \quad (O, a_n)$$

where the offset O is a 16 bit number in the range -32768...32767, is a variation on address register indirect. In this case the address contained in the address register is offset by means of a fixed displacement in order to determine the final address of the operand.

The address register indirect with displacement mode is extremely useful in accessing elements in records and in accessing local variables within a Pascal procedure or function.

We can load the value which is addressed as being offset four bytes from **a2** into **d0** with the instruction:

```
move.w   4(a2),d0
```

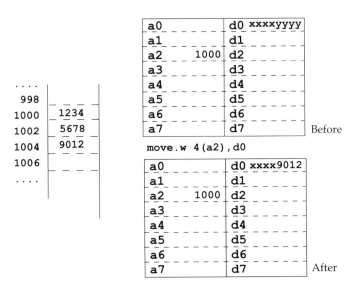

Figure A.4 *Address register indirect with offset*

A.6 Address register indirect with post-increment

This addressing mode which is written as:

(a_n) +

is a variation on address register indirect, except that the address register in question is *incremented* after the address is calculated. The amount that the address register is incremented depends on the size specifier of the instruction: for a byte size transfer 1 is added, for a word size operation 2 is added and 4 is added for a long operation.

For example, the instruction

```
move.w  (a3)+,d0
```

moves the word pointed at by address register **a3** into the lower half of **d0** and adds 2 to **a3**:

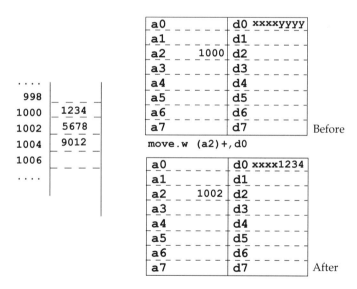

Figure A.5 *Address register indirect with post-increment*

It is not permissible for the system stack to be on an odd boundary; therefore if an instruction specifies a single byte transfer with post-increment mode involving **a7**, then a byte transfer takes place but the stack pointer in incremented by two. This avoids the system stack pointer being on an odd byte boundary.

The post-increment addressing mode can be used to implement block moves and, in conjunction with the pre-decrement addressing mode, is also used to implement expression stacks. For example, a string copy can be implemented with this addressing mode:

```
loop: move.b  (a0)+,(a1)+    ;move  1  byte
       dbra    d0,loop        ;until  end
       ...
```

A.7   Address register indirect with pre-decrement

This addressing mode is similar to the previous one, except that the address register is first decremented by an amount depending on the size specifier of the instruction. A pre-decrement operand is written as

$$-(a_n)$$

The instruction:

```
move.w  d0,-(a7)    ;push  d0
```

saves the word contents of data register **d0** on the system stack:

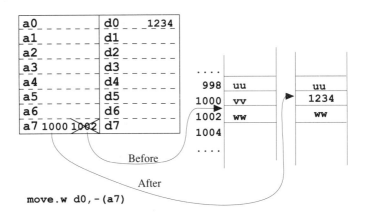

Figure A.6 *Address register indirect with pre-decrement*

In order to pop **d0** back off the stack we would use the instruction:

```
move.w  (a7)+,d0
```

Again, as with address register indirect with post-increment, if a byte sized transfer is specified using the system stack, then the **a7** register is decremented by two to avoid it being on an odd byte boundary. The contents of the extra byte are undefined. However, a push of a byte-sized quantity onto the system stack can be safely followed by a similar sized pop.

A.8 Address register indirect with index

The address register indirect with index addressing mode combines the use of an address register, a second register (to provide the index) and a displacement. It is most applicable to accessing elements of arrays (the index into the array will often be held as a data register and the array itself in an address register).

An operand using this mode is written:

$$\texttt{Off(a}_\texttt{x}\texttt{,r}_\texttt{y}\texttt{.w*s)} \qquad \text{or} \qquad \texttt{(Off,a}_\texttt{x}\texttt{,r}_\texttt{y}\texttt{.w*s)}$$

where $\texttt{a}_\texttt{x}$ is the address register and $\texttt{r}_\texttt{y}$ is the index register – it can be either an address register or more typically a data register – $\texttt{w}$ is the width specifier, $\texttt{s}$ is an optional *scale factor* and $\texttt{Off}$ is a displacement or offset.

The width specifier determines how much of the index register is to be used for the index width: it can be **w**ord or **l**ong. Typically, a programmer might use word length integers for the index of a small array which is less than 32 Kbytes long for example. By specifying a word length width on the index register the programmer does not need to ensure that the upper half of the index register has valid information in it. A long index uses the whole of the data register for computing the index.

The scale factor is the number by which the index is *multiplied* before use in the address computation. The scale factor can be 1, 2, 4 or 8. If the scale factor is missing then a factor of 1 is implied. The scale factor makes the implementation of certain arrays simpler: an entry in an array of long words, for example, can be indexed with a value which corresponds to the logical index of the entry within the array rather than its relative position in the array expressed as a byte offset. The scale factor is not available on the 68000/008/010 models.

The displacement is a quantity which is added to the address register base and the index offset. As with the address register indirect with displacement addressing mode this displacement makes access of arrays of records simpler.

The instruction:

```
move.l  d0,0(a2,d1.w*4)
```

stores the contents of **d0** into the small array of long words based at **a2** and indexed through **d1**:

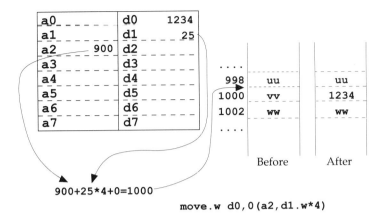

$$900+25*4+0=1000$$

move.w d0,0(a2,d1.w*4)

Figure A.7 *Address register indirect with index*

The form of this addressing mode is somewhat restricted on the 68000 compared to the later models: the scale factor is set to 1, and the displacement is restricted to the range -128...127 bytes.

On the 68020 it is possible to suppress one or more of the components. In particular it is possible to suppress the address register specification; if this is done then zero is assumed as the base address. The effect of this is to allow a 'data register indirect' addressing mode even though this is not specifically permitted.

A.9   Program counter with displacement

This addressing mode – often called program counter relative on other machines – uses the program counter instead of an address register but otherwise it is the same as address register indirect with displacement.

It is most often used in specifying sub-programs within a larger program but it can also be used for data transfer. The instruction

jmp   36(PC)

would, in effect, add 36 to the program counter and cause a jump to that new address. The instruction

move.w *+10,d3

uses an alternative notation for this addressing mode. The effect of this instruction would be to move the word which is 10 bytes further on *from the start of this instruction* into **d3**. It is up to the programmer, of course, to ensure that this address contains something meaningful – it is quite liable to contain program instruction words! Many assemblers generate this addressing mode automatically in preference to absolute addressing for variables which have been declared using the define storage directive **ds**.

A.10 Program counter with index

This addressing mode is analogous to address register indirect with index, except that the program counter is used rather than an address register. It is written as:

```
Off(PC,rn.w*s), (Off,PC,rn.w*s) or *+Off(rn.w*s)
```

or just

```
label(rn.w*s)
```

As with normal indexing the width of the index is specified with the index register and there is an optional scale factor (on the 68020).
The instruction

```
move.l  charray(d0.w*4),d1
```

moves a long word from a table built into the program (at relative address **charray**) into **d1**:

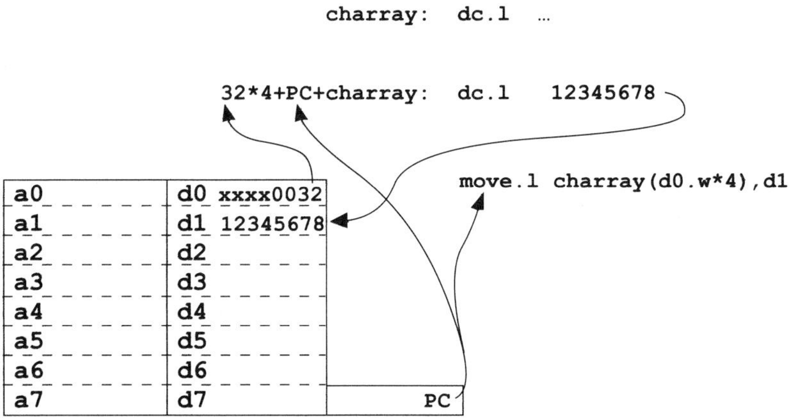

charray: dc.l   ...

32*4+PC+charray: dc.l   12345678

move.l charray(d0.w*4),d1

a0	d0 xxxx0032
a1	d1 12345678
a2	d2
a3	d3
a4	d4
a5	d5
a6	d6
a7	d7
	PC

Figure A.8 *Example of program counter with index*

As with the address register indexing mode the form of program counter relative indexing is restricted on the 68000 compared to the 68020/68030. In the 68000/68010 the displacement can only be short, i.e. in the range -128...127 bytes, and the scale factor is restricted to being just 1.

A.11 Memory indirect post-indexed

The memory indirect post-indexed addressing mode is a combination of address register indirect (with displacement) and indexing, except that the indexing is performed after accessing a value in memory specified by the address register.

It is written as

$$([Oi, a_n], r_m.w*s, Od)$$

The operand address is computed by first finding out the address [Oi, a_n], which is obtained in the same way as address register indirect with displacement, then taking the long word which is stored at this address, and using it with the appropriately scaled indexing register and the outer displacement Od.

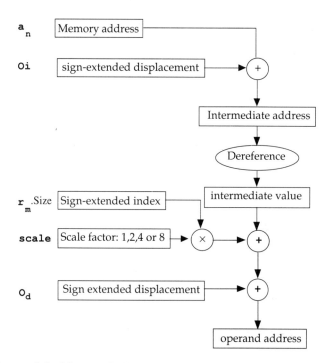

Figure A.9 *Memory indirect post-indexed address computation*

For example, the instruction

```
move.w  ([6,a2],d0.w*4,0),d1
```

accesses the long word at **6(a2)**, adds it to the contents of register **d0** (scaled to be a long word index) and the final offset of zero to compute the actual address:

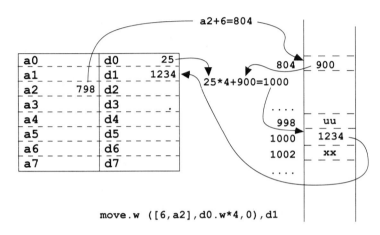

move.w ([6,a2],d0.w*4,0),d1

Figure A.10 *Memory indirect post-indexed addressing*

This addressing mode is not available on the 68000/008/010 models.

A.12 Memory indirect pre-indexed

This addressing mode is similar to the memory indirect post-indexed mode except that the indexing is performed first. So, if the operand is specified as:

$$([\text{Oi},\text{a}_n,\text{r}_m.\text{w*s}],\text{Od})$$

then the final value is obtained by computing the address at $(\text{Oi},\text{a}_n,\text{r}_m.\text{w*s})$ as with the address register indirect indexing mode. The long word at this address is then added to the outer displacement **Od** to get the final address of the operand.

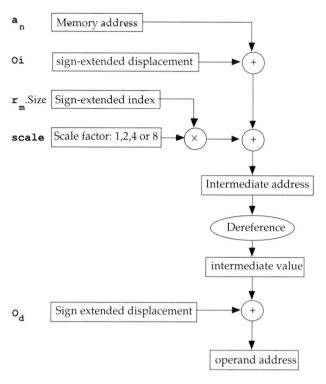

Figure A.11 *Memory indirect with pre-indexing address computation*

One possible application of this addressing mode is with arrays of pointers to records. The array would be indexed though the indexing component and the field in the record would be accessed via the memory indirection.

This addressing mode is not available on the 68000/008/010 models.

A.13 Program counter memory indirect with post-indexing

This addressing mode is similar to memory indirect with post-indexing; except that the program counter is used instead of an address register.

The syntax for this mode is:

$$([Oi, PC], r_n.w*s, Od)$$

This addressing mode is not available on the 68000/010/008 models.

A.14 Program counter memory indirect with pre-indexing

This addressing mode is similar to memory indirect with pre-indexing; except that the program counter is used instead of an address register.

The syntax for this mode is:

$$([Oi, PC, r_n.w*s], Od)$$

We can use this indexing mode to implement a single instruction case switch statement.

Assuming that the index value is in **d0**, and that the index table is a table of addresses, then the instruction:

```
        jmp     ([@0,PC,d0.w*4],0)
  @0    dc.l    lab1
        dc.l    lab2
        ...
        dc.l    labn
```

will cause a switch to one of labels **lab1**,...,**labn** depending on the value of **d0**.

This addressing mode is not available on the 68000/010/008 models.

The 680x0 instructions used in the text

Below are listed the instructions which are actually referred to in the main text. Where appropriate, related instructions are also listed.

The exact Motorola mnemonics are given – in many cases, we can use a generic mnemonic and allow the assembler to choose the correct one. For example, the **adda** instruction is a special case of **add** which adds to an address register; many assemblers automatically substitute for the correct mnemonics as necessary.

The list is not intended as a complete reference to all the 680x0 instructions; however the main instructions that application assembler programmers use are all covered; the omitted instructions tend to be for special system purposes and are often not available to the application programmer. The format of each description is:

name   **Title of the instruction**

syntax   name[.bwl]   <ea>$_1$,<ea>$_2$ **instruction format**

description: Description of the effects of the instruction, together with possible restrictions to note.

note: <ea> means one of the addressing modes as described in Appendix A. If the instruction has a size specifier associated with it then it may be one of **byte** , **w**ord or **l**ong word.

ccr: How each flag in the condition code register is affected.

see: A section in the main text which uses this instruction in an example, or explains it more fully

add	**Add source to destination**

syntax: add[.bwl]   <ea>,d$_n$

                add[.bwl]   d$_n$,<ea>

description: Add the source to the destination using binary arithmetic. The size of the operation can be byte, word or long.

ccr: N set if result negative, cleared otherwise
                Z set if result zero, cleared otherwise
                V set if overflow is generated, cleared otherwise
                C set if carry is generated, cleared otherwise
                X set as carry bit.

see: Section 4.2

adda	**Add to address register**

syntax: adda[.wl]   <ea>,a$_n$

description: Add source to destination **address** register. Operation can be word or long, in the case of word the entire destination is always used.

                Some assemblers automatically generate this instruction from the **add** mnemonic if the destination is an address register.

ccr: not affected

addi   Add immediate data

syntax: `addi[.bwl]  #<data>,<ea>`

description: Add immediate data to destination. This instruction is used when immediate data is specified with the **add** mnemonic.

ccr: N set if result negative, cleared otherwise
              Z set if result zero, cleared otherwise
              V set if overflow is generated, cleared otherwise
              C set if carry is generated, cleared otherwise
              X set as carry bit.

see: Section 4.2

addq   Add quick immediate data

syntax: `addq[.bwl]  #<data>,<ea>`

description: Add immediate data to destination. Data is in the range 1 to 8. This instruction is the one actually used when immediate data in the range 1..8 is specified with the **add** mnemonic.

ccr: N set if result negative, cleared otherwise
              Z set if result zero, cleared otherwise
              V set if overflow is generated, cleared otherwise
              C set if carry is generated, cleared otherwise
              X set as carry bit.

addx   **Add binary extended**

syntax: `addx[.bwl]  d`$_y$`,d`$_x$

`addx[.bwl]   -(a`$_y$`),-(a`$_x$`)`

description: Add source to destination along with the e**x**tend bit. This instruction is used to implement multi-word arithmetic.

Note the restrictions in the allowed addressing modes: either both operands are data registers or they are both address register predecrement.

ccr: N set if result negative, cleared otherwise
Z set if result zero, cleared otherwise
V set if overflow is generated, cleared otherwise
C set if carry is generated, cleared otherwise
X set as carry bit.

see: Section 9.2

and   **AND logical**

syntax: `and[.bwl]   <ea>,d`$_n$

`and[.bwl]   d`$_n$`,<ea>`

description: Logically 'and' the bit pattern in the source with that of the destination. Each bit in the destination is formed by and-ing it with the corresponding bit of the source operand.

note: Address register direct addressing is not permitted with this instruction.

ccr: N set to most significant bit of result.
Z set if result is zero, cleared otherwise
V always cleared
C always cleared
X not affected.

see: Section 6.1,6.2

andi ## AND immediate data

syntax: `andi[.bwl]   #data,<ea>`

description: Logically 'and' the bit pattern in the immediate data with that
of the destination. This instruction is used with the **and**
instruction when the source operand is a literal value.

note: Address register direct addressing is not permitted with this
instruction.

ccr: N set to most significant bit of result.
Z set if result is zero, cleared otherwise
V always cleared
C always cleared
X not affected.

andi ## AND immediate to ccr

syntax: `andi  #data,ccr`

description: Logically 'and' the bit pattern in the immediate data with the
condition code register. In effect this is used to mask out
certain flags in the **ccr**.

ccr: N cleared if bit 3 of data is zero, unaffected otherwise
Z cleared if bit 2 of data is zero, unaffected otherwise
V cleared if bit 1 of data is zero, unaffected otherwise
C cleared if bit 0 of data is zero, unaffected otherwise
X cleared if bit 4 of data is zero, unaffected otherwise.

asl	**Arithmetic shift left**

syntax: `asl[.bwl]   dx,dy`

`asl[.bwl]   #<data>,dx`

`asl  <ea>`

description: The destination is left shifted by `<count>` bits. The rightmost bit is replaced by 0.

In the case of a register count, amount of shift is the contents of the register, modulo 64.

In the case of an immediate count, range of shifts is 1 to 8.

In the case of a memory instruction the operation is limited to word length and shifts of one bit only.

ccr: N is set to most significant bit of result
Z is set if result is zero, cleared otherwise
V is set if the most significant bit is changed at any time during the shift operation, cleared otherwise.
C set to the last bit shifted out of the operand. Cleared for a zero shift count.
X set to the last bit shifted out of the operand. Unaffected for a zero shift count.

see: Section 5.2, 6.1

`asr`	**Arithmetic shift right**

syntax: `asr[.bwl]`   `dx,dy`

                `asr[.bwl]`   `#<data>,dx`

                `asr <ea>`

description: The destination is right shifted by `<count>` bits. The leftmost (i.e. most significant) bit is duplicated. In effect this instruction implements a division by a power of 2.

In the case of a register count, amount of the shift is the contents of the register, modulo 64.

In the case of an immediate count, range of shifts is 1-8.

In the case of a memory instruction the operation is limited to word length and shifts of one bit only.

ccr: N is set to most significant bit of result
Z is set if result is zero, cleared otherwise
V is set if the most significant bit is changed at any time during the shift operation, cleared otherwise.
C set to the last bit shifted out of the operand. Cleared for a zero shift count.
X set to the last bit shifted out of the operand. Unaffected for a zero shift count.

see: Section 6.1

b_{cc}   **Branch conditionally**

syntax: b_{cc}[.swl]   **label**

description: If the specified condition is met then program execution continues at **label**. There are three forms of this instruction: **s**hort (or byte), **w**ord and **l**ong. (Long format is not available on the 68000/008/010.) These refer to the length of displacement of the instruction and therefore to the distance of the label from the instruction. A **s**hort displacement is ±127 bytes from the instruction, a **w**ord displacement is ±32,767 bytes from the instruction and a **l**ong displacement is ±2,147,483,647 bytes.

The branch is taken if the condition **cc** is satisfied. The available conditions are:

CC — carry clear	¬C		CS — carry set	C
EQ — equal/zero	Z		NE —unequal/non zero	¬Z
MI — minus	N		PL — plus	¬N
VC — overflow clear	¬V		VS — overflow set	V
GE — greater or equal	N•V+¬N•¬V		LT — less than	N•¬V+¬N•V
GT — greater than	¬Z•N•V+¬Z•¬N•¬V		LE — less or equal	Z+N•¬V+¬N•V
HI — high	¬C•¬Z		LS — low or same	C+Z

ccr: condition codes are not affected.

note: A short branch to the immediately following instruction cannot be formed as that code is reserved for word branch.

see: Section 7.1

bchg Test a bit and change

syntax: bchg d$_n$, <ea>

bchg #<data>, <ea>

description: A bit in the destination is tested, complemented and copied to the Z flag in the **ccr**. The complemented bit is returned to the destination. If the destination is a data register then the numbering of the bits is modulo 32 which allows any bit in the register to be manipulated; if the destination is memory then the numbering is modulo 8 and it is a byte operation.

The *least* significant bit of the byte or long word is bit 0.

ccr: Z is set to the new value of the corresponding bit. All other flags are unaffected.

bclr Test a bit and clear

syntax: bclr d$_n$, <ea>

bclr #<data>, <ea>

description: A bit in the destination is tested and copied to the Z flag in the **ccr**. The corresponding bit in the destination is then zeroed. If the destination is a data register then the numbering of the bits is modulo 32 which allows any bit in the register to be manipulated; if the destination is memory then the numbering is modulo 8 and it is a byte operation.

A 0 bit refers to the least significant bit of the byte or word.

ccr: Z is set if the old value of the corresponding bit was zero, reset otherwise. All other flags are unaffected.

see: Section 6.2

bfchg   **Test bit field and change**

syntax: `bfchg <ea>{offset:width}`

description: Sets the condition codes depending on the specified bit field and then complements the bit field.

The **offset** indicates the number of bits from the effective address to the start of the bit field, and the **offset** is the size of the field.

The offset to the bit field can be either given as a literal number in the range 0..31 bits, or it can be specified as the contents of a data register, in which case the offset range is $-2^{31}..2^{31}$ bits.

The **width** field can also be specified as a literal in the range 0..31, or through a data register in which case the contents of the data register are used modulo 32, with 0 meaning 32 bits.

ccr: N is set if the most significant bit of the field is 1, cleared otherwise; Z is set if the bit field is all 0's and is cleared otherwise; V and C are cleared and X is unaffected.

note: The address register direct, pre-decrement and post-increment addressing modes are not available for this instruction.

This instruction is not available on 68000/008/010 processors.

`bfclr` Clear bit field

syntax: `bfclr  <ea>{offset:width}`

description: Sets the condition codes depending on the specified bit field and then zeroes the bit field.

The `offset` indicates the number of bits from the effective address to the start of the bit field, and the `offset` is the size of the field.

The offset to the bit field can be either given as a literal number in the range 0..31 bits, or it can be specified as the contents of a data register, in which case the offset range is $-2^{31}..2^{31}$ bits.

The `width` field can also be specified as a literal in the range 0..31, or through a data register in which case the contents of the data register are used modulo 32, with 0 meaning 32 bits.

ccr: N is set if the most significant bit of the field is 1, cleared otherwise; Z is set if the bit field is all 0's and is cleared otherwise; V and C are cleared and X is unaffected.

note: The address register direct, pre-decrement and post-increment addressing modes are not available for this instruction.

This instruction is not available on 68000/008/010 processors.

bfexts   **Signed extraction of a bit field**

syntax: **bfexts <ea>{offset:width},d$_n$**

description: Sets the condition codes depending on the specified bit field
and extracts the bit field extended to a 32 bit signed number
into the data register.

The **offset** indicates the number of bits from the effective
address to the start of the bit field, and the **offset** is the size
of the field.

The offset to the bit field can be either given as a literal
number in the range 0..31 bits, or it can be specified as the
contents of a data register, in which case the offset range is
-2^{31}..2^{31} bits.

The **width** field can also be specified as a literal in the range
0..31, or through a data register in which case the contents of
the data register are used modulo 32, with 0 meaning 32 bits.

ccr: N is set if the most significant bit of the field is 1, cleared
otherwise; Z is set if the bit field is all 0's and is cleared
otherwise; V and C are cleared and X is unaffected.

note: The address register direct, pre-decrement and post-
increment addressing modes are not available for this
instruction.

This instruction is not available on 68000/008/010 processors.

see: Section 6.1

bfextu   Unsigned extraction of a bit field

syntax: `bfextu   <ea>{offset:width},d`$_n$

description: Sets the condition codes depending on the specified bit field
and extracts the bit field as a zero-extended 32 bit unsigned
number into the data register.

The **offset** indicates the number of bits from the effective
address to the start of the bit field, and the **offset** is the size
of the field.

The offset to the bit field can be either given as a literal
number in the range 0..31 bits, or it can be specified as the
contents of a data register, in which case the offset range is
$-2^{31}..2^{31}$ bits.

The **width** field can also be specified as a literal in the range
0..31, or through a data register in which case the contents of
the data register are used modulo 32, with 0 meaning 32 bits.

ccr: N is set if the most significant bit of the field is 1, cleared
otherwise; Z is set if the bit field is all 0's and is cleared
otherwise; V and C are cleared and X is unaffected.

note: The address register direct, pre-decrement and post-
increment addressing modes are not available for this
instruction.

This instruction is not available on 68000/008/010 processors.

see: Section 6.1

`bfffo`	**Find first one in a bit field**

syntax: `bfffo   <ea>{offset:width},d`$_n$

description: Searches the bit field for a 1 bit. The bit offset of that bit (i.e. the bit offset given in the instruction plus the offset within the field) is placed into the data register. If no 1 bit is found then the data register is loaded with the offset plus field width. The instruction also sets the condition codes depending on the specified bit field.

The **offset** indicates the number of bits from the effective address to the start of the bit field, and the **offset** is the size of the field.

The offset to the bit field can be either given as a literal number in the range 0..31 bits, or it can be specified as the contents of a data register, in which case the offset range is $-2^{31}..2^{31}$ bits.

The **width** field can also be specified as a literal in the range 0..31, or through a data register in which case the contents of the data register are used modulo 32, with 0 meaning 32 bits.

ccr: N is set if the most significant bit of the field is 1, cleared otherwise; Z is set if the bit field is all 0's and is cleared otherwise; V and C are cleared and X is unaffected.

note: The address register direct, pre-decrement and post-increment addressing modes are not available for this instruction.

This instruction is not available on 68000/008/010 processors.

bfins   Insert a bit field

syntax: bfins   d_n,<ea>{offset:width}

description: Inserts the value contained in the bottom **width** bits of the data register into the specified bit field. It also sets the condition codes depending on the inserted value of the bit field.

The **offset** indicates the number of bits from the effective address to the start of the bit field, and the **offset** is the size of the field.

The offset to the bit field can be either given as a literal number in the range 0..31 bits, or it can be specified as the contents of a data register, in which case the offset range is $-2^{31}..2^{31}$ bits.

The **width** field can also be specified as a literal in the range 0..31, or through a data register in which case the contents of the data register are used modulo 32, with 0 meaning 32 bits.

ccr: N is set if the most significant bit of the field is 1, cleared otherwise; Z is set if the bit field is all 0's and is cleared otherwise; V and C are cleared and X is unaffected.

note: The address register direct, pre-decrement and post-increment addressing modes are not available for this instruction.

This instruction is not available on 68000/008/010 processors.

see: Section 6.1

bfset   **Set bit field**

syntax: **bfset   <ea>{offset:width}**

description: Sets the condition codes depending on the specified bit field and then sets the bits in the bit field to all ones.

The **offset** indicates the number of bits from the effective address to the start of the bit field, and the **offset** is the size of the field.

The offset to the bit field can be either given as a literal number in the range 0..31 bits, or it can be specified as the contents of a data register, in which case the offset range is $-2^{31}..2^{31}$ bits.

The **width** field can also be specified as a literal in the range 0..31, or through a data register in which case the contents of the data register are used modulo 32, with 0 meaning 32 bits.

ccr: N is set if the most significant bit of the field was 1, cleared otherwise; Z is set if the bit field was all 0's and is cleared otherwise; V and C are cleared and X is unaffected.

note: The address register direct, pre-decrement and post-increment addressing modes are not available for this instruction.

This instruction is not available on 68000/008/010 processors.

bftst   **Test bit field**

syntax: `bftst  <ea>{offset:width}`

description: Sets the condition codes depending on the specified bit field.

The **offset** indicates the number of bits from the effective address to the start of the bit field, and the **offset** is the size of the field.

The offset to the bit field can be either given as a literal number in the range 0..31 bits, or it can be specified as the contents of a data register, in which case the offset range is $-2^{31}..2^{31}$ bits.

The **width** field can also be specified as a literal in the range 0..31, or through a data register in which case the contents of the data register are used modulo 32, with 0 meaning 32 bits.

ccr: N is set if the most significant bit of the field is 1, cleared otherwise; Z is set if the bit field is all 0's and is cleared otherwise; V and C are cleared and X is unaffected.

note: The address register direct, pre-decrement and post-increment addressing modes are not available for this instruction.

This instruction is not available on 68000/008/010 processors.

bra   **Branch always**

syntax: `bra[.swl]  <label>`

description: Program execution continues at `<label>`. The offset from the current program counter and the `<label>` must be within ±127 bytes for the short version of the instruction, and ±32767 bytes for the long version.

note: A short branch to the immediately following instruction (i.e. with offset 0) is not possible since offset 0 indicates a long branch.

see: Section 7.1

bset   Test a bit and set

syntax: `bset  d`$_n$`,<ea>`

          `bset  #<data>,<ea>`

description: A bit in the destination is tested and reflected in the state of the Z flag in the **ccr**. The corresponding bit in the destination is set to one. If the destination is a data register then the numbering of the bits is modulo 32, if the destination is memory then the numbering is modulo 8 and it is a byte operation.

ccr: Z is set if the old value of the corresponding bit was zero, reset otherwise. All other flags are unaffected.

see: Section 6.2

bsr   Branch to subroutine

syntax: `bsr[.swl]  <label>`

description: The long word address of the immediately following instruction is saved on the system stack (**a7**). Program execution continues at `<label>`. The offset from the current program counter and the `<label>` must be within ±127 bytes for the short version of the instruction, and ±32767 bytes for the long version.

note: A short subroutine branch to the immediately following instruction (i.e. with offset 0) is not possible since offset 0 indicates a long subroutine branch.

btst	**Test a bit**

syntax: btst d_n,<ea>

             btst #<data>,<ea>

description: A bit in the destination is tested and its state is reflected in the Z flag in the **ccr**. If the destination is a data register then the numbering of the bits is modulo 32, if the destination is memory then the numbering is modulo 8 and it is a byte operation.

ccr: Z is set if the value of the corresponding bit was zero, reset otherwise. All other flags are unaffected.

see: Section 6.2

chk	**Check register against bounds**

syntax: chk[.wl] <ea>,d_n

description: Check the value of the data register d_n against the operand specified in <ea>. If $d_n < 0$, or is greater than the source operand (i.e. <ea>) then issue a TRAP which results in exception processing. The comparison is signed

ccr: N is set if $d_n < 0$, cleared if $d_n >$source, else is undefined.
             Z is undefined.
             V is undefined.
             C is undefined.
             X is unaffected.

chk2   **Check register against two bounds**

syntax: chk2[.bwl]   <ea>,r_n

description: Check the value of the register r_n against the bounds pair stored at location **<ea>**. The lower bound is the first byte, word or long word (depending on the size of the operation) and the upper bound is the second location.

                If the checked register is a data register, and the operation is byte or word then the appropriate lower part of the register is checked. If the checked register is an address register then the bounds are sign extended to 32 bits in order to make the comparison.

                If r_n is outside the bounds then issue a TRAP.

ccr: N is undefined.
                Z is set if r_n is equal to either bound, cleared otherwise
                V is undefined.
                C is set if r_n is out of bounds, cleared otherwise
                X is unaffected.

note: Not available on the 68000/008/010 processors

clr   **Clear an operand**

syntax: clr[.bwl]   <ea>

description: Clear the destination to all zeroes

ccr: Z is set, X is unaffected and all other flags are cleared.

cmp   Compare

syntax: cmp[.bwl]   <ea>,d$_n$

description: Subtract the source from the destination, using binary arithmetic, only setting the flags in the condition codes register. The size of the operation can be byte, word or long.

ccr: N set if result negative, cleared otherwise
Z set if result zero, cleared otherwise
V set if overflow is generated, cleared otherwise
C set if borrow is generated, cleared otherwise
X not affected.

see: Sections 4.2, 7.1

cmpa   Compare addresses

syntax: cmpa[.wl]   <ea>,a$_n$

description: Subtract the source from the destination address register, using binary arithmetic, but just set the flags in the condition codes register. The size of the operation can be word or long.

This instruction is often generated by the assembler for the **cmp** instruction when the destination is an address register.

ccr: N set if result negative, cleared otherwise
Z set if result zero, cleared otherwise
V set if overflow is generated, cleared otherwise
C set if borrow is generated, cleared otherwise
X not affected.

cmpi   Compare immediate

syntax: `cmpi[.bwl]  #data,<ea>`

description: Subtract the immediate data from the destination using binary arithmetic. Just set the flags in the condition codes register. The size of the operation can be byte, word or long.

This instruction is often generated by the assembler for the **cmp** instruction when the source is immediate data. Note that this can be used to compare *any* destination, compared to just registers for **cmp** and **cmpa**.

ccr: N set if result negative, cleared otherwise
Z set if result zero, cleared otherwise
V set if overflow is generated, cleared otherwise
C set if borrow is generated, cleared otherwise
X not affected.

cmpm   Compare memory

syntax: `cmpm[.bwl]   (Ay)+,(Ax)+`

description: Subtract the memory location addressed by **Ay** from the memory location addressed by **Ax** – incrementing both registers as for post-increment addressing – using binary arithmetic. Just set the flags in the condition codes register. The size of the operation can be byte, word or long.

This instruction is often used, as part of a loop, when performing a string comparison.

ccr: N set if result negative, cleared otherwise
Z set if result zero, cleared otherwise
V set if overflow is generated, cleared otherwise
C set if borrow is generated, cleared otherwise
X not affected.

cmp2   **Compare register against bounds**

syntax: `cmp2[.bwl]   <ea>,`r_n

description: Compare the register r_n (it can be a data or address register) against the values stored successively at `<ea>`. The size of these bounding values depends on the size of the operation of the instruction: a word bounds check requires two word values. The first location contains the lower bound, and the second contains the upper bound.

The condition codes are set by this comparison as follows:

ccr: N Undefined
Z set if r_n is equal to either bound, cleared otherwise
V Undefined
C set if r_n is out of bounds, cleared otherwise
X not affected.

note: Not available on the 68000/008/010 processors

see: Section 4.2

db$_{cc}$ ## Test condition, decrement and branch

syntax: db$_{cc}$ d$_n$, label

description: If the condition $_{cc}$ is satisfied then continue with the next instruction; otherwise decrement the register **d$_n$** (lower half only) and if the register is ≠ -1 then branch to the label else continue.

The condition $_{cc}$ can be any of

CC — carry clear	¬C		CS — carry set	C
EQ — equal/zero	Z		NE —unequal/non zero	¬Z
MI — minus	N		PL — plus	¬N
VC — overflow clear	¬V		VS — overflow set	V
GE — greater or equal	N•V+¬N•¬V		LT — less than	N•¬V+¬N•V
GT — greater than	¬Z•N•V+¬Z•¬N•¬V		LE — less or equal	Z+N•¬V+¬N•V
HI — high	¬C•¬Z		LS — low or same	C+Z

ccr: Not affected

see: Sections 5.1, 7.1.3

dbra   ## Decrement and branch

syntax: dbra   d$_n$, label

description: Decrement the register (as a word value) and if the register is ≠ -1 then branch to the label.

ccr: Not affected

see: Sections 5.1, 7.1

divs	**Signed division**

syntax:
$$\text{divs.w} \quad \text{<ea>,} d_n \qquad 32/16 \rightarrow 16r:16q$$
$$\text{divs.l} \quad \text{<ea>,} d_q \qquad 32/32 \rightarrow 32q$$
$$\text{divs.l} \quad \text{<ea>,} d_r:d_q \qquad 64/32 \rightarrow 32r:32q$$
$$\text{divsl.l} \quad \text{<ea>,} d_r:d_q \qquad 32/32 \rightarrow 32r:32q$$

description: Divide the destination data register(s) by the source. There are several forms of this instruction:

1) Signed divide of a 32 bit data register by a 16 bit source, giving the quotient as a 16 bit quantity in the lower part of the result data register, and the remainder in the upper 16 bits. This is the only form available on the 68000/008/010.

2) Signed divide of a 32 bit destination by a 32 bit source. The remainder is discarded and the destination replaced by the quotient.

3) Signed divide of a 64 bit number – represented by two data registers d_r/d_q – by a 32 bit source. The 32 bit quotient is placed in d_q and the 32 bit remainder in d_r.

4) Signed divide of a 32 bit number in d_r by a 32 bit source; the quotient is left in d_q and the remainder in d_r.

If a division by zero is attempted then a trap occurs, otherwise the condition codes are set by this comparison as follows:

ccr: N set if quotient is negative, cleared otherwise. Undefined if divide by zero or overflow.
Z set if quotient is zero, cleared otherwise. Undefined if divide by zero or overflow.
V set if overflow occurred and/or the quotient is > 16/32 bits.
C always cleared
X not affected.

see: Section 4.2

`divu`	**Unsigned division**	

syntax:	`divu.w   <ea>,d`$_n$	`32/16→16r:16q`
	`divu.l   <ea>,d`$_q$	`32/32→32q`
	`divu.l   <ea>,d`$_r$`:d`$_q$	`64/32→32r:32q`
	`divul    <ea>,d`$_r$`:d`$_q$	`32/32→32r:32q`

description: Divide the destination data register(s) by the source. There are several forms of this instruction:

1)   Unsigned divide 32 bit data register by a 16 bit source, giving the quotient as a 16 bit quantity in the lower part of the result data register, and the remainder in the upper 16 bits.

   This is the only form available on the 68000.

2)   Unsigned divide of a 32 bit destination by a 32 bit source. The remainder is discarded and the destination replaced by the quotient.

3)   Unsigned divide of a 64 bit number – represented by two data registers d_r/d_q – by a 32 bit source. The quotient is placed in d_q and the remainder in d_r.

4)   Unsigned divide of a 32 bit number in d_r by a 32 bit source; the quotient is left in d_q and the remainder in d_r.

   If a division by zero is attempted then a trap occurs, otherwise the condition codes are set by this comparison as follows:

ccr: N set if quotient is negative, cleared otherwise. Undefined if divide by zero or overflow.
Z set if quotient is zero, cleared otherwise. Undefined if divide by zero or overflow.
V set if overflow occurred and/or the quotient is > 16/32 bits.
C always cleared
X not affected.

eor   **Exclusive OR**

syntax: `eor[.bwl]`   `d`$_n$`,<ea>`

description: Logically 'exclusive or' the bit pattern in the source with that of the destination. Each bit in the destination is formed by exclusive or-ing it with the corresponding bit of the source data register.

Note: The source of the instruction must be a data register. Address register direct addressing is not permitted with this instruction.

ccr: N set to most significant bit of result.
Z set if result is zero, cleared otherwise
V always cleared
C always cleared
X not affected.

eori   **Exclusive OR immediate data**

syntax: `eori[.bwl]`   `#data,<ea>`

description: Logically 'exclusive or' the bit pattern in the immediate data with that of the destination. This instruction is used in place of the **eor** mnemonic when the source operand is a literal value.

ccr: N set to most significant bit of result.
Z set if result is zero, cleared otherwise
V always cleared
C always cleared
X not affected.

`eori`   Exclusive OR to condition codes register

syntax: `eori  #data,ccr`

description: Logically 'exclusive or' the bit pattern in the immediate data with the condition code register. In effect this is used to complement certain flags in the **ccr**.

ccr: N changed if bit 3 of data is one, unaffected otherwise
Z changed if bit 2 of data is one, unaffected otherwise
V changed if bit 1 of data is one, unaffected otherwise
C changed if bit 0 of data is one, unaffected otherwise
X changed if bit 4 of data is one, unaffected otherwise.

`exg`   Exchange registers

syntax: `exg r`$_x$`,r`$_y$

description: Exchange the 32 bit registers **r**$_x$ and **r**$_y$ (which can be either address or data).

ccr: Not affected.

ext   **Sign extend data register**

syntax: `ext[.wl]` d_n

             `extb.l` d_n

description: Sign extend the lower byte (or word) in the data register to a valid word (or long word) quantity. This involves replicating the most significant bit in the byte (or word) throughout the upper byte (or word) of the register.

                  The `extb.l` instruction extends a byte quantity into a long word quantity.

ccr: N set if result is negative, cleared otherwise.
                  Z set if result is zero, cleared otherwise
                  V always cleared
                  C always cleared
                  X not affected.

see: Section 4.2

jmp   **Jump**

syntax: `jmp <ea>`

description: Program execution address continues at `<ea>`

note: Only memory addressing is allowed for this instruction.

ccr: Not affected.

see: Section 7.2

jsr	**Jump to sub-routine**

syntax: `jsr <ea>`

description: Call sub-routine located at **`<ea>`**; this involves pushing the address of the following instruction and subsequent program execution address continues at **`<ea>`**.

note: Only memory addressing modes are allowed for **`<ea>`**.

ccr: Not affected.

see: Chapter 8

lea	**Load effective address**

syntax: `lea <ea>,a`$_n$

description: Load the memory address specified by **`<ea>`** into address register **a**$_n$. This in contrast with the **move** instruction which would move the *contents* of the memory location.

note: Only memory addressing modes are valid for **`<ea>`**.

ccr: Not affected.

see: Section 5.1, 5.2

link	**Link and allocate**

syntax: `link     a`$_n$`,#data`

description: Allocate space on the system stack and link address register **a**$_n$ to it. This involves pushing the old value of **a**$_n$ onto the stack, setting **a**$_n$ to point to its old value on the stack, and adding **#data** to the system stack. (**Data** is normally negative.)

ccr: Not affected.

see: Section 8.1

lsl	**Logical shift left**

syntax: lsl[.bwl]   d$_x$,d$_y$

             lsl[.bwl]   #<data>,d$_y$

             lsl <ea>

description: The destination is left shifted by *count* bits where *count* is either
#data or the least significant 6 bits of **d$_x$**. The rightmost bits
are replaced by 0, and the leftmost bit shifted out is placed
into the e**X**tend and **C**arry flags.

In the case of a register count, amount of shift is modulo 64.

In the case of an immediate count, range of shifts is 1-8.

In the case of a memory instruction the operation is limited
to word length and shifts of one bit only.

ccr: N is set to most significant bit of result
Z is set if result is zero, cleared otherwise
V is set if the most significant bit is changed at any time
during the shift operation, cleared otherwise.
C set to the last bit shifted out of the operand. Cleared for a
zero shift count.
X set to the last bit shifted out of the operand. Unaffected for
a zero shift count.

lsr	**Logical shift right**

syntax: lsr[.bwl]   dx,dy

             lsr[.bwl]   #<data>,dx

             lsr <ea>

description: The destination is right shifted by *count* bits where *count* is either **#data** or the least significant 6 bits of d_x. The leftmost bits are replaced by 0, and the rightmost bit shifted out is placed into the e**X**tend and **C**arry flags.

In the case of a register count, amount of shift is modulo 64.

In the case of an immediate count, range of shifts is 1-8.

In the case of a memory instruction the operation is limited to word length and shifts of one bit only.

ccr: N is set to most significant bit of result
Z is set if result is zero, cleared otherwise
V is set if the most significant bit is changed at any time during the shift operation, cleared otherwise.
C set to the last bit shifted out of the operand. Cleared for a zero shift count.
X set to the last bit shifted out of the operand. Unaffected for a zero shift count.

`move`	**Move data**

syntax: `move[.bwl] <ea>`$_1$`,<ea>`$_2$

description: Move the quantity indicated by `<ea>`$_1$ to the address indicated by `<ea>`$_2$. If the destination is a data register or memory then the condition codes are set accordingly; if the destination is an address register then they are *not affected*.

ccr: N set if result is negative, cleared otherwise.
Z set if result is zero, cleared otherwise
V always cleared
C always cleared
X not affected.

`movea`	**Move data to address register**

syntax: `move[.wl] <ea>,a`$_n$

description: Move the quantity indicated by `<ea>` to the address register. This instruction is normally automatically generated by the assembler in place of a `move` instruction where the destination is an address register.

ccr: Not affected.

`move`	**Move from ccr**

syntax: `move ccr,<ea>`

description: Moves the `ccr` (zero extended to 16 bits) to `<ea>`.

ccr: Not affected.

move   **Move to ccr**

syntax: `move <ea>,ccr`

description: Moves the least significant byte at `<ea>` to the `ccr`.

ccr: N set to bit 3 of data in `<ea>`
           Z set to bit 2 of data in `<ea>`
           V set to bit 1 of data in `<ea>`
           C set to bit 0 of data in `<ea>`
           X set to bit 4 of data in `<ea>`.

movem   **Move multiple registers to/from memory**

syntax: `movem[.wl] <ea>,register list`

             `movem[.wl] register list,<ea>`

description: Move the registers in the list to memory or from memory. The `<ea>` specifies the starting address in memory for the transfer of the registers.

ccr: Not affected.

see: Section 8.2

moveq   **Move quick immediate data**

syntax: `moveq #<data>,`d_n

description: Moves a long immediate data to destination. `<data>` is in the range 1 to 8. This instruction is the one actually used when immediate data in the range 1..8 is specified with the **move** mnemonic.

ccr: N set if result negative, cleared otherwise
           Z set if result zero, cleared otherwise
           V always cleared
           C always cleared
           X not affected
           X set as carry bit.

`muls`	**Signed multiply**

syntax:

`muls.w`	`<ea>,`d_n	$16 \times 16 \rightarrow 32$
`muls.l`	`<ea>,`d_n	$32 \times 32 \rightarrow 32$
`muls.l`	`<ea>,`$d_h:d_l$	$32 \times 32 \rightarrow 64$

description: Multiply two signed quantities, giving a signed result. There are three forms of this instruction:

1)   A 16 bit multiplication, giving a 32 bit result. This is the only form on the 68000.

2)   A 32 bit multiplication, giving a 32 bit result.

3)   A 32 bit multiplication – `<ea>`$\times d_l$ – giving a 64 bit result in d_h and d_l.

ccr: N set if result is negative, cleared otherwise.
Z set if result is zero, cleared otherwise
V always cleared
C always cleared
X not affected.

see: Section 4.2

`mulu`	**Unsigned multiply**

syntax: `mulu.w  <ea>,d`$_n$ $16 \times 16 \rightarrow 32$

         `mulu.l  <ea>,d`$_n$ $32 \times 32 \rightarrow 32$

         `mulu.l  <ea>,d`$_h$`:d`$_l$ $32 \times 32 \rightarrow 64$

description: Multiply two unsigned quantities, giving an unsigned result. There are three forms of this instruction:

1) A 16 bit multiplication, giving a 32 bit result. This is the only form on the 68000.

2) A 32 bit multiplication, giving a 32 bit result.

3) A 32 bit multiplication – `<ea>`$\times$`d`$_l$ – giving a 64 bit result.

ccr: N set if result is negative, cleared otherwise.
Z set if result is zero, cleared otherwise
V always cleared
C always cleared
X not affected.

`neg`	**Negate operand**

syntax: `neg[.bwl]  <ea>`

description: Negate the operand specified in `<ea>`. This is the 2's complement of the number; equivalent to subtracting it from 0.

ccr: N set if result is negative, cleared otherwise.
Z set if result is zero, cleared otherwise
V always cleared
C always cleared
X not affected.

`negx`   ## Negate operand with eXtend

syntax: `negx[.bwl]  <ea>`

description: Negate the operand specified in `<ea>`. This involves subtracting it from 0 and also subtracting the e**X**tend flag value.

ccr: N set if result is negative, cleared otherwise.
Z set if result is zero, cleared otherwise
V always cleared
C always cleared
X not affected.

`not`   ## Complement operand

syntax: `not[.bwl]  <ea>`

description: Complement the operand specified in `<ea>`. This involves complementing each bit in `<ea>`.

ccr: N set if result is negative, cleared otherwise.
Z set if result is zero, cleared otherwise
V always cleared
C always cleared
X not affected.

or   **Inclusive OR**

syntax: `or[.bwl]  <ea>,dₙ`

                `or[.bwl]  dₙ,<ea>`

description: Logically OR the bit pattern in the source with that of the destination. Each bit in the destination is formed by or-ing it with the corresponding bit of the source operand.

Note: Address register direct addressing is not permitted with this instruction.

ccr: N set to most significant bit of result.
Z set if result is zero, cleared otherwise
V always cleared
C always cleared
X not affected.

see: Section 6.1, 6.2

ori   **Inclusive OR with immediate data**

syntax: `ori[.bwl]  #data,<ea>`

description: Logically OR the bit pattern in the immediate data with that of the destination. This instruction is used with the `or` instruction when the source operand is a literal value.

ccr: N set to most significant bit of result.
Z set if result is zero, cleared otherwise
V always cleared
C always cleared
X not affected.

`ori`	**Inclusive OR immediate to ccr**

syntax: `ori  #data,ccr`

description: Logically OR the bit pattern in the immediate data with the condition code register. In effect this is used to set certain flags in the `ccr`.

ccr: N set if bit 3 of data is one, unaffected otherwise
Z set if bit 2 of data is one, unaffected otherwise
V set if bit 1 of data is one, unaffected otherwise
C set if bit 0 of data is one, unaffected otherwise
X set if bit 4 of data is one, unaffected otherwise.

`pea`	**Push effective address**

syntax: `pea  <ea>`

description: Push the memory address specified by `<ea>` onto the system stack. This in contrast with the `lea` instruction which would load the address into a address register.

ccr: Not affected.

see: Section 8.1

| rol | **Rotate left** |

syntax: `rol[.bwl]` d_x, d_y

           `rol[.bwl]`   `#<data>`, d_y

           `rol <ea>`

description: The destination is rotated left by by *count* bits where *count* is either `#data` or the least significant 6 bits of d_x. The leftmost bits are inserted into the rightmost bit positions, and the leftmost bit shifted out is placed into the Carry flag.

In the case of a register count, amount of shift is modulo 64.

In the case of an immediate count, range of shifts is 1-8.

In the case of a memory instruction the operation is limited to word length and shifts of one bit only.

ccr: N is set to most significant bit of result
Z is set if result is zero, cleared otherwise
V always cleared.
C set to the last bit shifted out of the operand. Cleared for a zero shift count.
X not affected

ror   **Rotate right**

syntax: ror[.bwl] d_x, d_y

             ror[.bwl]   #<data>, d_y

             ror <ea>

description: The destination is rotated to the right by by *count* bits where
             count is either #**data** or the least significant 6 bits of d_x. The
             rightmost bits are inserted into the leftmost bit positions, and
             the rightmost bit shifted out is placed into the Carry flag.

             In the case of a register count, amount of shift is modulo 64.

             In the case of an immediate count, range of shifts is 1-8.

             In the case of a memory instruction the operation is limited
             to word length and shifts of one bit only.

ccr: N is set to most significant bit of result
             Z is set if result is zero, cleared otherwise
             V always cleared.
             C set to the last bit shifted out of the operand. Cleared for a
             zero shift count.
             X not affected

roxl   **Rotate left with eXtend**

syntax: `roxl[.bwl]` d_x, d_y

              `roxl[.bwl]`   `#<data>`, d_x

              `roxl`   `<ea>`

description: The destination is rotated left by *count* bits, where *count* is either **#data** or the least significant 6 bits of d_x, through the eXtend flag. As each bit is rotated, the eXtend flag is shifted into the rightmost bit of the destination, and the leftmost bit is shifted into the eXtend flag. The last bit shifted out is placed into the Carry flag.

In the case of a register count, amount of shift is modulo 64.

In the case of an immediate count, range of shifts is 1-8.

In the case of a memory instruction the operation is limited to word length and shifts of one bit only.

ccr: N is set to most significant bit of result
Z is set if result is zero, cleared otherwise
V always cleared.
C set to the last bit rotated out of the operand. Set to the value of the eXtend flag for a zero shift count.
X Set according to the last bit rotated out of the operand; not affected for a zero rotate count.

roxr	## Rotate right with eXtend

syntax: `roxr[.bwl]`   `d`$_x$`,d`$_y$

                     `roxr[.bwl]`   `#<data>,d`$_y$

                     `roxr`   `<ea>`

description: The destination is rotated right by *count* bits, where *count* is either **#data** or the least significant 6 bits of **d**$_x$, through the eXtend flag. As each bit is rotated, the eXtend flag is shifted into the leftmost bit of the destination, and the rightmost bit is shifted into the eXtend flag. The last bit shifted out is placed into the Carry flag.

                In the case of a register count, amount of shift is modulo 64.

                In the case of an immediate count, range of shifts is 1-8.

                In the case of a memory instruction the operation is limited to word length and shifts of one bit only.

ccr: N is set to most significant bit of result
                Z is set if result is zero, cleared otherwise
                V always cleared.
                C set to the last bit rotated out of the operand. Set to the value of the eXtend flag for a zero shift count.
                X Set according to the last bit rotated out of the operand; not affected for a zero rotate count.

rtd	## Return and deallocate parameters

syntax: `rtd #displacement`

description: Return from subroutine and adjust system stack, by adding **displacement** to the **a7** register after popping the return address, to deallocate parameters.

ccr: Not affected.

Note: Not available on the 68000/008/010 processors.

see: Section 8.1

rts	**Return from sub-routine**

syntax: rts

description: Return from subroutine.

ccr: Not affected.

see: Section 8.1

s$_{cc}$	**Set according to condition**

syntax: s$_{cc}$ <ea>

description: If the condition is satisfied then set byte value at <ea> to true: all ones; otherwise set byte at <ea> to false: all zeroes.

The condition $_{cc}$ can be any of

CC — carry clear	¬C		CS — carry set	C
EQ — equal/zero	Z		NE —unequal/non zero	¬Z
MI — minus	N		PL — plus	¬N
VC — overflow clear	¬V		VS — overflow set	V
GE — greater or equal	N•V+¬N•¬V		LT — less than	N•¬V+¬N•V
GT — greater than	¬Z•N•V+¬Z•¬N•¬V		LE — less or equal	Z+N•¬V+¬N•V
HI — high	¬C•¬Z		LS — low or same	C+Z

ccr: Not affected

see: Section 6.2, 7.1

sub   **Subtract source from destination**

syntax: sub[.bwl] <ea>,d$_n$
              sub[.bwl] d$_n$,<ea>

description: Subtract the source from the destination using binary
             arithmetic. The size of the operation can be byte, word or
             long.

ccr: N set if result negative, cleared otherwise
             Z set if result zero, cleared otherwise
             V set if overflow is generated, cleared otherwise
             C set if borrow is generated, cleared otherwise
             X set as carry bit.

see: Section 4.2

suba   **Subtract from address register**

syntax: suba[.wl] <ea>,a$_n$

description: Subtract source from a destination address register. The
             operation can be word or long; in the case of word, the source
             operand is sign extended to 32 bits prior to subtracting from
             the destination register.

             Some assemblers automatically generate this instruction
             from the **sub** mnemonic if the destination is an address
             register.

ccr: not affected

`subi`   **Subtract immediate data**

syntax: `subi[.bwl]   #<data>,<ea>`

description: Subtract immediate data from destination. This instruction is the one actually used when immediate data is specified with the **sub** mnemonic.

ccr: N set if result negative, cleared otherwise
Z set if result zero, cleared otherwise
V set if overflow is generated, cleared otherwise
C set if borrow is generated, cleared otherwise
X set as carry bit.

`subq`   **Subtract quick immediate data**

syntax: `subq[.bwl]   #<data>,<ea>`

description: Sub immediate data from destination. **data** is in the range 1 to 8. This instruction is the one actually used when immediate data in the range 1..8 is specified with the **sub** mnemonic.

ccr: N set if result negative, cleared otherwise
Z set if result zero, cleared otherwise
V set if overflow is generated, cleared otherwise
C set if borrow is generated, cleared otherwise
X set as carry bit.

subx   **Subtract with extend**

syntax: subx[.bwl] d_y, d_x

               subx[.bwl] $-(a_y)$, $-(a_x)$

description: Sub source from destination along with the e**X**tend bit. This instruction is used to implement multi-word arithmetic.

               Note the restrictions in the allowed addressing modes: either both operands are data registers or they are both address register predecrement.

ccr: N set if result negative, cleared otherwise
               Z set if result zero, cleared otherwise
               V set if overflow is generated, cleared otherwise
               C set if borrow is generated, cleared otherwise
               X set as carry bit.

swap   **Swap register halves**

syntax: swap d_n

description: Swap upper half of data register d_n with its lower half.

ccr: N set if result negative, cleared otherwise
               Z set if result zero, cleared otherwise
               V always cleared
               C always cleared
               X not affected.

tst   **Test an operand**

syntax: tst <ea>

description: Test the operand and set condition codes accordingly

ccr: N set if result negative, cleared otherwise
               Z set if result zero, cleared otherwise
               V always cleared
               C always cleared
               X not affected.

`unlk`   **Deallocate**

syntax: `unlk        `a_n

description: Unlink address register a_n and deallocate space from stack. This involves setting the system stack pointer to a_n and popping into it its old value of the register from the stack.

ccr: Not affected.

see: Section 8.2

Answers to selected exercises

Exercises 2.2.4

1. a) $1000 = 1*512+1*256+1*128+1*64+1*32+1*8$

    $= 1*2^9+1*2^8+1*2^7+1*2^6+1*2^5+0*2^4+1*2^3+0*2^2+0*2^1+0*2^0$

    b) $\left|-1000\right|_{65536} = 65536-1000 = 64536$

2. There are 7 numbers in the range 20...26. The fewest number of bits that can represent 7 numbers is 3 bits (which can represent up to 8 numbers).

3. Let $M=2^m$ be the modulus, a power of 2. The binary expansion of M is:

    M $= 1*2^m+0*2^{m-1}+0*2^{m-2}+...+0*2^0$

    $= 1*2^{m-1}+1*2^{m-2}+...+1*2^0 + 1$

    Let A, an arbitrary number in the range $0...2^{m-1}$, be represented by the expansion:

    A $= a_{m-1}*2^{m-1}+a_{m-2}*2^{m-2}+...+a_0*2^0$

    where each a_i is either 0 or 1. If we subtract A from M we get:

M-A $= 1*2^{m-1}+1*2^{m-2}+...+1*2^{0} + 1 - (a_{m-1}*2^{m-1}+a_{m-2}*2^{m-2}+...+a_0*2^0)$

   $= (1-a_{m-1})*2^{m-1}+(1-a_{m-2})*2^{m-2}+...+(1-a_0)*2^0 + 1$

Where each term of the form $(1-a_i)$ is actually the complement of a_i: if $a_i=0$ then $(1-a_i)=1$, and if $a_i=1$ then $(1-a_i)=0$. Finally the +1 term at the end signifies that we must add 1 after complementing the individual terms in the expansion.

6. Our solution is written as a Pascal program; although considering the extent of bit manipulations involved an assembler program might be clearer! **mult** is a recursive function with declaration:

```
function   mult(a,b,n:integer):integer;
var   a0,b0,a1,b1,temp,a0b0,a1b1,n0,n2:integer;
```

The base case of the recursion involves multiplying two 1 bit numbers, which is the same as 'and':

$0 \times 0 = 0$ $0 \times 1 = 0$

$1 \times 0 = 0$ $1 \times 1 = 1$

This can be expressed as the Pascal code fragment:

```
    if  n=1  then
        mult  := a & b
    else  ...
```

otherwise, for the recursive case we have to split our two numbers, recurse and then recombine. Splitting can be done by a mask and shift operation. In standard Pascal this appears to be quite expensive since it involves a multiplication in its own right; however if we temporarily borrow some 'C' notation we can express it more directly:

```
begin
    n2   :=n/2;                mask  :=  (1<<n2)-1
    a0  :=  (a & mask); a1  := a >> n2;
    b0  :=  (b & mask); b1  := b >> n2;
    a0b0  :=  mult(a0,b0,n2);
    a1b1  :=  mult(a1,b1,n2);
    temp  :=  mult(a0+a1,b0+b1,n2)
              -a0b0-a1b1;
    mult:=a0b0+(temp<<n2)+(a1b1<<n);
end;
```

Actually, there are some extra complications regarding the generation of carries in the partial additions **a0+a1** and **b0+b1**; therefore a more correct program is

```
begin
    if  odd(n)  then      { make  sure  n  is  even }
        n := n + 1;
    n2  :=  n>>1;
    mask  :=  (1<<n2)  - 1;
    a0  := a & mask;      a1  := a>>n2;
    b0  := b & mask; b1  := b>>n2;
    a0b0  :=  mult(a0,  b0,  n2);
    a1b1  :=  mult(a1,  b1,  n2);
    if ((a0 + a1) & mask) <> a0+a1) or
            ((b0+b1) & mask) <> b0+b1) then
        n0  :=  n2+2
    else
        n0  :=  n2;            { adjust for carry }
    temp  :=  mult(a0+a1,b0+b1,n0)  -
                    a0b0 - a1b1;
    mult  :=  a0b0 + temp<<n2 + a1b1<<n;
end;
```

In each pass of this algorithm there are three recursive calls to **mult**. On the other hand, the size of the subsidiary problems is half the number of bits. Therefore, the average depth of recursion will be $\log_2 N$ for an N-bit multiplication. The complexity of this algorithm is, then, $O(N\log_2 N)$ which is less than $O(N^2)$ for the conventional multiplication algorithm. However, this algorithm is considerably more complex to implement and it would require very careful coding or implementation in silicon to achieve a speed-up.

Exercises 2.3.4

1. In a binary system, 0.5 would be represented as $0.1000000000000000B$. The sequence of squares that we get in binary are:

    $0.1000000000000000^2 = \quad 0.0100000000000000$

    $0.0100000000000000^2 = \quad 0.0001000000000000$

    $0.0001000000000000^2 = \quad 0.0000000100000000$

    $0.0000000100000000^2 = \quad 0.0000000000000000$

    Therefore, we have lost the significant digit by the fourth successive square.

    In a floating point system, the sequence would be represented as

    $(0.1000\ldots \times 2^0)^2 \qquad = \qquad 0.1000\ldots \times 2^{-1}$

    $(0.1000\ldots \times 2^{-1})^2 \qquad = \qquad 0.1000\ldots \times 2^{-3}$

    $(0.1000\ldots \times 2^{-3})^2 \qquad = \qquad 0.1000\ldots \times 2^{-7}$

    The sequence would only end when we could no longer represent a sufficiently small exponent. If we had 9 bits to represent the exponent then the smallest power of 2 would be:

    $0.1000\ldots \times 2^{-255}$

    We would get to this number in two further steps. Continuing the squaring after this would lead to the same degeneration of the result as with a fixed point number.

2. If we are to divide two fixed point numbers, a and b (say) with a fixed point at k bits, then we can express the numbers as:

    $a = \mathcal{A}*2^{-k}$

    and

    $b = \mathcal{B}*2^{-k}$

    Dividing a by b gives us:

    $a \div b \quad = (\mathcal{A}*2^{-k}) \div (\mathcal{B}*2^{-k})$

    $\quad = ((\mathcal{A} \div \mathcal{B}) \div 2^{-k})*2^{-k}$

    Thus we can divide the integer part of a by the integer part of b, and divide that by 2^{-k} to give us the correct result with a fixed binary point at k. Dividing a number by 2^{-k} amounts to a left shift of k bits:

    $a \div b \quad = ((\mathcal{A} \div \mathcal{B}) << k)*k$

    As with fixed point multiplication, this left shift may lose significant bits from the answer. In this case however, any bits that we lose are liable to be the *most* significant bits rather than the least significant bits that we lose in multiplication.

3. We can 'convert' the problem of representing a number of the form 2^{-x} into one of representing numbers of the form 5^x as follows:

    $2^{-x} \quad = 10^x \times 2^{-x} \times 10^{-x}$

    $\quad = (10^x / 2^x) \times 10^{-x}$

    $\quad = 5^x \times 10^{-x}$

    Clearly, 5^x is representable finitely in decimal numbers and a multiplication by 10^{-x} is simply a 'right shift' of the decimal number by x places.

    (This solution was suggested to the author by K.Broda and G. Ringwood in private communications.)

Exercises 3.3.3

2.   The decimal number **100000** is **186A0** in hexadecimal, whereas **200000** is **30D40** in hexadecimal. The third **move** instruction only moves the least significant 16 bits of **d0** into the least significant 16 bits of **d1**, the remaining bits of **d1** are untouched. Therefore, **d1** is left with **$386A0** in it, which is **231072**.

3.   We shall use **d2** as the third register:

```
move.l   d0,d2
move.l   d1,d0
move.l   d2,d1
```

4.   The key observation here is that exclusive or is its own inverse, i.e. that

$$X \oplus Y \oplus X = Y$$

So, we can swap X and Y as follows:

$X := X \oplus Y$ $\qquad\qquad$ $X = X_0 \oplus Y_0$

$Y := X \oplus Y$ $\qquad\qquad$ $Y = (X_0 \oplus Y_0) \oplus Y_0 = X_0$

$X := X \oplus Y$ $\qquad\qquad$ $X = (X_0 \oplus Y_0) X_0 = Y_0$

The instructions to do this are:

```
eor.l    d0,d1
eor.l    d1,d0
eor.l    d0,d1
```

The execution time for these three instructions is the same as for the three **move** instructions in the previous exercise.

Exercises 4.2.3

1.   u - v - w + x - y

⟹ | u v - | - w + x - y

→ | u v - w - | + x - y

⟹ | u v - w - x + | - y

⟹ | u v - w - x + y - |

The instructions which implement this sequence are:

```
move.w   u,-(a7)
move.w   v,d0
sub.w    d0,(a7)      ;subtract  v  from  u
move.w   w,d0
sub.w    d0,(a7)      ;subtract  w  from  u-v
move.w   x,d0
add.w    d0,(a7)      ;add  x  to  u-v-w
move.w   y,d0
sub.w    d0,(a7)      ;subtract  y
```

2. a)   (u+v) / (u-15)

⟹ | u v + | / | u 15 - |

⟹ | u v + u 15 - / |

b) Instructions implementing the expression using the system stack:

```
move.w   u,-(a7)
move.w   v,d0
add.w    d0,(a7)
bov      overflow_error
move.w   u,-(a7)
move.w   #15,d0
sub.w    d0,(a7)
bov      overflow_error
beq      divide_zero_error
move.w   (a7)+,d1
move.w   (a7)+,d0
ext.l    d0
divs.w   d1,d0
bov      overflow_error
move.w   d0,-(a7)
```

c) Instructions using data registers to simulate a stack:

```
move.w   u,d7
add.w    v,d7
bov      overflow_error
move.w   u,d6
sub.w    #15,d6
bov      overflow_error
beq      divide_zero_error
ext.l    d7
divs.w   d6,d7
bov      overflow_error
```

3. The expression converted into reverse polish form is:

```
u  32  *  u  v  /  +  w  **
```

We shall use registers **d7**, **d6** and **d5** to simulate an expression stack. The basic code, without error checking is:

```
        move.w  u,d7
        move.w  #32,d6
        muls    d6,d7       ;u 32 *
        move.w  u,d6
        move.w  v,d5
        ext.l   d6          ;extend  dividend
        divs    d5,d6       ;u v /
        add.w   d6,d7       ;u 32 * u v / +
        move.b  w,d6        ;start  exponentiation
        move.l  #1,d0       ;compute exp.  into  d0
        cmp.b   #0,d6       ;end of  loop
        beq.s   @2
@1      muls    d7,d0       ;multiply
        sub.w   #1,d6
        bne.s   @1
@2      move.l  d0,d7       ;store  final  answer
```

With error checking, the code is somewhat longer:

```
        move.w  u,d7
        move.w  #32,d6
        muls    d6,d7 ;u 32 *
        bov     overflow_error
        move.w  u,d6
        move.w  v,d5
        ext.l   d6              ;extend  dividend
        beq     zero_divide
        divs    d5,d6           ;u v /
        bov     overflow_error
        add.w   d6,d7           ;u 32 * u v / +
        bov     overflow_error
        move.b  w,d6            ;start  exponentiation
        move.l  #1,d0           ;compute exp.  into  d0
        cmp.b   #0,d6           ;end of  loop
        beq.s   @2
@1      muls    d7,d0           ;multiply
        bov     overflow_error
        sub.w   #1,d6
        bne.s   @1
@2      move.l  d0,d7           ;store  final  answer
```

Exercises 5.1.4

1. We can implement

    ```
    fbp^.foop:=fbp^.foop^.foop;
    ```

    in three instructions:

    ```
    move.l  fbp,a0
    move.l  foop(a0),a1
    move.l  foop(a1),foop(a0)
    ```

2. The first record:

    ```
    d_entry  =  record
          mark:boolean;        { 1 byte }
          t:(a_tag,b_tag);     { 1 byte }
          n:^d_entry;          { 4 bytes }
       end;
    ```

    requires 6 bytes, but the second record requires up to two filler bytes:

    ```
    e_entry  =  record
          mark:boolean;        { 1 byte }
                               { filler }
          n:^e_entry;          { 4 bytes }
          t:(a_tag,b_tag);     { 1 byte }
                               { filler }
       end;                    { 8 bytes }
    ```

    Whether the compiler should automatically substitute one for the other is mostly a philosophical point. By performing the replacement a 25% saving in space can be achieved; furthermore, since the compiler is left to allocate space as it pleases (unlike a packed record), it may be assumed that the compiler could optimise the representation if it saw the opportunity. Certainly, a substitution of a code sequence by an equivalent optimized code sequence would be perfectly permissible.

    However, if this record is used in the definition of a file, as in:

    ```
    f:file of d_entry;
    ```

then the data in the record file may be accessible from *outside* the system: the program containing this definition may access data from other programs or even other operating systems. These other programs may be compiled using compilers which did not make the same optimizations, therefore the program may not operate correctly over the data file.

Perhaps an appropriate solution would be for the Pascal compiler to *inform* the programmer that a small reorganization of the record would yield the improvement: this leaves the actual decision to the programmer.

Exercises 5.2.3

1. The assignment:

```
jjp^[x].jar[y]:=jjn;
```

involves two array accesses.

```
move.w   x, d0
cmp.w    #1,d0      ;1<x?
blt      array_error
cmp.w    #5,d0      ;5>x?
bgt      array_error
move.l   jjp, a0
sub.w    #1,d0      ;cant use offset
mulu     #42,d0     ;size of a jamjar
lea      jar(a0,d0.w),a0
move.w   y, d0
cmp.w    #1,d0      ;1<y?
blt      array_error
cmp.w    #10,d0     ;10>y?
bgt      array_error
add.w    d0,d0      ;*2
move.w   jjn,-2(a0,d0.w)   ;...:=jjn
```

2. The shift'n add style of multiplying by a constant depends on the breakdown of a number into its binary expansion. So if we want to multiply an unknown M by a known I, then we examine the binary expansion for I:

$$I = I_0 * 2^0 + I_1 * 2^1 + I_2 * 2^2 + \ldots + I_n * 2^n$$

assuming that I is a positive number number less then 2n+1. To multiply M by I results in the expansion:

$$I * M = M * I_0 + (M<<1) * I_1 + \ldots + (M<<n) * I_n$$

There is a significant term in this expansion for every non-zero bit in the binary expansion for I. So, to determine the effectiveness of using the shift'n add style, we have to count the number of bits in I. For each non-zero bit in I, there is a shift and an add instruction; so the total cost of the multiplication sequence is

$$6 * \mathcal{B}_I$$

where $\mathcal{B}_I$ is the number of non-zero bits in I. For the code to be faster than the general purpose **mulu** instruction, this must be less than 29, i.e.:

$$\mathcal{B}_I < 29 \div 6 \qquad \text{or} \qquad \mathcal{B}_I < 4.8333333333$$

If there are more than four significant bits in I then we are better to use the **mulu** instruction. Note that this restriction does *not* refer to the size of I; if we are multiplying by 32 then there is only one non-zero bit in I, but if we want to multiply by 31 then there are five non-zero bits in I and it would be better to use **mulu**.

3. Suppose that we wanted to access the two-dimensional array:

```
bi:array[0..20,1..10] of integer;
```

using this technique. We would have a table of offsets to rows in the array **bi** defined somewhere within our program. In fact each entry in the offset table would consist of the length of the array so far:

```
bioff dc.w     0          ;first  row  at  offset  0
      dc.w     20         ;each  row  is  20  bytes
      dc.w     20*2       ;larger  arrays  might
      ...                 ;need  long  offsets
      ...
      dc.w     20*20      ;the  21st  row
```

Access to the element of the array involves accessing this table as well as the array itself.

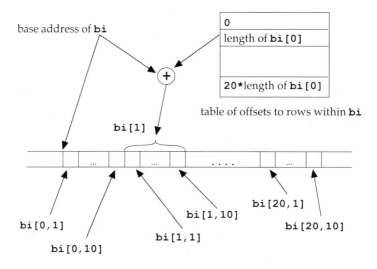

To implement **bi[x,y]:=bi[y,x];** we would use the sequence:

```
lea      bioff,a1   ;table  of  row  offsets
move.w   y,d0            ;bi[y,x]...
move.w   0(a1,d0.w*2),d0      ;68020  code
lea      bi,a0           ;base  of  bi
lea      0(a0,d0.w),a0   ;add  row  offset
move.w   x,d0            ;column  x
move.w   -2(a0,d0.w*2),d1     ;d1=  bi[y,x]

move.w   x,d0            ;start  bi[x,y]
move.w   0(a1,d0.w*2),d0 ;offset  to  bi[x,]
lea      bi,a0
lea      0(a0,d0.w),a0   ;add  row  offset
move.w   y,d0            ;column  y
move.w   d1,-2(a0,d0.w*2)     ;...:=bi[y,x]
```

Exercises 6.2.3

1. Suppose that we wanted to implement the assignment:

    ```
    i_set:=i_set+[I];
    ```

    then we could use the **bfset** instruction directly, without needing to calculate byte offsets, because the bit field offset can be specified in a data register:

    ```
    move.w   I,d0
    ext.l    d0           ;convert to long
    bfset    i_set{d0:1}
    ```

    This sets a bit field – of width 1 – to 1's. We need to convert the word length index *I* to a long value because the **bfset** instruction uses a long value to specify the bit field's offset. We can also set a sub-range of the set in one instruction also:

    ```
    i_set:=i_set+[I..I+4];
    ```

    becomes

    ```
    move.w   I,d0
    ext.l    d0           ;convert to long
    bfset    i_set{d0:5}
    ```

2. A subset test, such as J⊃I can be re-expressed as follows:

    J⊃I ⇔ I∩J=I

    So, in 68000 instructions, when testing a large set such as **i_set**, each segment of the test becomes:

    ```
    move.l  (a0),d0    ;I  fragment
    and.l   (a1),d0    ;I ∩ J
    cmp.l   (a0),d0    ;=?
    bne     not_subset
    ```

and the complete test is implemented using a loop:

```
        lea     i_set, a0
        lea     j_set, a1
        move.w  #31, d1
@ 1     move.l  (a0), d0      ; I  fragment
        and.l   (a1)+, d0     ; I ∩ J
        cmp.l   (a0)+, d0     ; = ?
        bne     not_subset
        dbra    d1, @1
        ... ...               ; yes,  i_set<=j_set
```

3. i) The expression can be converted to reverse polish form as follows:

x * (y+1)

=>   x * | y 1 + |

=> | x y 1 + * |

ii) z := z + [x * (y+1)] ;

using **a7** as an expression stack:

```
        move.w  y, -(a7)
        move.w  #1, -(a7)
        move.w  (a7)+, d0
        add.w   (a7)+, d0
        bov     overflow_line_xxx
        muls    x, d0
        bov     overflow_line_xxx
        cmp.w   #0, d0          ; range  check
        blt     range_error_xxx
        cmp.w   #1023, d0
        bgt     range_error_xxx
        move.w  d0, d1
        lsr.w   #3, d1          ; compute  byte  offset
        bset    d0, 0(a1, d1)
```

Exercises 7.1.5

1. The instructions needed to implement this **while** loop are:

```
         bra      @4               ;go  round  body
@0       move.w   i,d0
         add.w    d0,d0            ;2*i
         cmp.w    j,d0             ;2*i>j?
         bgt      @1               ;yes,  early  exit
         cmp.w    #10,j            ;j>10?
         ble      @2
@1       lea      ai,a0
         move.w   i,d0
         add.w    d0,d0
         move.w   j,-2(a0,d0.w)
         bra      @3
@2       lea      ai,a0
         move.w   j,d0
         add.w    d0,d0
         move.w   i,-2(a0,d0.w)
@3       sub.w    #1,i
@4       move.w   i,d0
         cmp.w    j,d0             ;i>j?
         bgt      @0
```

2. To implement conditional expressions is simply a matter of evaluating the conditional part of the expression within a normal expression calculation as opposed to within a conditional or loop construct. The branches of the conditional are expressions rather than statements, but otherwise their implementation is the same as conditionals.

```
            bra     @1
    @0      lea     ai, a0
            move.w  i, d0
            add.w   d0, d0
            move.w  -2(a0, d0.w), i
    @1      move.w  i, d0
            cmp.w   j, d0         ; i < j?
            blt     @2
            move.w  j, d0
    @2      add.w   d0, d0        ; d0 = i or j
            lea     ai, a0
            cmp.w   #10, -2(a0, d0.w)
            blt     @0
```

Index

F